Persons and Things

Barbara Johnson

and Persons
THINGS

HARVARD UNIVERSITY PRESS   Cambridge, Massachusetts, and London, England

Copyright © 2008 by the President and Fellows of Harvard College
All rights reserved
Printed in the United States of America

First Harvard University Press paperback edition, 2010

Library of Congress Cataloging-in-Publication Data

Johnson, Barbara, 1947–
   Persons and things / Barbara Johnson.
     p. cm.
   Includes bibliographical references and index.
   ISBN 978-0-674-02638-4 (cloth)
   ISBN 978-0-674-04628-3 (pbk.)
   1. Literature—Philosophy.   2. Human beings in literature.
   3. Objects (Philosophy) in literature.   I. Title.
   PN49.J55 2007
   809'.9335—dc22   2007037448

Pages 251–252 constitute an extension of the copyright page.

To the many wonderful students
who have made teaching Persons and Things
such a delight in the past few years

Contents

The Personhood of Things

Persons

When he returned he sought the image of his maid, and bending over the couch he kissed her. She seemed warm to his touch. Again he kissed her, and with his hands also he touched her breast. The ivory grew soft to his touch and, its hardness vanishing, gave and yielded beneath his fingers, as Hymettian wax grows soft under the sun and, moulded by the thumb, is easily shaped to many forms and becomes usable through use itself.

—Ovid, *Metamorphoses*

How can I describe my emotions at this catastrophe, or how delineate the wretch whom with such infinite pains and care I had endeavoured to form? His limbs were in proportion, and I had selected his features as beautiful. Beautiful!—Great God! His yellow skin scarcely covered the work of muscles and arteries beneath; his hair was of a lustrous black, and flowing; his teeth were of a pearly whiteness; but these luxuriances only formed a more horrid contrast with his watery eyes, that seemed almost of the same colour as the dun white in which they were set, his shrivelled complexion and straight black lips.

—Mary Shelley, *Frankenstein*

Prologue

Which of us has not had this dream: an object shaped by our desire and lovingly formed by our fantasy until its inanimate face perfectly reflects our own wishes suddenly shudders, awakens, breathes, and becomes warm. Pygmalion had it, surely, when he fell in love with the work of his own hands and, miraculously, the thing came to life: "The lips he kisses are real indeed, the ivory girl can feel them, and blushes and responds, and the eyes open at once on lover and heaven . . ." Yet also, which of us has not had this nightmare: an object crafted with loving attention to resemble life shudders, awakens, breathes, becomes warm—and suddenly what was an object becomes a subject whose gaze turns *us* into an object and who escapes our control. This is the horror Victor Frankenstein feels when the monster whom he has spent months creating finally opens its eyes.

From artificial intelligence to Deep Blue, the variety of tests to which objects are submitted implies that the aim is to achieve so perfect a resemblance to persons that the viewer mistakes things for human beings. Yet each time they fail to attain this, humanity breathes a sigh of relief. The simulacrum may be *better* than what it simulates (think of little David in the what is this? but further, even if it does exist, *do* we project what we think it is?

2   *Prologue*

film *AI*), but it is not yet (and may never be) indistinguishable. Persons retain some ineffable humanness that things have not captured.

The difficulties of establishing proper definitions of "person" and "thing" in this study are, of course, at the heart of the study. But one caveat can be formulated: something defined as not one of them is not *therefore* the other. It is important to explore the category of *non-person* separately from that of *thing*. Many entities that could be—or later are—defined as persons are represented as non-persons in the eyes of the law: slaves and fetuses and corporations, for example. Does this mean they are things? Not necessarily. Are corpses persons or things? Are human-like objects (statues, for example) altogether like computers in their inanimateness? Are dead bodies inanimate in the same way that something that was never animate is? Shakespeare's play *The Winter's Tale* plays with these questions when the statue of a dead woman reveals itself to have been a living being all along. The phrase "treating someone like a thing" could be a condemnation if it means "treating someone like a tool of one's own desire," but treating *oneself* like a thing may not be so easy to define nor so morally clear.

The more I thought about this asymptotic relation between things and persons, the more I realized that the problem is not, as it seems, a desire to treat things as persons, but a difficulty in being sure that we treat *persons* as persons. In other words, the relations between persons and things might be the *norm* in human relations already and not the object of an impossible quest. A study of persons and things might reveal all of the ways we already treat persons as things, and how humanness is mired in an inability to do otherwise. Rather than trying to invent a humanoid thing capable of passing ever more sophisticated Turing tests, in other words, our real impossible dream is precisely to learn to live in a world where persons treat persons as persons. It is in many ways *that* project that occupies the pages of this book.

plurality of
person and
thinghood...

(things to explore...)

Chapter One

Toys R Us

LEGAL PERSONS, PERSONAL PRONOUNS, DEFINITIONS

What are the origins and aims of this book? It is not organized chronologically, although it may well be about the anxiety and the excitement of being historical. After all, according to Marx, human beings become historical the moment they start to work, and the first "thing" they produce is— the concept of "human beings." The book is not about literary movements, although what defines such movements may well be the way they see the relationships between persons and things. It is not about science and literature, although the relation between man and machine has preoccupied all those who live in a Newtonian universe; the distinction between "persons" and "things" may here be a legacy of the Enlightenment in the twenty-first century.

There are three dimensions I will try to keep constantly in mind when I talk about the relations between persons and things: the reality of desire, the reality of materiality, and the reality of rhetoric. Each of these domains has an image of the relation between persons and things that ignores the others: to dream about a statue coming to life is to situate the real in fantasy, not materiality. To concentrate on rocks and trees and stones is to forget the

[margin note: 3 dimensions… in relations of Persons & Things]

slumber and its dreams. And to talk as if concepts and abstractions act and feel and intend as people do implies that one knows how people act, when in fact those beliefs may inhere in a linguistic system of which its users are not conscious. In other words, while all three dimensions are part of my subject, they may not be compatible among themselves.

This book may also have its origins in two personal epiphanies, whose idiosyncrasies should not obscure their general applicability. One occurred to me as a suburban child; the other as a Yale graduate student. The first concerned my inability to eat anything that had a face. Not anything that *had had* a face: I was not an incipient vegetarian and was perfectly happy to devour a hamburger, but I could not bring myself to consume anything that might be looking at me while I ate it or that continued to smile cheerfully as parts of its body disappeared into my mouth—gingerbread men or jack o' lantern candies. This fear of cannibalism, or overinvestment in the face, will recur. The other epiphany was the realization that deconstruction gravitated to the inanimate: Paul de Man was happiest when proving that what we take as human nature is an illusion produced by mechanical means. Jacques Derrida's first seminar at Yale was called The Thing, and I have been thinking about it ever since. It was from that seminar that I came to know Heidegger—and Ponge. Both of these preoccupations—the face and the thing—lie beneath everything in this book.

One of the most persistent questions children ask is, "Where do babies come from?" On the one hand, they are asking about the very origins of life, a question that has preoccupied philosophers and theologians ever since philosophers and theologians existed. But on the other hand, they may be curious to know which organ fits where, and how the baby gets into the mother's body to begin with. They know it has something to do with the relationship between their parents: which itself is a mystery they spend their lives trying to penetrate. But perhaps the idea of combining organs is what leads to a toy like Socket Poppers. The box proclaims that there are "Over 15 Quadrillion Combinations. Create Countless Creatures! All Body Parts Move . . . Even to Other Bodies!" Inside the box are creatures from wrestlers to mutants, each revealing to the user how, for example, a rock singer becomes a dinosaur. Each of the figures is on the same scale as the others, so that everything is both changeable and interchangeable. There may be 15 quadrillion combinations, but every one of them is male. If one is looking to the mathematical sublime for an understanding of sexual difference, one is bound to be disappointed. And even if these toys might clue one in to the secrets of male-male coupling, they promise a spectacle only out of the transformation of a single figure, not out of the relationships between them.

Another toy that mobilized children's attention a few years ago was called a "transformer": each of them had the potential to change something inanimate into something animate. An insect became a motorcycle; a robot became a lizard; a dog became a car: all with the flick of a wrist. What was mesmerizing about them was the use of exactly the same materials to produce a living thing or a machine: it was a matter of transformation. There was no fundamental incompatibility between life and machines; they were continuous if you knew the right moves. This magic of "transformers" may underlie Ovid's use of the very same word to name his tales of transformation: *Metamorphoses*. It may also be why Nathaniel Hawthorne entitled the first edition of his *Marble Faun* "The Transformation." Under the spell of shape-changing, anything can become anything at any moment, and the world around us may contain the ghosts of the stories that we no longer know. The relation between person and things grows more uncanny.

The question of what counts as a "person," which often seems intuitively obvious, has had some interesting legal moments over the years. In 1871, with the Civil War in the past but Reconstruction in shambles and the prospect of turning three-fifths of a person (which was how a former slave had been counted for purposes of representation) into a whole rights-bearing person nowhere in sight, suddenly Congress passed the Dictionary Act, a glossary of terms Congress might use in any act, stating that the word "person" "may extend and be applied to bodies politic and corporate." In other words, control of political rights and corporate property had become more central to the constitutional functioning of the United States than the mere stories of individuals. In 1973 the courts again had to decide what counted as a person, in deciding whether the rights of pregnant women seeking abortions violated the rights of the unborn under the Fourteenth Amendment (equal protection). In the landmark decision in *Roe v. Wade,* it was decided that, since it was impossible to pin down the exact moment a human being was "animated," or brought to life, a fetus was not a "person" under the law. Again, the question of where babies come from—or rather, the question of when persons form out of non-persons. And again, the border-

Handwritten margin notes: "Transforming Toys"; "legal complications of the 'person'"; "corporate"; "abortion"; "Gen 2"

line between persons and things involves the very origins of life. Yet this issue remains contested and complex: in *Black's Law Dictionary,* the entry for *unborn child* under "person" reads as follows:

> *Unborn child.* Word "person" as used in the Fourteenth Amendment does not include the unborn. Roe v. Wade, 410 U.S. 113, 93 S.Ct. 705, 729, 35 L. Ed. 2nd 147. Unborn child is a "person" for purposes of remedies given for personal injuries, and child may sue after his birth. Weaks v. Mounter, 88 Nev.118, 493 P. 24 1307, 1309. In some jurisdictions a viable fetus is considered a person within the meaning of the state's wrongful death statute, *e.g.* Summerfield v. Superior Court, 144 Ariz. 467, 693 P. 2nd 712, and within the meaning of the state's vehicular homicide statute, *e.g.* Comm. v. Cass, 392 Mass. 799, 467 N.E. 2nd 1324.

A well-known linguist had something to say about the presence or absence of "persons" in his discussion of personal pronouns. Addressing himself to "problems in general linguistics," Emile Benveniste averred: "The situation of the personal pronouns should be considered first. It is not enough to distinguish them from the other pronouns by a denomination that separates them. It must be seen that the ordinary definition of the personal pronouns as containing the three terms *I, you,* and *he,* simply destroys the notion of 'person.' 'Person' belongs only to *I/you* and is lacking in *he.*"[1] In other words, the notion of "person" has something to do with presence at the scene of speech and seems to inhere in the notion of *address.* "I" and "you" are persons because they can either address or be addressed, while "he" can only be talked *about.* A person who neither addresses nor is addressed is functioning as a *thing* in the same way that being an *object* of discussion rather than a *subject* of discussion transforms everything into a thing.

There seems to be an easy way to treat a thing as a person, then: address it, turn it into an interlocutor or at least a listener through the rhetorical power of language. I would like to explore here the major rhetorical figures by which this act of animation is achieved. The first and most pervasive of these rhetorical figures is *apostrophe,* the calling out to inanimate, dead, or absent beings. Other definitions of this well-known figure bring out its main characteristics: "A digression in discourse. Esp. a turning away from an audience to address an absent or imaginary person. (Gk *apo,* away; *strephein,* to turn)"; "a figure of speech which consists in addressing a dead or absent person, an animal, a thing, or an abstract quality or idea as if it were alive, present, and capable of understanding."[2] Apostrophe situates its fictive entities in the field of direct address, so that the spoken voice is what knits the utterance together. This figure of address has come to be almost synonymous with lyric poetry itself: as Paul de Man puts it, "Now it is certainly beyond question that the figure of address is recurrent in lyric poetry, to the point of constituting the generic definition of, at the very least, the ode (which can, in its turn, be seen as paradigmatic for poetry in general)."[3] This figure is found in some of the most canonical poems—"To Intellectual Beauty," "To a Nightingale," "To a Skylark," "To Duty," "To the West Wind"—as well as some of the most consciously "unpoetic" ones—"To a Mouse," "To a Louse," "To a Steamroller."

William Wordsworth's famous "Boy of Winander" (published both as part of *The Prelude* and as a poem in itself) begins almost as a poem about apostrophe. The Boy seems to be a virtuoso at getting the natural world to respond to his call. He weaves his fingers together and makes sounds:

> Uplifted, he, as though through an instrument,
> Blew mimic hootings to the silent owls,
> That they might answer him.—And they would shout
> Across the watery vale, and shout again,
> Responsive to his call,—with quivering peals,
> And long halloos, and screams, and echoes loud
> Redoubled and redoubled; concourse wild
> Of jocund din!

It is not unusual to find the poet's skill compared to playing an instrument. Mallarmé thinks of language and the self as instruments in his discussion of free verse and the nature of poetic language: "Mon sens regrette que le discours défaille à exprimer les objets par des touches y répondant en coloris et en allure, lesquelles existent dans *l'instrument* de la voix, parmi les langages et quelquefois chez un" (My senses regret that language fails to express objects by qualifiers that correspond to them in coloring or in bearing, which exist in the linguistic *instrument*, among languages, and sometimes in one).[4] Coleridge, in his poem "The Eolian Harp," sees the poet as being a sounding board for the voice of nature: "The mute still air / Is Music slumbering on her instrument."[5] In these poems, the question of where poetry comes from—often figured by a Muse—has a paradoxical answer. The poet's voice depends on the other voices that *play him.* In his celebrated "Ode to the West Wind," Shelley asks the wind to blow new life into him and his work, saying, "Drive my dead thoughts over the universe. . . . Be thou me!"—or, in effect, "I'll animate *you* if you'll animate *me.*" The mystery of poetic power is often the seemingly involuntary transformation of something material into an instrument capable of sounding the depths of humanity.

So central to the poetic function is apostrophe that in Whitman's 1860 edition of *Leaves of Grass,* a poem called "Apostroph" prefaced the section titled "Chants Democratic," as if an apostrophe were a kind of strophe. Giving voice to its revolution in poetic language, the poem is a long series of exclamations designed to touch everything with a new form of address. Here is an excerpt:

> O equality! O organic compacts! I am come to be your born poet!
> O whirl, contest, sounding and resounding! I am your poet, because I am
>   part of you;
> O days by-gone! Enthusiasts! Antecedents!
> O vast preparations for These States! O years!
> O what is now being sent forward thousands of years to come!
> O mediums! O to teach! To convey the invisible faith!
> To promulgate real things! To journey through all The States!
> O creation! O to-day! O laws! O unmitigated adoration!

By addressing anything and everything, Whitman thus turns this *apostrophe ad absurdum* into a democratic ideal.

In an interesting essay on apostrophe in *The Pursuit of Signs,* Jonathan Culler notes that apostrophe differs from other figures of speech that seek greater vividness in that apostrophe "makes its point by troping not on the meaning of a word but on the circuit or situation of communication itself."[6]

Apostrophe provides the poet with two immediate advantages, the second of which is seldom seen as such: (1) it brings the whole surrounding world into the speech event, and (2) it simplifies the poet's grammar. Instead of stating something (as one would have to do in description), the implicit whole sentence is stripped down, as if the poet were ringing each entity like a bell as he speaks of it; as if that *were* the poetic experience, and not a condition for it. The poetic performance suggests not that the poet is more intense than other people, but actually that he says less. The complete thought he utters is not "X is Y," but "I invoke X." The problem of poetic authority does not depend on what the poet says but on his capacity to *call*. He doesn't even have to say anything about X; he merely has to "ring" it. In fact apostrophe can be mere sound, amplified by the laws of sound waves, "redoubled and redoubled" or "sounding and resounding."

If we recall now what Benveniste says about personal pronouns, we can say that apostrophe enables the poet to transform an "I-it" relationship into an "I-thou" relationship, thus making a relation between persons out of was in fact a relation between a person and non-persons.

[margin note: I-it to I-thou]

As Jonathan Culler summarizes Quintilian, there is a curious indirectness in apostrophe that is something other than persuasion: Quintilian calls apostrophe "a diversion of our words to address someone other than the judge." In general, he advises against it "since it would certainly seem to be more natural that we should particularly address ourselves to those whose favor we desire to win." Nevertheless, sometimes "some striking expression of thought is necessary . . . which can be given point and vehemence when addressed to some other person than the judge."[7]

If we now recall the famous statement by J. S. Mill that "eloquence is heard; poetry is overheard," lyric poetry seems defined by this indirectness: neither direct communication nor direct persuasion, it is something other than an argument and is heard by someone other than the one it is addressed to. Neither the judge nor the addressee is really the object of the poetic utterance, but rather someone who witnesses both and registers the quality of speech from the subject, not the effect on the object. The speech situation—presence—is about the poet, and his or her feelings about the object; addressing something reveals the nature of the subject, not of the object, but the object is nevertheless affected, drawn into the speech event with the poet. The poet may simply be making that being-with happen. The poet is in the final analysis a subject as an object for the overhearer. So important is address for the poet, so important is it to supply his living voice, that Rousseau, in his account of the origin of languages, wonders why there is not a punctuation mark for the vocative: "The question mark, which we have, would be much less necessary, since a question is recognizable by its structure alone, at least in our language. . . . But how is one to distinguish, in writing, between a man one mentions and a man one addresses. There really is an equivocation which would be eliminated by a vocative mark."[8]

[margin note: Poetry, Address and Audience ↓ hm...]

Apostrophe thus has the same power, if not the same institutional back-ing, as Althusser's concept of ideology; *l'interpellation*—the hail—is an ad-dress to which one cannot not respond. Apostrophe turns toward anything the poet throws his voice to, and in so doing magnetizes a world around his call.

English (and all languages derived from Latin forms) gives no informa-tion about "I" and "you." Gender and number enter only with third person. "I" and "you" are pure shifters, purely positions in a discourse, and symmet-rical ones. The third person or non-person is not a pure shifter, in fact not a participant in the speech situation. Is it an accident that gender enters only with the non-person? Are the "I" and the "you" ungendered? In some lan-guages "I" and "you" *are* gendered: a female "you" would use different verb forms than a male. In those languages, therefore, gender is a function of the person, not just the non-person, and the role of pure shifter—address with-out gender or any other characteristics—does not exist. Does this make a difference? In a love lyric in English, any gender can address a poem to any gender, but in Hebrew, say, the poem cannot be hijacked for uses it has not authorized from the beginning. But one might ask whether it is true that the gender and race of a speaker are present only when they are grammatical.

To change the subject abruptly, as Wordsworth does, what happens when the Winander Boy unexpectedly dies?

> This boy was taken from his mates, and died
> In childhood, ere he was full twelve years old.
> Pre-eminent in beauty is the vale
> Where he was born and bred: the churchyard hangs
> Upon a slope above the village school;
> And through that churchyard when my way has led
> On summer-evenings, I believe that there
> A long half-hour together I have stood
> Mute—looking at the grave in which he lies!

This is quite a sudden and baffling turn of events. The personification of apostrophe dies, is buried, and Wordsworth pronounces his epitaph. What is Wordsworth doing here?

Wordsworth in fact wrote three essays on epitaphs. Samuel Johnson, too, wrote an essay about the subject, and appended to the section on Pope in his *Lives of the Poets* a discussion of Pope's contributions to the genre. Writing an essay on epitaphs seems like a minor but canonical thing for a poet—at least since Johnson—to do. Epitaphs were a poetic genre, in other words, and had two functions: to protect the corpse from desecration, and to monumentalize the memory of the deceased. Johnson emphasizes the identificatory importance of the deceased's proper name: "My name is Ozymandias, King of Kings! Look on my works, ye mighty, and despair!" However much Shelley may surround his king of kings with irony, at the heart of his "Ozymandias" is a classic epitaph. Interestingly, an epitaph centers on the proper name of the deceased and not that of the poet. Wordsworth sums up the epitaph's two major rhetorical styles: "Epitaphs . . . often personate the Deceased, and represent him as speaking from his own Tomb-stone"; and, "What is said comes from the Survivors directly . . . [when] the Survivors speak in their own Persons."[9] One of the constraints on the genre is that it should be short enough to be inscribed on a tomb, which not only excludes the lengths often gone to in other poems but excludes their agility, too. An epitaph is inscribed on a monument to the deceased, and as such it cannot display the virtuosity and the rapid ironies of the longer elegies—an important part of the works of individual poets. As the *Princeton Encyclopedia of Poetry and Poetics* has it, the epitaph is "a literary production suitable for placing on the grave of someone or something, though this need not actually be done or even intended." The stone as substrate enters into the thematic content of what is said in any case; the stone is unprotected, outdoors, exposed to the elements and impossible to keep free of—life. Inevitably, moss begins to grow on the tombstone. Many of the most uncanny lyrics take place in a mossy tomb:

Epitaphs
⇩

> I died for beauty, but was scarce
> Adjusted in the tomb,
> When one who died for truth was laid
> In an adjoining room. . . .
>
> And so, as kinsmen met a night,
> We talked between the rooms,
> Until the moss had reached our lips,
> And covered up our names.[10]

The moss chokes speech, but the stone is not destroyed by natural processes, just rendered unreadable.

Audre Lorde, too, evokes the grave as a mossy stone: in her poem, "There Are No Honest Poems about Dead Women," she asks, "Do we want / mossy quiet stealing over our scars."[11] In Toni Morrison's *Beloved,* the proper name of the ghost woman comes from the priest's ceremonial vocative:

> The welcoming cool of unchiseled headstones; the one she selected to lean against on tiptoe, her knees wide open as any grave. Pink as a fingernail it was, and sprinkled with glittering chips. Ten minutes, he said. You got ten minutes I'll do it for free.
>
> Ten minutes for seven letters. With another ten could she have gotten "Dearly" too? She had not thought to ask him and it bothered her still that it might have been possible—that for twenty minutes, a half hour, say, she could have had the whole thing, every word she heard the preacher say at the funeral (and all there was to say, surely) engraved on her baby's headstone: Dearly Beloved. But what she got, settled for, was the one word that mattered. She thought it would be enough, rutting among the headstones with the engraver, his young son looking on. . . . Not only did she have to live out her years in a house palsied by the baby's fury at having its throat cut, but those ten minutes she spent pressed up against dawn-colored stone studded with star-chips, her knees wide open as the grave, were longer than life, more alive, more pulsating than the baby blood that soaked her fingers like oil.[12]

Prosopopeia
⇓

The tendency of monuments to call out to the passing stranger brings to the fore the second rhetorical figure: *prosopopeia.* "Voice assumes mouth, eye, and finally face," says Paul de Man in an important essay that links Wordsworth's writings on epitaphs to autobiography and monuments; "a chain that is manifest in the etymology of the trope's name, *prosopon poien,* to confer a mask or a face."[13] The word *poiein* is from the same root as "poem," a made thing, a personification—creating a person, making a thing act like a person as a fiction or disguise. But also, poetry is an attempt to capture the cadences of speech, the feeling of meantness, of intention, and not merely grammatical correctness.

Wordsworth says several times that the meaning and impulse in the epitaph can come only from a conviction of man's immortality, but other poets label immortality itself a literary effect:

> Or I shall live your epitaph to make,
> Or you survive when I in earth am rotten,

From hence your memory death cannot take,
Although in me each part will be forgotten.
Your name from hence immortal life shall have,
Though I, once gone, to all the world must die.
The earth can yield me but a common grave,
When you entombed in men's eyes shall lie.
Your monument shall be my gentle verse,
Which eyes not yet created shall o'er-read,
And tongues to be your being shall rehearse,
When all the breathers of this world are dead.
    You still shall live—such virtue hath my pen—
    Where breath most breathes, ev'n in the mouths of men.

(Shakespeare, Sonnet 81)

Prosopopeia, the voice from beyond the grave, speaks *from* the grave. The epitaph uses rhetorical strategies that animate the dead and thus blur the boundary between life and death. It is precisely the person who has just died that is most alive. While waiting for Judgment Day, many poets hedge their bets: writing has a temporality that is not dependent on mortality.

Both Wordsworth and Johnson stress the coincidence of epitaphs with writing. Johnson: "Epitaphs seem entitled to more than common regard, as they are probably of the same age with the art of writing."[14] Wordsworth:

> It needs scarcely be said, that an epitaph presupposes a Monument, upon which it is to be engraven. Almost all nations have wished that certain external signs should point out the places where their Dead are interred. Among savage Tribes unacquainted with letters, this has mostly been done either by rude stones placed near the graves, or by Mounds of earth raised over them. . . . As soon as Nations learned the use of letters, Epitaphs were inscribed upon these Monuments.[15]

The impulse to epitaph is thus the same as the impulse to write: to mark something that can communicate with any passer-by. The epitaph is occasioned by a death and inscribed on a tomb, and the mourner himself or herself can and will also die: the grave will continue to be marked regardless of the mortality of the mourner. Sometimes the deceased is addressed by survivors, but an epitaph must be short (short enough to be carved on a tomb), and must mark memory, not display the mourner. The author must write like every mourner. In an elegy, a longer and more expressive genre, the poem can be the portrait and feelings of an individual mourner. In an epitaph, the opposite is true. What is marked and what calls out to the passerby has the proper name of the deceased, and the proper name of the mourner is not relevant.

Prosopopeia does not create a mouth here so much as reanimate one: rhetorically, the dead come alive, and the talking grave reverses the progress toward death. The deceased is animated, however, only to warn the traveler of mortality—the corpse speaks, but only of death. The solemnity of the speaking site that warns of the approach of death would affect the traveler less if one were certain of eternal life, yet the animate corpse speaks only of the grave, not of resurrection. The corpse does come back to life after death, perhaps, but the eternity he now enters consists entirely of a consciousness of the shortness of life.

Thus epitaphs, like all lyric poetry, depend on the creation of a poetic *voice.* However much a poem may be written or read *in fact* on the page, common wisdom says the "real" poem is spoken. This means that understanding the poem and hearing (or overhearing) the voice go together, and that the poem should not ultimately be up to something that cannot be assumed by a voice, a living speaker, a human mind. As Paul de Man puts it, "The principle of intelligibility, in lyric poetry, depends on the phenomenalization of the poetic voice. Our claim to understand a lyric text coincides with the actualization of a speaking voice."[16] An epitaph uses the fiction of life to animate a corpse and have it speak. For lyric poetry, it transforms a genre that depends on writing into the living and speaking presence of the deceased. What an epitaph accomplishes, then, is what all literature has to accomplish: to make poetry that convinces the reader that the poet speaks, that the poem gives access to his living voice—even though the individual author may have been buried for more than two hundred years. This is the immortality of literature brought about by *reading*—to bring alive the voice of a dead author. A text "speaks." This is how texts in general are assumed to work: they "say" something. Prosopopeia is thus *the* figure for reading. People who want to summarize *Of Grammatology* try to explain what Derrida "says." The meaning of a text is supposed to be conformable with structures of speech: when Derrida writes in an "unspeakable" grammar, when his sentences are something no one would say, when the writing

[margin note: voice as animating force behind epitaphs ⇓]

[margin note: literature as epitaph]

follows rhythms other than those of breath, that fact alone makes them seem obscure, although they transgress no grammatical rules.

The pedagogy of lyric poetry is constantly insisting (and readers are constantly forgetting) that the "I" in a poem should be called the "speaker" or the "persona," and should not be conflated with the biographical author. Many poets have made a point of considering this "speaker" as a function of the poem, and not the other way around. Emily Dickinson (to Higginson): "When I state myself, as the representative of the verse, it does not mean me, but a supposed person."[17] John Berryman (note on *The Dream Songs*): "The poem, then, whatever its wide cast of characters, is essentially about an imaginary character (not the poet, not me) named Henry, a white American sometimes in blackface, who has suffered an irreversible loss and talks about himself sometimes in the first person, sometimes in the third, sometimes even in the second; he has a friend, never named, who addresses him as Mr Bones and variants thereof. Requiescant in pace."[18]

The next figure that plays a prominent but not always recognized role in the relation between persons and things is *anthropomorphism*. Anthropomorphism—having a human-like character or form—is a rhetorical figure that sometimes allows authors to imagine things by projection, but is often part of language itself as an unconscious constraint on imagination. Anthropomorphisms are often catachreses: there is no other way to refer to a table leg, clock hand, or chair arm. When people noticed that their image of God was made in man's likeness, the whole religious world was jolted. By imagining God as a human, with benign or wrathful intentions and emotions, one unknowingly also imagines Him as having a color and a gender. Here is where the supposed difference between I/you and the third person nevertheless implies that one cannot assume address without gender and race.

Here is how the problem is discussed by two black women in Alice Walker's epistolary novel *The Color Purple:*

> Then she say: Tell me what your God look like, Celie.
> . . . Okay, I say. He big and old and tall and graybearded and white. He wear white robes and go barefooted.
> . . . Then she tell me this old white man is the same God she used to see when she prayed. If you wait to find God in church, Celie, she say, that's who is bound to show up, cause that's where he live.

How come? I ast.

Cause that's the one that's in the white folks' white bible.

Shug! I say. God wrote the bible, white folks had nothing to do with it.

How come he look just like them, then? She say. Only bigger? And a heap more hair. How come the bible just like everything else they make, all about them doing one thing and another, and all the colored folks doing is gitting cursed?

I never thought bout that.

. . . Ain't no way to read the bible and not think God white, she say. Then she sigh. When I found out I thought God was white, and a man, I lost interest. You mad cause he don't seem to listen to your prayers. Humph! Do the mayor listen to anything colored say? . . .

I know white people never listen to colored, period. If they do, they only listen long enough to tell you what to do.

Here's the thing, say Shug. The thing I believe. God is inside you and everybody else. You come into the world with God. But only them that search for it inside find it. And sometimes it just manifest itself even if you are not looking, or don't know what you looking for. . . .

It? I ast.

Yeah, It. God ain't a he or a she, but a It.

But what do it look like? I ast.

Don't look like nothing, she say. It ain't a picture show. It ain't something you can look at apart from everything else, including you. . . . My first step from the old man was trees. Then air. Then birds. Then other people. But one day when I was sitting quiet and feeling like a motherless child, which I was, it come to me: that feeling of being part of everything, not separate at all.[19]

Anthropomorphism is built into common expressions, whether they are willed for an occasion or not. Or the human reactions of natural phenomena may be part of the point a poet is making. The human drama is so strong that even inanimate things are affected. When Lamartine remembers his love for Elvire, whom he now mourns in his poem "Le Lac," he addresses a plea to the surroundings, imploring "everything" to say that "they have loved." In a typical epitaph, the tombstone itself is seen as being expressive—it weeps for the deceased, too.

Wisława Szymborska's poem "Conversation with a Stone" perfectly illustrates the booby traps that figurative language can lay for those who think they are avoiding it. Six times the speaker of the poem knocks on the stone's front door, and six times the stone refuses to let the speaker in. Despite the care taken to describe the lack of violence he or she will commit inside the stone and the avoidance of anthropocentric assumptions in the speaker's desire to get inside, the stone says, in effect, "I have no inside." When the speaker knocks on the stone's door a final time, the stone ends the quest by saying, "I don't have a door." The warning against projecting onto the non-human an inside/outside relation that characterizes the human is loud and clear, but all the while *that* is not the anthropomorphism the speaker is taking for granted. The stone finally growls at the speaker, "I don't even accept your assumption that I present a place to knock, or that you are left outside something that I can open." In a poem that expresses the desire to experience the thingness of a stone without anthropomorphic projections, Szymborska shows that such knowledge is even harder to obtain than the humble speaker thinks. Having a conversation with another presumed not to communicate is already something that only a human can imagine. Far from answering "No," the stone should not enter into dialogue in the first place. When the stone answers, "You're still anthropomorphizing me," the stone is right, but by speaking *at all* it stands up against anthropomorphism precisely by using it. The stone can't defend itself against anthropomorphism without resorting to anthropomorphism.

A related figure of speech, and one more self-consciously literary, also central to the relationship between persons and things, is of course *personification,* defined by the *American Heritage Dictionary* as "A. A person or thing typifying a certain quality or idea: an embodiment or exemplification: 'He's invisible, a walking personification of the Negative' (Ralph Ellison). B. A figure of speech in which inanimate objects or abstractions are endowed with human qualities or represented as having human form, as in Hunger sat shivering on the road or Flowers danced about the lawn. Also called prosopopeia. C. Artistic representation of an abstract quality or idea as a person."[20] The central function in this definition is "to represent": to endow a quality with a psychology, to confer on an idea a human form. Whereas anthropomorphism may also draw on the charms of treating the non-human as human, both figures seem to be in no doubt as to what "human form" consists of. Personification purposely represents an abstraction as a person. A quality that might form a part of a whole person becomes the whole around which a person is shaped.

The proper names of personifications are often keys to their meanings. The arbitrary relation that unites most signs to their referents does not obtain. The story of any character in a narrative seems to be crystallized in its name, the motivated suggestiveness of which is one of the first clues to the allegorical meaning of the text. Thus it is no accident that the heroine in Walt Disney's *Beauty and the Beast* is called Belle. In John Bunyan's *Pilgrim's Progress,* a character named Pliable becomes impatient and the margin glosses, "It's not enough to be pliable." Another character in *Pilgrim's Progress* named Talkative discourses fluently, but his speech turns out to be empty. Even the main character, Christian, represents a kind of everyman undertaking an indoctrination into Christianity. *Pilgrim's Progress* literalizes all the figures often used for the passage to Christianity—for example, Christian has to pass through a narrow gate—and raises to personified status all the qualities Christian possesses or rejects along the way. The distance between common and proper names is reduced: characters derive their names from the qualities they embody.

Figures for abstractions—the Statue of Liberty, for example—often owe their gender to the genders of the Latin nouns that lie behind them; abstractions in Romance languages are often female because the form abstractions take is often grammatically feminine. The elaborate femininity of many figures is therefore derived not from any femininity that is naturally associated with the ideas they embody, but from a grammatical property that begins with Latin.

Personification and anthropomorphism have an important thing in common: they are figures of being, not address. What matters in them is their predicates, not their voices. Instead of the phenomenalization of human speech, they endow the world with meaning centered around the representation of human being.

[margin note: But is voice also a predicate?]

While prosopopeia may sometimes seem contrived and old-fashioned in poetry, it is robust and necessary in advertising, where speaking things seem to be de rigueur. Let us therefore take a talking Barbie as an illustration of prosopopeia. It is well known that Barbie is not anatomically correct—there are no nipples on her breasts and no sexual organs beneath her underwear. This makes the pink button in the middle of her back seem like a sexual organ, all the more obscene for being accessible through a hole cut into the box. This seems to suggest a close association between sexual organs and vocal organs, between sexual potency and vocal potency, as a traditional understanding of the power of eloquence has always assumed. When the button is pressed, Barbie speaks, saying something about partying after the game on the weekend or some other fixture of high school life in the United States. Through Barbie's cheery voice, the user is thus acculturated into the proper role, schedule, and diet of the American girl, and, as befits this type of ideological acculturation, the 100,000 sentences Barbie can utter may be, admits the box, "similar." Vociferous protests forced Mattel to put "math is hard" under erasure, but nothing else was changed. The box also positions the doll in the most hair-inflated and welcoming ("feminine") way, and surrounds her with accessories and pink cardboard. The box states: "Costume may vary from that shown. Socks not included. Doll cannot stand alone." It is interesting to note how often direct address is used to call attention to the product. The box proclaims: "I say 100,000 different things! Try me!" "We should get a pizza after the game this weekend with Midge!" Barbie chirps.

In the world of doll collectors, a Barbie still in her original box is apparently worth much more than one without, and not only because she remains in better condition. The packaging is part of what the consumer buys: not only can Barbie not stand without the box, but in it she is positioned for maximum effect. Some dolls come in boxes that almost function like mirrors: the commodity is surrounded by a gleaming aura that adds glamour to its appeal. Indeed, it would be interesting to know just how packaging influences consumer choices. The failure of generic packaging suggests one answer.

A speaking thing can sell itself; if the purchaser responds to the speech of the object, he or she feels uninfluenced by human manipulation and therefore somehow not duped. We are supposed not to notice how absurd it is to be addressed by the Maalox Max bottle, or Mr. Clean, or Mrs. Butterworth, or the Quaker Oats man, or Aunt Jemima, or the Elidel man, or the Aflac duck. Lumière and Mrs. Potts would not be produced by the influence of a magic spell; they would be part of the everyday reality of consumerism. It is as though the relation between buyer and commodity were the entrance to a relationship—*res ipsa loquitur.* The beauties of the product are spoken about by that product, or by the animation and articulateness of a cat, a duck, a cow, a nose, a set of dentures. In one particularly daring use of prosopopeia, talking weeds in a television ad express the pathos of being sprayed by weed killer as they die. It is not necessary that the speaking thing be the product itself: those that the product gets the better of are objects of identification, too. The Juggernaut-like strength of the product is all the more believable if you are made to identify with its victims. The purchaser may be enlisting on his side a power that transcends representation while exulting over the defeat of a merely human-like rival. Alternatively the container or trademark person speaks for the commodity. Animation and voice give consumers a psychology and a humanness to identify with when buying heartburn remedies, cleaning fluids, pesticides, health drinks. It is as though the purchaser is seduced into feeling that buying the product is, in fact, carrying out the wishes of the product itself.

Karl Marx decried this tendency to feel a human relation with the product and to forget the human labor that produced it; he called the misguided transference of humanness from the maker to the product the "fetishism of the commodity":

> A commodity is therefore a mysterious thing, simply because in it the social character of men's labor appears to them as an objective character stamped upon the product of that labour; because the relation of the producers to the sum total of their own labour is presented to them as a social relation, existing not between themselves, but between the products of their labour. This is the reason why the products of labour become commodities, social things whose qualities are at the same time perceptible and imperceptible by the senses.[21]

This "solidifying" of human relations into intimacy with things may depend on figures of the animation of the inanimate, but the opposite trajectory is usually depicted as catastrophic. People turning to stone hardly inspire the positive feelings triggered by statues coming alive. The "foul Propoetides" that surround and disgust Pygmalion have so little shame that they unblushingly turn first to prostitution and then to stone. Medusa's naked glance turns men to stone, so that her beheader, Perseus, gets the upper hand only by looking at her in a mirror. Even given the confusion between the vocabulary of death and the vocabulary of sex (both a corpse and a penis are "stiff"; testicles are often referred to as "stones" and erections as "bones"; orgasm is known as "the little death"; the ecstasy of "going outside oneself" suggests that the most intense moments of life resemble non-life most closely), a person turning to stone is usually bad, while a stone coming to life is desirable. But perhaps it is the confusion of the two realms that is really, and unavowedly, attractive. Walter Benjamin, in his study of the Paris

arcades and the rise of commodity capitalism, speaks often of "the sex appeal of the inorganic."[22] The fetishism of the commodity might well reveal
the side of desire that neither Marx nor Pygmalion can face.

It is no surprise, therefore, to find that the terms that depict a process of
turning something nebulous into something solid are not rhetorical terms
but names for an involuntary and lamented process. Rhetorical terms aid
in the expression of desire; no one seeks new ways to say what is *not* desired. "Reification," for instance, seems the mirror image of "anthropomorphism"—becoming-thing versus becoming-man—except that the impulse
to find a name for such a process has totally different motivations. Whereas
treating a thing like a man locates it in a human world, treating a man like a
thing locates human beings in the realm of the inhuman. There could be
something sobering and lucid about this realm, but it is never welcomed,
never consciously fantasized as an object of desire. In a dictionary of Marxist
terms, "reification" is defined as follows:

> The act (or result of the act) of transforming human properties, relations, and
> actions of man-produced things which have become (and which are imagined
> as originally independent) of man and govern his life. Also transformation of
> human beings into thing-like beings which do not behave in a human way
> but according to the laws of the thing-world. Reification is a "special" case of
> ALIENATION, its most radical and widespread form characteristic of modern
> capitalist society.[23]

In imagining a speaking thing, then, one transfers the social character of labor into a sociability among objects, sucking the humanness out of the
makers and injecting it into the products. The makers' role is reduced to
that of adjunct to the product. The elevation of a quality to a psychology in
personification is reversed: here a psychology is reduced to a quality, and the
only part that matters is the one needed to produce the thing. The human
being is alienated from its whole self and becomes a mere producing mechanism. Benjamin's fascination with Baudelaire as a symptom of this phase is
summed up in his famous 1938 letter to Horkheimer: "Baudelaire's unique
importance consists in having been the first one, and the most unswerving,
to have apprehended, in both senses of the word, the productive energy of
the individual alienated from himself—agnosticized and heightened through
concretization."[24] There is in the modern capitalist world, in other words, a

productiveness of self-alienation that Baudelaire makes poetry out of, and that one denies to humanness at one's peril.

Benjamin several times notes the process of concretization in linguistic usage. What begins as an abstraction solidifies into a thing. So, for example, he says of souvenirs: "The things sold in the arcades are souvenirs [*Andenken*]. The 'souvenir' is the form of the commodity in the arcades. One always buys only mementos of the commodity and of the arcade. Rise of the souvenir industry."[25] A memory in the mind hardens into a memento; a trip to the Eiffel Tower becomes a plastic image of it. The comforter that begins by designating the Holy Ghost ends up as an item of bedding. Perhaps this is why turning to stone is so dire: the process of being hardened, externalized, mass produced, and sold is the *normal* story of a commodity.

Marx nevertheless tries to protest against it, seeing in such processes of reification precisely the dehumanization he decries in capitalism. He associates this type of fetishism with all that is irrational in religion and mysticism. He likens the "fetishism of the commodity" to the false worship of things, and to the desire for magic and mystery that mature human beings should outgrow. Therefore it is astonishing to see him sum up his case by imagining things speaking: "Could commodities themselves speak, they would say . . ." He then has them voice the delusion they foster, but this scene of prosopopeia is nevertheless a sign that the very thing he is arguing against is too strong for him. It is simply irresistible to imagine the social life of commodities without people.

Aimé Césaire fulminates against a related process of turning persons into things:

> No human contact, but relations of domination and submission which turn the colonizing man into a classroom monitor, an army sergeant, a prison guard, a slave driver, and the indigenous man into an instrument of production.
>
> My turn to state an equation: colonization = "thingification" [*chosification*].[26]

Both capitalism and colonization (which are tied closely together) tend to turn persons into things so that everything serves the needs and centrality of commodities. Here, colonized man loses his humanity and becomes a thing to extend the reach of capitalism itself.

The rhetorical figures that confer on things some properties of persons are thus *apostrophe, prosopopeia, anthropomorphism,* and *personification.* The parallel processes of turning persons into things does not offer itself in the form of a figure, but suggests that figures that increase humanness are by nature working against a decline of humanness and a thingification that go on all the time and have only accelerated with commodity capitalism.

Summary...

Things

Chapter Two

The Poetics of Things

MARIANNE MOORE AND FRANCIS PONGE

Modern poems often set out to capture what is at the farthest remove from humanness—the world as it really is and not the world inflected by human interests or, still less, shaped by aesthetic forms. When William Carlos Williams claimed that in poetry there should be "no ideas but in things," he was not only mandating that poems should find the perfect concrete image to communicate every idea, but also suggesting that ideas without things are empty fantasies, concepts dreamed up by human minds that might correspond to no reality.

This concept of a thing untainted by human perception is itself a tenacious fantasy throughout history. Immanuel Kant called it the *Ding an sich*—"the thing in itself." In his *Critique of Pure Reason* he asks whether non-empirical (that is, "pure") knowledge is possible. Most of human knowledge is derived from experience, but Kant begins with a priori non-empirical forms (time and space) that are not objects for empirical knowledge but that make empirical knowledge itself possible. All empirical knowledge depends on perception by sense organs, but Kant wonders whether there can be pure intelligible understanding independent of the senses (knowledge of God). The senses can perceive only the appearance of the object, not the object in

[margin, handwritten:] Kant: Is "pure" knowledge possible?

itself. God or an object in itself would be intelligible, not sensible, knowl-edge. Kant calls objects of the senses *phenomena* and objects that might be known only by the mind *noumena*. Because human knowledge does not ex-tend beyond appearances that can be perceived by the senses, we can know nothing beyond the mere existence of such noumena. God and the *Ding an sich* remain unknown. Nevertheless, poetry often attempts to present this impossible knowledge of the thing whose face is turned away."

We will begin our investigation of things in poetry with an address to a self-consciously *unpoetic* object in a poem by Marianne Moore. This is not so much a thing ignored by history as a thing that hasn't been poetically addressed before. The classical moves around the thing bring it into the history of poetry, but only to emphasize how *in*appropriate it is for poetic address. The poem consists of telling the thing why poets have not sung about it before. The poem is a tirade against the object it addresses. The poem's animus against its object extends so far that even if some poetic cliché chooses to fraternize with the ungainly object, the addresser will not change his mind about it, but only admit the attention of its opposite as a possibility.

In what precedes, I have been attempting to paraphrase Marianne Moore's lyric apostrophe "To a Steamroller," which reads:

The illustration
is nothing to you without the application.
        You lack half wit. You crush all the particles down
        into close conformity, and then walk back and forth on them.

Sparkling chips of rock
are crushed down to the level of the parent block.
        Were not "impersonal judgment in aesthetic
        matters, a metaphysical impossibility," you

might fairly achieve
it. As for butterflies, I can hardly conceive
        of one's attending on you, but to question
        the congruence of the complement is vain, if it exists.[1]

The aim of the steamroller's action is "close conformity," an aim that, like an aesthetic aim, has as its center—at the heart of the word, in fact—the shap-

conclusion: we can only know phenomenon... no pure knowledge...

ing of a "form." No matter what the steamroller starts with, it produces   steamroller
"close conformity" by the end, and ends up making a "form" that will per-   ⇩
haps call for a "close reading." Everything "illustrative" is pressed into service as an "application": Moore takes the etymology of "application," meaning "pressure on a folded surface to make it flat," as being literally what a
steamroller does. "You walk back and forth on them," however, is an anthropomorphism: steamrollers don't have legs. But humans don't literally
"walk all over" those they dominate, either: the expression, while it does
imply legs, is figurative in the human's case so that the human's action is
more like that of a machine. A human being crushes other people *as if* walking on them, but doesn't actually walk; what the human does resembles   ✓
nothing so much as the action of a steamroller. The poem here uses an anthropomorphism that refers to human form all right, but it is humanity
behaving like a machine. "You lack half wit," too, expresses a difference between persons and things that becomes tangled in confusion: if someone is a
half-wit, he is without the normal brain of a human, but to *lack* half
wit implies that its opposite would be "wit." "You lack half wit" could
mean "you don't even have the brains of an idiot," or it could mean "you
can't even laugh at the ridiculous figure you make" or even "you lack self-
consciousness."

Marianne Moore's poetry is full of embedded quotations, which she
calls "flies trapped in amber." Life becoming stone is exactly the process
the steamroller aims to achieve, so that there is a resemblance between
Marianne Moore grinding other people's words into her poetry and the
steamroller crushing all particles down to the level of the parent block. The
quotation in these lines comes from an article by Lawrence Gilman on the
music of Leo Ornstein—hardly a well-known text. Moore's collection of
quotations resembles a magpie's nest more than a traditional list of prior
greatest hits ready to be used in allusions. What Moore achieves by the use
of quotations is a disowning of sentiments that does not necessitate discard-
ing them. In this case the assertion that "impersonal judgment in aesthetic
matters is a metaphysical impossibility" is never made, not even by Gilman,
who claims to have judged Ornstein impartially "were not impersonal judgment in aesthetic matters a metaphysical impossibility." Gilman and Moore,
in other words, do not claim this belief as their own but need it in someone
else's mouth in order to complete their aesthetic picture. Yet impersonal
judgment in aesthetic matters is just what Moore seems to hold against the

steamroller: by reducing everything to close conformity, the steamroller treats everything alike. Only a "person" would be able to make the discriminations without which aesthetic judgment is an absurdity.

Moore's stanzas begin by obeying grammatical form, but by the end, "you," "it," and "I" start to appear chaotically, hanging out of the stanzas and making the reader notice them. The poem is very nonchalant about introducing its final surprise. It says, "As for butterflies. . ." as if one had been talking about them all along, instead of introducing them here. If a butterfly—one of nature's most fleeting and fragile creatures—should happen to alight on the steamroller, the poet will neither question the appropriateness of its being there nor establish a whole poetics to accommodate it. She will just observe its anomalous beauty and do nothing.

What is the form and effect of address in this poem? It seems as though Moore has chosen the most traditional form to write about the most untraditional object. She teases the addressee with familiarity as well as insult: "You lack half wit," and so on, implies that they have had this disagreement before and will have it again, that they represent known sides in an argument. When, in the third stanza, the poet introduces an "I," the grammar reinforces the bantering tone: "I can hardly conceive of one's attending on you." To include the "I" in the act of addressing a "you" is either not done (most of Shelley's "Ode to Liberty") or concerns the poet alone ("Do I wake or sleep?") and not the relationship between the poet and the addressee. Such a relationship presumes and perpetuates a certain intimacy; Moore's poetics will be affected by questions that the addressee makes one raise. The "I" and the "you" maintain their differences while paradoxically getting to know each other better. The "I" and the "you" behave like persons, in other words, while the butterfly, if it exists, remains a non-person. But there is no attempt to hide, in this poem, the human stakes represented by things—the poem is not interested in getting to the thingness of the thing by stripping away the human presence.

Such an effort cannot be ruled out from a collection of poems that claim to take the side of things. Francis Ponge, in entitling his volume *Le Parti pris des choses,* would seem to be from the outset on the side of the non-human. But once the reader looks into the volume, things are not quite so clear. We will take Ponge's poem about an oyster as a representative example. The poem begins, "L'huître, de la grosseur d'un galet moyen, est d'une apparence plus rugueuse, d'une couleur moins unie, brillament blanchâtre." The first thing the reader might remark is that the poem does not *address* its object; it

describes it. Indeed, it is careful to seem to do so objectively and without pre-
conception. A relation of call and response does not humanize the poem;
neither is the object described as being in any way anthropomorphic. As the
poem goes on, however, what is described are the difficulties of opening, the
satisfactions of eating, and the delight of observing an oyster from a decidedly human point of view. This is hardly an oyster in the wild, and *homo
sapiens* is taken for granted as the appropriate even though inept figure
for whom the oyster exists. Are human beings, then, excluded or the rai-
son d'être for taking the side of things? It is time, perhaps, to quote the entire poem:

L'huître, de la grosseur d'un galet moyen, est d'une apparence plus rugueuse,
d'une couleur moins unie, brillamment blanchâtre. C'est un monde
opiniâtrement clos. Pourtant on peut l'ouvrir: il faut alors la tenir au creux
d'un torchon, se servir d'un couteau ébréché et peu franc, s'y reprendre à
plusieurs fois. Les doigts curieux s'y coupent, s'y casse les ongles: c'est un travail grossier. Les coups qu'on lui porte marquent son enveloppe de ronds
blancs, d'une sorte de halos.

A l'intérieur l'on trouve tout un monde, à boire et à manger: sous un
firmament (à proprement parler) de nacre, les cieux d'en-dessus s'affaissent
sur les cieux d'en-dessous, pour ne plus former qu'une mare, un sachet
visqueux et verdâtre, qui flue et refloue à l'odeur et à la vue, frangé d'une
dentelle noirâtre sur les bords.

Parfois très rare une formule perle à leur gosier de nacre, d'où l'on trouve
aussitôt à s'orner.[2]

*   *   *

"THE OYSTER"

The oyster, about as big as a fair-sized pebble, is rougher, less evenly colored,
brightly whitish. It is a world stubbornly closed. Yet it can be opened: one
must hold it in a cloth, use a dull jagged knife, and try more than once. Avid
fingers get cut, nails get chipped: a rough job. The repeated pryings mark its
cover with white rings, like haloes.

Inside one finds a whole world, to eat and drink; under a *firmament* (properly speaking) of nacre, the skies above collapse on the skies below, forming
nothing but a puddle, a viscous greenish blob that ebbs and flows on sight
and smell, fringed with blackish lace along the edge.

Once in a rare while a globule pearls in its nacre throat, with which one
instantly seeks to adorn oneself.[3]

In an interview with Philippe Sollers, Ponge tells an anecdote about reading his poetry at the University of Chicago. After his talk, a professor
who had written on Robbe-Grillet accused him of sneaking a bit of anthropomorphism into the description of things, which the professor assumed
should be opaque to humans: "Mais enfin, avouez, dans votre huître, nous
avons, par exemple, 'C'est un monde opiniâtrement clos': Enfin, voilà bien
de l'anthropomorphisme! L'huître n'est pas opiniâtre! Opiniâtre, c'est un
caractère humain!'" ("But you have to admit that in your oyster is a 'stubbornly closed world': that's an anthropomorphism! The oyster is not stub-
born! Stubbornness is a human trait!")[4]

Ponge answered with annoyance that he had chosen a lot of words that
ended with -^tre because of the word *huître,* and that this was one of them.
Instead of defining poetry as something containing rhyming words at the
ends of lines, Ponge had written a prose piece with words that "rhyme"
with the object. He chose them for their letters, not their sense. Even the
pronouns used signify that the human presence is both impersonal and general. Ponge uses *on* (or the more euphonious *l'on*) as the pronoun for the
perceiver. This is a third person that *intends* to be a non-person, and takes
the poem still farther out of the realm of direct address.

Still, if the sense of words seems to bring in an anthropomorphic dimension, this does not upset Ponge; such human flavorings are unavoidable in
human language. He replies to the Chicago professor, "Comment ne pas
être anthropomorphe? Cela, c'est une très grande question, mais vous n'avez
tenu aucun compte de l'analyse *littérale* que j'ai faite de mon texte." ("How
can one not be anthropomorphic? That's a big question, but you haven't
taken any account of the *literal* analysis I performed on my text.") In discussing the phrase "brillamment blanchâtre," Ponge notes that the word
brillamment has a positive connotation, while *blanchâtre* pulls toward the
negative, without any intention of *his*. "Evidemment, nous sommes dans
l'anthropomorphisme à partir du moment où nous constatons objective-
ment que les mots sont affectés d'un coefficient moral," he sighs.[5] ("Ob-
viously, we're in anthromorphism from the moment we understand that
words have a moral coefficient.") *Moral,* in French, is much more encompassing than "moral" in English. As soon as words have a coloration of feeling—which is often part of their definition as well as their usage—the human shaping presence is there. To eliminate anthropomorphism would in
essence be to eliminate language itself: what other species uses it?

'Feeling'
in
Language

One of the aspects of language Ponge draws on to produce his often witty poems about things is literality. Upon opening an oyster, the consumer is presented with a whole world in which to part the waters below from the waters above. The word *firmament* is used in its etymological sense as a solid top and bottom to the world, an upper and lower dome that certain ancients believed composed the cosmos. "Firmament," says Ponge in the same interview, "c'est donc un peu pédant. On ne m'a pas fait ce reproche; on aurait pu me le faire."[6] ("Firmament is a bit pedantic. I haven't been subjected to that reproach, but I could have been.") With the mixed clichés ("trouver un monde," "à boire et à manger"), the learned etymologies ("le firmament"), the double meanings ("l'expression," when it is a matter of squeezing an orange), Ponge puts language through all its tricks, and that is his aim. Taking the side of things is really a way of playing with words.

The poem's last paragraph is short and concerns an experience the consumer rarely has: a pearl is lodged in the oyster's throat. "Une formule perle à leur gosier de nacre." Ponge uses the verb "to pearl" and not the noun "pearl" to stress the similarity between the poet and the oyster: both have something in their throat. "Formula," like "firmament," is being used in its etymological sense: "a little form." The pearl, an ornament, is a little form. But the word "form," again, suggests an aesthetic domain. Like Moore's "close conformity," Ponge's *formule* suggests that, however distant or inappropriate an object may seem, the poet of things—at least in these two cases—is still working on "form."

? · · · · ·

form ?

Is presence itself the basis of address, inferred by the way we "speak" w/o voice?

Chapter Three

Monuments

T he adjective "monumental" normally means "huge" or, as one might say colloquially, "awesome." And many monuments—Mount Rushmore, Crazy Horse Memorial, Bunker Hill Monument, Washington Monument—are indeed colossal. It is there that we learn how many tons of rock have been blasted or carved for a national memory. A monument usually stands for a collective memory, and viewers are meant to behold them with subservience and awe. Statues honoring Confederate heroes—plus Arthur Ashe—are the pride of Richmond, Virginia: what was, and perhaps still is, honored there is a glorious "lost cause" that divided rather than unified the nation. But the memorials still have a collective, even political, air.

In Alfred Hitchcock's film *North by Northwest,* tiny human actors scamper about on the giant brows of Mount Rushmore. The humor and irony in the treatment of the plight of a tiny, disabused human caretaker devoted to a gigantic but unmanageable monument is beautifully captured in Sylvia Plath's "Colossus":

> I shall never get you put together entirely,
> Pieced, glued, and properly jointed.

Mule-bray, pig-grunt and bawdy cackles
Proceed from your great lips.
It's worse than a barnyard.

Perhaps you consider yourself an oracle,
Mouthpiece of the dead, or of some god or other.
Thirty years now I have labored
To dredge the silt from your throat.
I am none the wiser.

Scaling little ladders with gluepots and pails of Lysol
I crawl like an ant in mourning
Over the weedy acres of your brow
To mend the immense skull plates and clear
The bald, white tumuli of your eyes. . . .[1]

The fascination of climbing on a huge being undoubtedly goes back to earliest childhood, and, indeed, the easy, demystified intimacy in Plath's poem corresponds to the performance of a filial duty. A monument is a parent, then, or perhaps the ideology of filial obligations. The more one lacks respect for the monument, the more one doesn't buy into whatever collective ideal it represents.

The idea of a ruined monument seems to have great appeal; it signals, at least, the death of a collective belief. At the end of the film *Planet of the Apes,* the huge hand of a buried Statue of Liberty tells of a human catastrophe in the past.

When one searches "monument" on the Internet, one finds many companies offering "monuments and grave markers." The commemoration thus takes place in the face of death. "Monument" is another word for "tombstone." Monuments often commemorate the war dead; when they honor the memory of a battle, it is as likely to be a defeat as a victory.

Hence the irony of a ruined monument to greatness like that commemorated in Shelley's "Ozymandias." The sneering prosopopeia is meant as a taunt from the dead monarch—"Look on my works, ye mighty, and despair!"—his voiced epitaph keeping him forever alive. If the king is thus impervious to history, however, his works and surroundings are not: "Nothing beside remains." The "despair" of the mighty at Ozymandias's example is diametrically opposite to what it was before: once it was perhaps impossible to equal Ozymandias's greatness, but now the mighty should tremble even more before the ruins of anything subject to time. If even Ozymandias

is devastated, what hope is there of leaving a permanent memory of greatness?

Nevertheless, the poem's center is the sculptor's ability to read, and reproduce, the king's facial expressions in a work of art, a monument to his
monarchy.

> . . . its sculptor well those passions read
> Which yet survive, stamped on these lifeless things,
> The hand that mocked them. . .

Indeed, the poem's message hangs on the relation between the transitive and
the intransitive meanings of the verb "survive." If the verb is intransitive, the
poem is talking about now, but if the verb is transitive, it speaks about
stone's ability to outlast its sculptor. Both readings say something about
mortality, but not at all the same thing. One reading identifies the weakness
of the poet's contemporaries; the other makes a comparison between the inanimate and the mortal. Mortals can either be dead or exhibit the same
flaws as Ozymandias's contemporaries; the monument may outlast the sen-
timent it commemorates and at the same time it may itself be subject to the
laws of matter.

Because monuments are so often huge, there is a certain piquancy in
their miniaturization in a sonnet. "The Sonnet" by Dante Gabriel Rossetti
self-consciously works the paradox of size to locate in a small thing the
two faces of a monument: one turned toward death; the other turned toward life.

> A Sonnet is a moment's monument,—
>   Memorial from the Soul's eternity
>   To one dead deathless hour. Look that it be,
> Whether for lustral rite or dire portent,
> Of its own arduous fullness reverent:
>   Carve it in ivory or in ebony,
>   As Day or Night may rule; and let Time see
> Its flowering crest impearled and orient.
>
> A Sonnet is a coin: its face reveals
>   The soul—its converse to what Power 'tis due:
> Whether for tribute to the august appeals
>   Of Life, or dower in Love's high retinue,

It serve; or, 'mid the dark wharf's cavernous breath,
In Charon's palm it pay the toll to Death.

Rossetti's description of the moment commemorated by the sonnet—"one
dead deathless hour"—is not just a paradox but the very paradox of literature. It already forms the argument of that other maker of sonnets: Shakespeare. The superiority of writing as a monument lies in the fact that its materiality is not subject to the ravages of time. Shakespeare writes explicitly:
"Not marble, nor the gilded monuments / Of princes, shall outlive this
powerful rhyme." It is an accident of history if monuments survive (in both
the transitive and the intransitive senses), but writing transcends its material
base. Stone survives the sculptor, but writing survives the stone. "Life" becomes deathless: "You live in this, and dwell in lovers' eyes." A sonnet can
confer eternal life.

Of course, Shakespeare himself inspired many monuments, many of
which are sonnets. This one by Matthew Arnold honors Shakespeare as the
anchor and ideal of canonical authority:

"SHAKESPEARE"
Others abide our question. Thou art free.
We ask and ask—thou smilest and art still,
Out-topping knowledge. For the loftiest hill,
Who to the stars uncrowns his majesty,

Planting his steadfast footsteps in the sea,
Making the heaven of heavens his dwelling place,
Spares but the cloudy border of his base
To the foiled searching of mortality;

And thou, who didst the stars and sunbeams know,
Self-schooled, self-scanned, self-honored, self-secure,
Didst tread on earth unguessed at.—Better so!

All pains the immortal spirit must endure,
All weakness which impairs, all griefs which bow,
Find their sole speech in that victorious brow.

Despite the apparent abjection of the celebrant, the sonnets by Arnold and
Rossetti turn away from their object in two ways. Their form is that of a
French or Petrarchan sonnet; Rossetti's has the classic continental form of a

major and minor premise, and the first and second quatrains are joined in a common rhyme scheme. Yet both these sonnets end with two rhyming lines, in the tradition of the Shakespearean sonnet. Their ambivalence is even more notable in the fluctuations of their address. Rossetti sometimes wants to define the sonnet ("A Sonnet is . . .") and sometimes to address its would-be makers ("Look that it be . . . Carve it in . . ."). He wants both to say what a sonnet *is* and to give advice about writing one. Arnold wants both to talk to Shakespeare and to contemplate him from a distance. His sonnet starts out with a bold address: "Others abide our question. Thou art free." But by the end he says, "Find their sole speech in *that* victorious brow," not "*thy* victorious brow." The word "brow" is a sure sign of a monument: derived from hugeness, it also connotes respectful distance. One of the attributes of Shakespeare's genius, according to the poem, is silence: "thou smilest and art still." In other words, if people are inspired by Shakespeare, it is neither to address nor to hear him. The poem is addressed to him because he "out-tops" anything its author can know. Admirers find their voices by *contemplating the figure,* not hearing the speech, of Shakespeare.

This would seem to be one of the reasons behind a monument: the figure or structure is there to express the inexpressible, to remember the unarticulable. The heart-stopping and language-stopping loss in mourning would explain why there are so many monuments to the dead. It is canonical to say that the real thing is ineffable: "Heard melodies are sweet, but those unheard are sweeter," and so on.

Milton's poem about Shakespeare affirms this, although in a backhanded way. It begins:

> What needs my Shakespeare for his honored bones
> The labor of an age in piléd stones?
> Or that his hallowed relics should be hid
> Under a star-ypointing pyramid?
> Dear son of Memory, great heir of fame,
> What need'st thou such weak witness of thy name?

Stone monuments enclose the relics of the person, but it is Shakespeare's *text,* not Shakespeare's *bones* that make the real monument: "Thou in our wonder and astonishment / Hast built thyself a livelong monument." "Astonishment," which I first assumed had some "stony" etymology, comes from "thunder"—to be astonished is to be thunderstruck. And "livelong," which may be playing on the same false origin I attributed to it, comes not from "life" but from the Old English *leof,* "dear." While reading and remembering the text as if it were an oracle ("Those delphic lines with deep impression took") may be a better and more living monument than the stones it is starting to resemble, the poem holds out as a lure the crossing of properties that it accomplishes in subsequent lines: "Then thou, our fancy of itself bereaving, / Dost make us marble with too much conceiving;" which for Paul de Man, we recall, evokes the latent threat in any animation of the inanimate, "that the living are struck dumb, frozen in their own death."[2] Reading Shakespeare may be a better monument than stone, but it may also immobilize the reader in his own death, making reading "dead" instead of commemoration "alive."

A monument, then, is supposed to confer on a memory the immortality that only inanimate things can possess. It seeks, through "slow-endeavoring art," to honor something mere living memory might forget, or something that demands a collective, not an individual, response. Yet the durability and decontextualization involved in canonical art makes it often function like a monument, as in these lines by Gwendolyn Brooks dedicating the "Chicago Picasso": "Does man love Art? Man visits Art, but squirms. / . . . / We do not hug the Mona Lisa."[3] The poem begins with an epigraph from the *Chicago Sun-Times,* emphasizing the public nature of the ceremony, and possibly its private doubts: "Mayor Daley tugged a white ribbon, loosing the blue percale wrap. A hearty cheer went up as the covering slipped off the big steel sculpture that looks at once like a bird and a woman."

The difficulty of understanding a monument if one does not share the memory it preserves, if one sees it as a "thing," is beautifully evoked in a poem by Elizabeth Bishop, in which a narrator takes another person on a walk designed to afford a view of the monument the narrator has happened upon. When the other person catches sight of the nondescript object, he or she exclaims,

"Why did you bring me here to see it?
A temple of crates in cramped and crated scenery,
what can it prove?

I am tired of breathing this eroded air,
this dryness in which the monument is cracking."[4]

The monument, then, is affected by the elements around it; the friend acts as though a monument shouldn't be. The speaker goes mentally down the list of things that make this wooden thing a monument:

The monument's an object, yet those decorations,
Carelessly nailed, looking like nothing at all,
Give it away as having life, and wishing;
Wanting to be a monument, to cherish something.
The crudest scroll-work says "commemorate" . . .

The same "purposiveness without purpose" that makes a thing a work of art makes up a monument: "It is the beginning of a painting, / A piece of sculpture, or poem, or monument." And yet, fantasies of a tomb make it public, political:

An ancient principality whose artist-prince
Might have wanted to build a monument
To mark a tomb or boundary . . .
. . . . .
It may be solid, may be hollow.
The bones of the artist-prince may be inside . . .

If a monument marks the boundary between life and death, it does so by making the dead belong to the public. The line between public and private corresponds to the line between life and death. Although mourning might seem like an intensely private experience, *group* experience would be inconceivable if it were impossible to share a corpse. And memory is always, eventually if not immediately, memory of the dead. Doesn't one refer to the dead when one says "in *memory* of"?

Monuments to ideas suffer from many of the same constraints as allegory: many allegorical personae are feminine because most abstract entities in Latin-derived languages are feminine. Many abstract ideas, in other words, are feminine not because the concept is feminine but because the *word* is.

"reality
of
rhetoric"

We may recognize the fictitiousness of the femininity of certain ideas, but it still requires some certainty about what a woman is. In Delacroix's painting *Liberty Leading the People,* Liberty is a sexually active "free woman," whose wardrobe malfunction is a sign of her sexiness, just as "liberty" takes on a sexual connotation. In the Statue of Liberty, however, the burden of representing U.S. ideals instead of the French Revolution, along with the Eiffel engineering of her hugeness,[5] transforms her into "a staid and matronly conception of the wild thing," writes Marina Warner.[6]

This "mighty woman," this "Mother of Exiles," as Emma Lazarus puts it in her poem emblazoned on the statue's pedestal, is the flip side (or perhaps the same) of the Parnassian "bad mother": she is the fantasy of the "good mother," indeed the phallic mother, the authority-tenderness of early childhood, the figure Baudelaire evokes in his poem "La géante." He would like to:

Parcourir à loisir ses magnifiques formes;
Ramper sur le versant de ses genoux énormes,
Et parfois en été, quand les soleils malsains,
Lasse, la font s'étendre à travers la campagne,
Dormir nonchalamment à l'ombre de ses seins,
Comme un hameau paisible au pied d'une montagne.

*   *   *

Wander at leisure over her magnificent forms,
Crawl on the slope of her enormous knees,
And sometimes, in summer, when unhealthy suns,
Make her stretch out, exhausted, across the countryside,
Sleep nonchalantly in the shade of her breasts,
Like a peaceful hamlet at the foot of a mountain.

(Translation mine.)

Intimacy with a giant can begin as adoration: "Marble-heavy, a bag full of God, / Ghastly statue with one gray toe," intones Plath to her hated-loved Daddy before getting out her pail of Lysol to dedicate herself to a huge wreck she knows isn't worth worshipping.[7] The transformation of an idol of childhood into an aesthetic of lack is for both these poets compensation for and anger at the disappearance of the gigantic divinities of childhood.

While Baudelaire laments a lost life as irretrievable but regretted, Plath (in her poem "In Plaster") describes the allure of the needed, and the fear of doing without it.

> This new absolutely white person and the old yellow one
> And the white person is certainly the superior one.
> She doesn't need food, she is one of the real saints.
> At the beginning I hated her, she had no personality—
> She lay in bed with me like a dead body
> And I was scared, because she was shaped just the way I was
> Only much whiter and unbreakable and with no complaints.
> I couldn't sleep for a week, she was so cold.
> . . . . .
> . . . she thought she was immortal . . .[8]

While Plath wants to annihilate any temptation to monumentality, Baudelaire incorporates the worship of the past into his aesthetic ideal: "Les poètes, devant mes grandes attitudes, / Que j'ai l'air d'emprunter aux plus fiers monuments" ("Poets, before my impressive attitudes / That I seem to have borrowed from the proudest monuments" [translation mine]), says Beauty. In *Les Fleurs du mal,* then, monuments stand as an ideal for art; in Plath's poems, as an unhealthy temptation.

Marina Warner's treatment of New York's Statue of Liberty does neither of these things, but rather describes in detail the experience of visiting it in its material hugeness. Rather than being an idea or an ideal, the statue presents sheets of copper, green paint, narrow stairways. The chapter of her *Monuments and Maidens* devoted to the Statue of Liberty begins with an address to the visitor:

> Climb inside her head and look out of one of the jewels in her crown, and you will see a helicopter hovering opposite, and the stargazing bowls of camera lenses staring back at you. The passengers are waving, delighted by human puniness beside the looming face of the colossus.[9] But unlike them, you are inside her and cannot tell how small you seem. . . .
>
> The notices at the bottom of the one hundred and seventy-one steps warn that the view is best from Liberty's pedestal, and that far above, inside her seven-pointed crown, vision is restricted. But everyone swarms up to the top inside her, for the voyage obeys imagination's logic and requires ascent into the heart and mind of Liberty. Departure, sailing across the ocean, docking at

a small leafy haven, gazing up at the colossus who is benign and approachable, and then, to enter her, to find that she is enfolding, even pregnable: these are the phases of a common dream of bliss.[10]

The fantasy is at once being a fetus inside the mother, and finding her "pregnable" to entry from the outside. The colossal mother offers both intrauterine existence and the fantasy of total potency for the child. Although both sexes long to be in the womb while able to possess the mother, these fantasies remain for the little boy dominant fantasies for his whole life, while to master the correct social imagination, the little girl must oppose those fantasies with others. But to both sexes, the monument offers the satisfactions of regression: the fetus inside the mother can scale her insides with the skill and consciousness of someone who has already been born. This fantasy—of being the fetus and not the mother—is part of the reason for the strength of antiabortion rhetoric; monuments thus collude with the fetus's right to life. The liberty being celebrated by the Statue of Liberty belongs to the fetus, not to the mother.

The fact that the statue serves as a navigational aid and was originally under the jurisdiction of the United States Lighthouse Board is no accident. Given to the United States to celebrate the friendship between the United States and France, it has always held its torch for the foreigner, for the immigrant. In all the years of immigration controversy, it is as though the Statue of Liberty represents some "home" population that defines the nation and welcomes the outsider. Yet not only is this a nation of immigrants but even the concept of liberty may be taken from elsewhere—from France, for example. The nervousness of the United States about what might be considered its own is well expressed in the prosopopeia coming from Liberty's mouth in Emma Lazarus's sonnet:

"Keep, ancient lands, your storied pomp!" cries she
With silent lips. "Give me your tired, your poor,
Your huddled masses yearning to breathe free,
The wretched refuse of your teeming shore.
Send these, the homeless, tempest-tost to me.
I lift my lamp beside the golden door!"

And what is the model she is rejecting? The beginning of the sonnet is explicit: "Not like the brazen giant of Greek fame." The poem's title is "The

New Colossus." Greece is again the origin, but the newness of the "new world" now becomes what is not wanted in the old. By offering a "world-wide welcome" to the refuse of the rest of the world,[11] the United States presents itself as a land of opportunity and riches ("golden door") that poverty can never exhaust, and as morally superior (more charitable) to the rest of the world. It wins without competing. Its strength lies in its open door.

The Thingliness of Persons

Chapter Four

Ego Sum Game

One of the most obvious assumptions we make is that the human "self" is a person, not a thing. But might this assumption be more problematic than it appears? We have seen how necessary transitional objects are to the development of a person. But is "knowing oneself" as deadly for every human being as it proved to be for Narcissus?

Narcissus, it will be recalled, was born to the water nymph Leirope, who asked the blind seer, Tiresias, whether her son would have a long life. "If he ne'er know himself," was the seer's reply according to Ovid, who tells the story in his *Metamorphoses*. Tiresias had been blinded by an irate Juno for having said that women enjoy sex more than men do. Juno and Jove had submitted their sexual query ("Who has more pleasure—men or women?") to Tiresias, who was the only mortal who had lived as both a woman and a man. Jove, who lamented Tiresias's blinding but could not undo it, gave him the gift of prophecy as compensation.

The problem would seem to arise when the "self" becomes known— known as an object of knowledge. But if the "self" becomes an object of knowledge, it can *only* be known as an object among other objects, and not

to know "the self is to make it an object

as a subject. "The self then, quite analogous to representations of objects," writes Heinz Kohut—one of the most important practitioners of American self-psychology, speaking against a common assumption about studying the "self"—the self, then, "is a content of the mental apparatus but is not one of its constituents, i.e., not one of the agencies of the mind."[1] Kohut calls *self-objects* other people who are treated as if they were parts or extensions of the self. The difference between self and other becomes very murky if one comes to know oneself only when what appears to be another is revealed to be the self. This is what Narcissus comes to recognize, much to his rue. It is no accident that the patients Kohut studies are those who have difficulty telling self from other—patients he has dubbed "narcissistic personalities."

Rather than inflicting their perfection and self-admiration on others, Kohut's narcissistic personalities are far more likely to use other people to shore up their own defects or to possess talents that they do not have. The tyranny of such people comes from their fear of others' freedom and their investment in others' capacity to compensate for what they believe they lack, not from some sense of their own superiority. But one would never guess this from the story Ovid tells of Narcissus, a youth who withheld himself from everyone who was smitten by his unusual beauty, men and women alike, until the day he fell passionately in love with his own image.

The narrative voice that tells the tale seems to know about Narcissus's delusion before Narcissus does. At the height of Narcissus's passion, the narrator steps forward and addresses his character thus: "O fondly foolish boy, why vainly seek to clasp but a fleeting image? What you seek is nowhere; but turn yourself away, and the object of your love will be no more. That which you behold is but the shadow of a reflected form and has no substance of its own."[2] The dramatic irony of the situation seems to be too much for the narrator, but, apparently not hearing this sagacious warning, Narcissus persists in his delusion, addressing the image as an unresponsive youth, and then shouting out, "Oh, I am he!"—"*iste ego sum*"—in recognition as he expires. It is at the moment of apostrophizing the figure he comes to know as an inanimate object that Narcissus starts to die. In other words, Narcissus now recognizes that the *other* is himself, and that love is impossible between them not because they cannot come together but because they cannot get far enough apart: "What I desire," laments Narcissus, "I have; the very abundance of my riches beggars me. Oh, that I might be parted from my own body! And, strange prayer for a lover, I would that what I love were absent from me!" Note that Narcissus says nothing about delusions or insubstantialities. What he regrets is not being able to merge with what he already is.

The narrator, however, is from the beginning as good an empiricist as the young chimpanzee will later be for Jacques Lacan. He makes a point of not being taken in for a minute by Narcissus's delusion and knows all the time where reality is. No matter what emotional event is taking place, he always pays attention to what is going on behind the curtain of fantasy. Desire and delusion, shadow and substance, must be distinguished at all costs. In order not to be duped by desire, it is good to be securely grounded in the real.

Here, for instance, is how the narrator-witness describes Narcissus's first encounter with his image, the youth having lain down to quench his thirst in a beautiful hidden pool while hunting: "While he seeks to slake his thirst another thirst springs up, and while he drinks he is smitten by the sight of the beautiful form he sees. He loves an unsubstantial hope and thinks that substance which is only shadow." Note how the narrator hastens to tell us the real truth of the case, to make sure we know right away that Narcissus is suffering from a delusion. There is almost a taboo against sharing in that delusion, remaining in the space of desire, taking a shadow for a substance. Falling in love with a beautiful form, however, suggests more than emptiness: it suggests a realm of aesthetics. Could it be that the aesthetic and the fantasmatic are related, or at least equally indifferent to the empirical difference between "real" and "not real"?

It is not just that Narcissus recognizes that the other is the self; he also recognizes that the self is another: "iste *ego sum*," "je *est un autre*." In other words, Narcissus, in his climactic recognition scene, shouts not "the other is *here*" but "I am *there*." *Iste* is a there-word, not a here-word: "*Iste,* ista, istud, istius (pronoun). That of yours; (*law*) your client, the plaintiff, the defendant; (*contemptuous*) the fellow; that, such." *Iste,* says the dictionary, is thus a distancing, almost dismissive, word, and the self recognized "over there" is a self that has become an object. By becoming an object, though, it lends itself to the confusions from which Narcissus suffers. A self-image can suffer all the distortions to which any *image* is susceptible, but it can be known only as an object, not a subject. A subject can only cry out, "I am that!"—which does not at all imply that the subject can *be* that.

The claim that the subject has *being* seems to be taken for granted as springing from Descartes. In his discovery scene in the second meditation, he details the process of radical doubt, and then realizes that even if he is deceived in everything, he cannot doubt the fact that he doubts. "*Cogito ergo sum*" is what we all learn he says at that moment (although he says it nowhere in that form): "I think, therefore I am." The content of thought—its truth or falsity—is not relevant; what gives the subject being is the fact that, while thinking about this problem, he exists. It is interesting to note that in Latin, the language the *Meditations* were first published in, and in 1647 still the language of serious scholarship, the pronouns are not necessarily included because they are redundant if one can tell who is speaking from the conjugation of the verb. In translating Freud into English, in contrast, Alex Strachey and his team *added* Latin pronouns—*ego, id,* and *superego*—where Freud had merely used the nominalization of the German pronouns—*das Ich, das Es,* and so on. The ego, id, and superego seem to be either excessive or lacking—and not just in a figurative sense but in every context where their nature is discussed.

The ego, the id, and the superego, in spite of their differences from anything experienced, says Kohut, are agencies of the mind, whereas the "self," more synthetic, more directly similar to what is experienced, is a mere "content" of the mental apparatus. Ego, id, and superego constantly struggle for control over the subject, whereas the "self" is something the subject treats as an object, constantly fine-tuning its perceived nature. "Ego, id, and superego are the constituents of a specific, high-level, i.e., experience-distant, abstraction in psychoanalysis: the psychic apparatus. . . . The self, however, emerges in the psychoanalytic situation and is conceptualized, in the mode of a comparatively low-level, i.e., comparatively experience-near, psychoanalytic abstraction, as a content of the mental apparatus."

Can the subject, then, have a descriptive qualifier of any kind and remain a subject? Does a predicate transform the subject into an object? Does a subject have to be unqualified to remain a subject? On the one hand, to describe is to view from a distance; on the other, an agent can tell certain things about himself. He certainly does not see himself as being "without qualities." But can a subject articulate its own predicate, or is that one of those things that ground a subject but cannot be articulated by the "I" who speaks, without endangering the status of subject? Are these questions that can be answered on the empirical or simply the rhetorical level? In other words, does it matter what is *known* about a subject, or only what is *said*?

To complicate things still further, one can ask, Is *being* a predicate? Is *be-*

ing something a subject can *have* and remain a subject? Let us return to Descartes for a moment. Is he saying more in formulating "I think, therefore I am" than simply using "I" properly: "I think, therefore 'I' is"? Does the sentence mean "I think, therefore I have being," or "I think, therefore I know the rules of grammar"?

Evidence that Descartes was profoundly worried about such things comes up when he has barely introduced his discovery: "I am, I exist, is necessarily true every time I pronounce it or conceive it in my mind. What then have I previously believed myself to be? Clearly, I believed myself to be a man. But what is a man?"[3] It is at this point that Descartes distinguishes between the evidence of the senses (which can always deceive me) and the evidence of reason (which, even if mistaken, *is*), and relies on the mind/body distinction to make his claim for the irrefutability of the existence of the thinking subject. Yet the question of what a man is continues to haunt him. Later in the essay, he writes, "Words impede me, and I am nearly deceived by ordinary language. . . . So I may by chance look out of a window and notice some men passing in the street, at the sight of whom I do not fail to say that I see men. . . . [A]nd nevertheless, what do I see from this window but hats and cloaks which might cover ghosts or automatons which move only by springs?"[4] A century later, a watchmaker in Neuchâtel, Switzerland, made an exquisite mechanical scribe capable of writing "I think, therefore I am" on a piece of paper spread out on his writing table. <u>Nothing Descartes writes proves that the being whose existence he had demonstrated was human: he discovered certainty only in the subject ("I am"), and not in any predicate ("I am X")</u>. The mechanism hiding beneath those hats and cloaks might only be the mechanics of language.

Over time, however, the psychology that has developed from Descartes's formula has tended to <u>conflate the ego with the self, the "content" of the mental apparatus, to take the subject for a substance.</u> American "ego psychology"—which combines the English translation of Freud with the ideology of the self-made man—works on reshaping the "ego" as if it were both mental *content* and mental *agency*, and as if it were the "self" who speaks about itself during a psychoanalytic session. The problem of any discordance between subject and self is not addressed, and the therapy has as its job to reshape the entity it is addressed by.

It is from American ego psychology that Jacques Lacan is most invested in distinguishing his own theories. He often uses Descartes as a clear example of the conflation of ego, self, and subject that is the delusion of which he would most like to rid psychoanalysis. For him, Freud's great discovery was the *non*-coincidence between consciousness and being, the split between the thinking subject and his unconscious. To make that distinction clear, he comes more and more to situate his theory of the human subject as a subject in language and to study the exact function of language in the split between subject and unconscious. An early text like "Le Stade du miroir" (1949) tries to isolate the moment when desire splits from reality; when the libidinal role of the non-coincidence between "I think" and "I am" is fixed. The text begins:

> La conception du stade du miroir . . . ne m'a pas paru indigne d'être rappelée à votre attention: aujourd'hui spécialement quant aux lumières qu'elle apporte sur la fonction du *je* dans l'expérience que nous en donne la psychanalyse. Expérience dont il faut dire qu'elle nous oppose à toute philosophie issue directement du *cogito.*[5]

> *   *   *

> The conception of the mirror stage . . . has since become more or less established in the practice of the French group. However, I think it worthwhile to bring it again to your attention, especially today, for the light it sheds on the formation of the *I* as we experience it in psychoanalysis. It is an experience that leads us to oppose any philosophy directly issuing from the *Cogito.*[6]

Later, in a 1957 lecture given, precisely, in the "amphithéâtre Descartes" at the Sorbonne, Lacan, being struck by the way in which Saussure-derived work in linguistics illuminated Freud and provided a clarification that was not available to Freud himself, expresses his distance from the *Cogito* in the following terms:

> *Je pense, donc je suis (cogito ergo sum). . .*
> La place que j'occupe comme sujet du signifiant est-elle, par rapport à celle que j'occupe comme sujet du signifié, concentrique ou excentrique? Voilà la question.
> Il ne s'agit pas de savoir si je parle de moi de façon conforme à ce que je suis, mais si, quand j'en parle, je suis le même que celui dont je parle. . . .
> C'est-à-dire que c'est peu de ces mots dont j'ai pu interloquer un instant mes auditeurs: je pense où je ne suis pas, donc je suis où je ne pense pas. . . .

Ce qu'il faut dire, c'est: je ne suis pas, là où je suis le jouet de ma pensée; je pense à ce que je suis, là où je ne pense pas penser. (516)

*   *   *

"I think, therefore I am" *(cogito ergo sum)*. . .

Is the place that I occupy as the subject of a signifier concentric or excentric, in relation to the place I occupy as subject of the signified?—that is the question.

It is not a question of knowing whether I speak of myself in a way that conforms to what I am, but rather of knowing whether I am the same as that of which I speak.

That is to say, what is needed is more than these words with which, for a brief moment I disconcerted my audience: I think where I am not, therefore I am where I do not think.

What one ought to say is: I am not wherever I am the plaything of my thought; I think of what I am where I do not think to think. (165–166)

But, according to the Lacan who wrote the account of "the mirror stage" in 1949 (after having introduced the term in 1936), the breakthrough occurred not as a commentary on a philosophical text but through a fact of comparative psychology:

Le petit d'homme à un âge où il est pour un temps court, mais encore pour un temps, dépassé en intelligence instrumentale par le chimpanzé, reconnaît pourtant déjà son image dans le miroir comme telle. . . .

Cet acte, en effet, loin de s'épuiser comme chez le singe dans le contrôle une fois acquis de l'inanité de l'image, rebondit aussitôt chez l'enfant en une série de gestes où il éprouve ludiquement la relation des mouvements assumés de l'image à son environnement reflété, et de ce complexe virtuel à la réalité qu'il redouble, soit à son propre corps et aux personnes, voire aux objets, qui se tiennent à ses côtés. (93)

*   *   *

The child, at an age when he is for a time, however short, outdone by the chimpanzee in instrumental intelligence, can nevertheless already recognize as such his own image in a mirror. . . .

This act, far from exhausting itself, as in the case of the monkey, once the image has been mastered and found empty, immediately rebounds in the case of the child in a series of gestures in which he experiences in play the relation between the movements assumed in the image and the reflected environment, and between this virtual complex and the reality it reduplicates—the child's own body, and the persons and things, around him. (1)

Lacan pursued his studies in psychiatry during the great age of behaviorism: experimenters with animals demonstrated how higher animals acquired conditioned reflexes that involved nothing mental at all. The experiments with dogs, cats, and rats presupposed an analogy between human beings and the species in question. The experiments were designed to demonstrate learned or developmental stages in all animals (including humans) that needed no psychic input: what looked like desire or intention could be explained by the pure mechanics of the body. Every form of salivation was Pavlovian. Freud had exaggerated the role of the psyche in human behavior along with the difference between human beings and other animals. Behaviorism was a welcome and demystifying corrective. Lacan's expression "le petit d'homme" is a sign of this mentality: it refers to a comparison between the "young" of two different animals; it is treating "man" as a species.

The little ape at first takes his image as another, and, when he recognizes that there is no other there, he loses interest. Dogs often bark at the dog in the mirror, while cats look for the other cat behind it. But the human baby's interest *increases* when he realizes that the other is himself; his fascination at seeing the "him" that others see leads him to test his movements against those of the image. In other words, it is not that his image is "merely" redundant as it is for other animals; it is the human image that now has reality in the world. Narcissus, therefore, made the mistake of the ape: he fell in love with his image *as if* it were another, and his tragedy was that his love was impossible if it were not. Narcissus, too, has no interest in his own image, and fades away as soon as he realizes that he loves himself. In a way, therefore, Narcissus is no narcissist: he gets no farther than the chimpanzee. His story is about the inability to become human. Normally, the human baby adopts as his "self" an image that shows him more unified and powerful than he is:

Cet événement peut se produire, on le sait depuis Baldwin, depuis l'âge de six mois, et sa répétition a souvent arrêté notre méditation devant le spectacle saisissant d'un nourisson devant le miroir, qui n'a pas encore la maîtrise de la marche, voire de la station debout, mais qui, tout embrassé qu'il est par quelque soutien humain ou artificiel (ce que nous appelons en France un trotte-bébé), surmonte en un affairement jubilatoire les entraves de cet appui, pour suspendre son attitude en une position plus ou moins penchée, et ramener, pour le fixer, un aspect instantané de l'image. (93–94)

*   *   *

This event can take place, as we have known since Baldwin, from the age of six months, and its repetition has often made me reflect upon the startling spectacle of the infant in front of the mirror. Unable as yet to walk, or even to stand up, and held tightly as he is by some support, human or artificial (what in France, we call a *trotte-bébé*), he nevertheless overcomes, in a flutter of jubilant activity, the obstructions of his support and, fixing his attitude in a slightly leaning-forward position, in order to hold it in his gaze, brings back an instantaneous aspect of the image. (1–2)

Lacan's attitude is markedly ambivalent about comparative biology. On the one hand, Lacan underlines what *differentiates* man from other species (this will only expand as Lacan explores the role of human language): whereas the chimpanzee loses interest when he realizes that the image is not "real," the human being comes to "know himself" through it. On the other hand, species that illustrate the developmental role of the double—pigeons or migratory locusts, for example—show that the mimeticism that seems at work uniquely in man exists elsewhere in nature. What is specific about humans can't be studied through other species, but if something that seems unnatural can be found in nature, that strengthens the argument for it.

What matters in the mirror stage, then, is not whether the image in the mirror is self or other, but how the subject recognizes that what the mirror promises to do is to give it a predicate. The subject jubilates because the image (which is now recognized to be the self) is *superior* to the little human who does the looking. The image seems to stand erect and to exemplify a wholeness that the little human, feeling weak and fragmentary, does not experience. Part of the image's perfection, indeed, inheres in the fact that *it does not feel.* Here is how Lacan describes that developmental moment:

Il y suffit de comprendre le stade du miroir *comme une identification* au sens plein que l'analyse donne à ce terme: à savoir la transformation produite chez le sujet, quand il assume une image,—dont la prédestination à cet effet de phase est suffisament indiquée par l'usage, dans la théorie, du terme antique d'*imago*.

L'assomption jubilatoire de son image spéculaire par l'être encore plongé dans l'impuissance motrice et la dépendance du nourrissage qu'est le petit

[handwritten top margin: ✱ Genesis 2 as infants/identification and growing out of child stage of dependence, precisely when the object turns subject and returns gaze back and the way this story is archetype of how this happens w/ all families and also in Zeus etc.]

homme à ce stade *infans,* nous paraîtra dès lors manifester en une situation exemplaire la matrice symbolique où le *je* se précipite en une forme primordiale. . . .

Cette forme serait plutôt au reste à désigner comme *je-idéal.* . . . Mais le point important est que cette forme situe l'instance du *moi,* dès avant sa détermination sociale, dans une lignée de fiction, à jamais irréductible pour le seul individu,—ou plutôt, qui ne rejoindra qu'asymptotiquement le devenir du sujet, quel que soit le succès des synthèses dialectiques par quoi il doit résoundre en tant que *je* sa discordance d'avec sa propre réalité.

C'est que la forme totale du corps par quoi le sujet devance dans un mirage la maturation de sa puissance, ne lui est donnée que comme *Gestalt,* c'est-à-dire dans une extériorité où certes cette forme est-elle plus constituante que constituée. (94–95)

*   *   *

[handwritten left margin: Mirror stage as an identification w/ image]

We have only to understand the mirror stage *as an identification,* in the full sense that analysis gives to the term: namely the transformation that takes place in the subject when he assumes an image—whose predestination to this phase-effect is sufficiently indicated by the use, in analytic theory, of the ancient term *imago.*

[handwritten left margin: ✱] This jubilant assumption of his specular image by the child at the *infans* stage, still sunk in his motor incapacity and nursling dependence, would seem to exhibit in an exemplary situation the symbolic matrix in which the *I* is precipitated in a primordial form. . . .

This form would have to be called the Ideal-I, if we wished to incorporate it into our usual register, in the sense that it will also be the source of secondary identifications, under which term I would place the functions of libidinal normalization. But the important point is that this form situates the agency of the ego, before its social determination, in a fictional direction, which will always remain irreducible for the individual alone, or rather, which will only rejoin the coming-into-being (*le devenir*) of the subject asymptotically, whatever the success of the dialectical syntheses by which he must resolve as *I* his discordance with his own reality.

The fact is that the total form of the body by which the subject anticipates in a mirage the maturation of his power is given to him only as *Gestalt,* that is say, in an exteriority in which this form is certainly more constituent than constituted. (2)

[handwritten left margin: Subject and Form/Being]

The subject, according to Lacan, identifies here with a form—not with *being*—a form that interests the subject precisely because it *anticipates* stages

But implicitly recognized is this "present" self.... before "ideal" self. The self that desires the "ideal".

of his development where he will be superior to what he is now. The subject, in other words, assumes an identity derived from the *discrepancy* between a present and an ideal self—and *that* is what is recognized with such jubilation. Henceforth the real self for the subject is the one in the mirror: the total form of a body standing erect and transcending all support. An idealization. A fiction. An object.

The unchanging and unfeeling image of this idealization will haunt the subject his whole life. No matter what he does, he can neither catch up to it nor equal it. He is not pursuing a "fair youth" like Narcissus; he is pursuing himself. The impossible coincidence from which Narcissus suffered, however, exists at the heart of the subject. The subject *is* this noncoincidence, this split between an "armor of alienating identity" from the mirror image and a "corps morcelé" that is "animated" by a trembling reality ("en opposition à la turbulence de mouvements dont il s'éprouve l'animer").

In other words, like Narcissus, the subject, too, has fallen in love with a form. The word "form" is used so often by Lacan to describe this moment that one cannot help thinking that the founding moment for the subject is its shift to an aesthetic—or fantasmatic—world where images, not substances, shape human beings. It does not matter to the subject whether the mirror image is "real"; what matters is the image it conveys of the self. In its fixity and persistance, it resembles a statue, and indeed Lacan refers to the "statue in which man projects himself," while Narcissus sits fascinated by his image "like a statue carved from Parian marble." For Jacques Lacan, the possibility of becoming a statue is not something that may or may not happen to a subject. It *must* happen if the little man is to become human. A baby cannot become a little human being without identifying with a statue. Michael Borsch-Jakobson, in his book *Lacan: The Absolute Master,* and particularly in its chapter "The Statue Man," accuses Lacan of treating the human infant as a thing and preferring form to affect; but Lacan's emphasis on the role of form and shape does not deny feeling: he studies, rather, what is distinctive in the human species. It is precisely the unreal that can seem not to foster the best use of feelings. Feelings are something that man shares with animals. What makes him human is something counterintuitive, something contrary to life.

statue of aesthetic self

Lacan on humanness

This dimension of loving a form is what differentiates, for Lacan, humans from other species. The world man creates ends up being populated by "automates," says Lacan. Descartes was right to wonder what was under those hats and coats. While all other animals measure information by its empirical usefulness, man alone does not have to connect a "substance" with a "form." Later, when it comes to formulating the difference between the "language of bees" and human language, Lacan will say that although bees have a very sophisticated set of signals to tell other bees where the honey is, they cannot say where it was yesterday, or tell the other bees a lie. It is the capacity *not* to tell the truth, to separate forms without substance from the tyranny of the referential, that characterizes the human. The human being differs from other animals because he submits to the judgment of those that measure him against an ideal image, not a reality.

In his earliest writings, indeed, Jacques Lacan was seeking to formulate the nature of this difference. When differentiating the human concept of family from that of other species, he called the human family "an institution" while for other species it was a biological group. Where animals have instincts, humans have complexes. At that time he attributed those differences to a difference between nature and culture. Later he would say that the human being learns desire at the same moment as prohibition, so that a "complex" is an image of the forbidden as desirable, the desirable as forbidden, a contradictory psychology which can only be imprinted through language.[7]

The identification with a beautiful form is an identification of life itself as imperfection. Only the inanimate has the fixity, the lack of feeling, the lack of need that corresponds to the unchanging ideal. While in love with an image that never had needs, Narcissus himself disregarded his own, and died behaving like the non-living thing he loved. In the poem that ends her volume of complete works, Sylvia Plath, too, seems to find that perfection in death:

> The woman is perfected.
> Her dead
>
> Body wears the smile of accomplishment. . . .[8]

Death, however, is not the only way to achieve the stillness of the ideal. What happens in the mirror stage is the self's identification with a still image, which then becomes the version of superiority that the living self will try to equal. In its fixity, it contrasts with the experience of weakness and fragmentation that is retrospectively established as the subject's present and actual reality. The image offers a fiction of wholeness that the subject will strive to resemble. <u>In other words, the subject comes into being in the gap of inferiority between a flawed viewer and the anticipated wholeness of an armor of fiction, an armor of inanimateness.</u> What happens in the mirror stage is the conflating of libidinal investments with beautiful forms: the <u>fantasmatic and the aesthetic are henceforth the "reality" of the self.</u> And the definition of "person" would then be: <u>the repeated experience of *failing to become a thing.*</u>

mirror stage

Person:
✓ *Failing to become a thing....*

That the mirror stage sets up the attractions and dangers of the aesthetic, fantasmatic domain is indicated in a surprising way by a medieval romance⟨ Guillaume de Lorris's⟩*Roman de la rose,* one of the earliest treatises of "courtly love" and the allegorical mechanics of desire. As the lover enters more deeply into the garden that will contain his beloved, he drinks from a fountain engraved warningly with the epitaph of Narcissus. Here died Narcissus, says the fountain, and (implicitly) here will die all those who suffer from the same delusion. The dreamer, however, has already caught sight of his beloved, on a rosebush—reflected in the water—on which the beautiful bud is growing. The object of desire is thus first perceived as an image reflected in what the text will call the "mireors périlleus."[9] The subject must drink from the waters of reflection in order to tie together libidinal and aesthetic fascination—in order to desire an image.

Roman de la Rose
⇓

In *Le roman de la rose* the text is narrated by a subject who tells his dream. The dream-narrative is a common allegorical device, and although the sleeper could not be telling us his dream while he is asleep, the presence of not two but *three* consciousnesses is not as marked as, say, in Ovid's tale of Narcissus, where the narrator warns, distances himself, and laments. In Lacan's account of the mirror stage, too, the narrator is a third—an observer who comments on the story he is telling. It is Lacan himself, trained observer that he is, who says:

> Cet événement peut se produire, on le sait depuis Baldwin, depuis l'âge de six mois, et sa répétition a souvent arrêté *notre méditation* devant le spectacle saisissant d'un nourisson devant le miroir. . . .
>
> . . . tout embrassé qu'il est par quelque soutien humain ou artificiel (ce que *nous* appelons en France un trotte-bébé). (93; emphasis added)

*   *   *

This event can take place, as we have known since Baldwin, from the age of six months, and its repetition has often made me reflect upon the startling spectacle of the infant in front of the mirror. Unable as yet to walk, or even to stand up, and held tightly as he is by some support, human or artificial (what in France, we call a *trotte-bébé*). (1)

Conscious of giving this talk in Zurich, and thus of presenting himself as a scientific researcher knowledgeable about French terms of art like *trotte-bébé,* Lacan presents the baby's joy as observed during his own astute "meditation," scientific and familial.

Thus the role of the "third" in these scenes is either identificatory (as in Ovid) or scientific (as in Lacan), but in both cases the libidinal investment is described as inhering wholly in what happens in the relation between the other person and his mirror image. In a short narrative by Heinrich von Kleist, however, the role of the "third" is hardly objective:

"About three years ago," I related, "I was swimming with a young man over whose physical form a marvelous grace seemed to shine. He must have been just sixteen or so, and only the first signs of vanity, induced by the favors of women, could be seen, as it were, in the farthest distance. It so happened that shortly before, in Paris, we had seen the famous statue called the Spinario, the youth removing a thorn from his foot—copies of it are familiar and can be found in most German collections. A glance in a large mirror recalled it to him at a moment when, in drying himself, he happened to raise his foot to a stool—he smiled and mentioned the discovery he had made. I indeed had noticed it too in the very same instant, but either to test the self-assurance of the grace with which he was endowed, or to challenge his vanity in a salutary way, I laughed and said he was seeing phantoms. He blushed and raised his foot a second time to prove it to me, but the attempt, as might easily have been foreseen, did not succeed. Confused, he raised his foot a third and fourth time; he must have raised it ten times more: in vain! He was unable to produce the same movement again. And the movements that he did produce had so comical an effect that I could barely suppress my laughter."[10]

Chapter Five

They Urn It

They make money the old-fashioned way: *they earn it.*

—Actor John Houseman for Smith Barney

I

What is a thing? "A jug is a thing," writes the philosopher Martin Heidegger
in an essay called "The Thing," and "a pair of peasant shoes," in an essay
called "The Origin of the Work of Art."

Looking at the titles of Heidegger's two essays, one is struck by the juxtaposition of things and art. A truly thingly thing—as one says a "manly
man"—should not be so close to art, we think. A mere thing is nothing like
a well-wrought urn, we insist. On the other hand, where but in art do we really encounter the materiality of daily life? Where but in Chardin's paintings
do we taste the peach skins, touch the cards, pluck the chicken? And even in
Jackson Pollock's paintings or other works of non-representational art, don't
we feel the nervousness of the painter, the texture of the paint, the pull of
gravity? Perhaps, after all, it takes art to bring out the thingliness of things.

Or philosophy. The first problem to solve is why Heidegger refers to the
"*made* things" that surround us, not to the "found things," the "thingly

"made" things vs. "thingly" things

"made things"
vs.
"found/thingly things"

✓

things," that they—and we—are made of. This is because, he writes, our traditional ways of approaching the thingness of the thing—as a subject with its predicate, as a manifold of sensations, as matter in a particular form—are fallacious ways of getting nearer to it. The moment we begin to talk about things at all, indeed, we find the structure of Latin grammar inadequately translating the Greek sense of being:

> According to current opinion, this definition of the thingness of the thing as the substance with its accidents seems to correspond to our natural outlook on things. No wonder that the current attitude toward things—our way of addressing ourselves to things and speaking about them—has adapted itself to this common view of the thing. A simple propositional statement consists of the subject, which is the Latin translation, hence already a reinterpretation, of *hupokeimenon* and the predicate, in which the thing's traits are stated of it. Who would have the temerity to assail these simple fundamental relations between thing and statement, between sentence structure and thing-structure? Nevertheless we must ask: is the structure of a simple propositional statement (the combination of subject and predicate) the mirror-image of the structure of the thing (of the union of substance with accidents)? Or could it be that even the structure of the thing as thus envisaged is a projection of the framework of the sentence?[1]

Influence of →
Realm of Rhetoric

Trying to think about things, one becomes enmeshed in the usual illusory insolubilities, and one often unthinkingly reflects the religious notion that in the beginning, God created made things, formed matter. And that pesky syntax.

Which points, perhaps, to a way of reading these baffling essays by Heidegger. "The thing things," he writes in one essay; "The world worlds," he writes in the other. In both cases, he relies on the structure of the sentence to stand as a statement, but not in the usual way, by adding a predicate to define the characteristics of the subject. Here, the verb says exactly the same thing as the subject. He has simply made a verb out of a noun, by manipulating it like those transformers mentioned earlier. The semantic content can be shaped one way—a noun!—and pulled the other way—a verb! But the message of completeness conveyed by the word's fulfillment of the structure makes the reader feel that something significant has been said. And to transform the nouns "thing" and "world" into verbs may be precisely what Heidegger is after. In any case, the "doing" of thing and world tells us

Heidegger:
"The thing things"
(verb)

Earth vs. World

no more than we learned from the noun—*except that the thing has now become an act.*

Another disconcerting aspect of Heidegger's writing is his subtle but total subversion of the protocols of philosophy. To take just one example, the realization that one is going in a circle is usually a sign that one should abandon that path. But when Heidegger realizes that origin, work, and art each presuppose the others, he writes: "Anyone can easily see that we are moving in a circle. Ordinary understanding demands that this circle be avoided because it violates logic . . . [But] . . . we are compelled to follow the circle. This is neither a makeshift nor a defect. To enter on this path is the strength of thought."[2]

Heidegger's subversion of philosophy — revealing its circularity

Heidegger decides to focus on the "things" by which we are surrounded, things that were expressly made to fit man's needs, things closest and most useful to us. He calls these useful items "equipment" and situates them between "mere" things and works of art:

A piece of equipment, a pair of shoes for instance, when finished, is also self-contained like the mere thing, but it does not have the character of having taken shape by itself like the granite boulder. On the other hand, equipment displays an affinity with the art work insofar as it is something produced by the human hand. However, by its self-sufficient presence the work of art is similar rather to the mere thing which has taken shape by itself and is self-contained. Nevertheless we do not count such works among mere things. As a rule it is the use-objects around us that are the nearest and authentic things. Thus the piece of equipment is half-thing, because characterized by thingliness, and yet it is something more; at the same time it is half art-work and yet something less, because lacking the self-sufficiency of the art work. Equipment has a peculiar position intermediate between thing and work, assuming that such a calculated ordering of them is permissible.[3]

equipment and art both human produced

art and mere thing both self-contained

Equipment as a "half-thing".

When analyzing the thing, one has ordinarily treated the thing, unwittingly, as equipment. The intermediate stage between work of art and thing is not so clear. The real opposition is between art and equipment. Equipment extends me, while art encompasses me. Equipment *is;* art represents. Equipment acts in the world; art re-creates the world.

art and equipment

Equipment, as thing, allows me to be at home in a world of things. A work of art shows me the world I inhabit; it shows me what a world is. If I analyze a piece of equipment, I can know how a world is made. A world can be made out of equipment only if the equipment's thingly character is allowed to act. Thus, Heidegger's essay called "The Thing" spends a great deal of time on the jug as an example of a thing, and on both of the senses of the expression: "its making." But the essay on the thing begins not with a thought about things but with a thought about the modern world's tendency to abolish all distances:

Heidegger on "the jug" ↓

What about nearness? . . . Near to us are what we usually call things. But what is a thing? . . . The jug is a thing. What is the jug? We say: a vessel, something of the kind that holds something else within it. . . . As a vessel the jug is something self-sustained, something that stands on its own. . . . As the self-supporting independence of something independent, the jug differs from an object. . . . [T]he thingly character of the thing does not consist in its being a represented object. . . . Clearly the jug stands as a vessel only because it has been brought to a stand. . . . The potter makes the earthen jug out of earth that he has specially chosen and prepared for it. . . .

The jug is a thing as a vessel—it can hold something. To be sure, this container had to be made. . . . But what shows itself here, the aspect (the *eidos,* the *idea*), characterizes the jug solely in the respect in which the vessel stands over against the maker as something to be made. . . .

. . . We become aware of the vessel's holding nature when we fill the jug. . . . When we fill the jug, the pouring that fills it flows into the empty jug. The emptiness, the void, is what does the vessel's holding. The empty space, this nothing of the jug, is what the jug is as the holding vessel. . . .

empty space of jug

Sides and bottom, of which the jug consists and by which it stands, are not really what does the holding. But if the holding is done by the jug's void, then the potter who forms sides and bottom on his wheel does not, strictly speaking, make the jug. He only shapes the clay. No—he shapes the void.[4]

It is no accident that a potter "throws" a pot, and that Heidgger's expression for our status on earth—*Geworfenheit*—means "thrownness."[5] The useful thing seems to shape a void, then; a "made thing" owes its existence to something missing. A work of art, too, is formed around something missing, but the void is its vanishing point, not its essence:

uh, does jug example extend beyond it? to a hammer similar? maybe in the sense that it inverts the emptiness like a sculptor shaving away marble to find the form of a man? the space around it becomes the empty void that defines its form.

The demands of beauty could not be reconciled with the pain in all its disfiguring violence. . . . The wide-open mouth, aside from the fact that the significance of Shape → form ?

purpose?

rest of the face is thereby twisted and distorted in an unnatural and loathsome manner, becomes in painting a mere spot and in sculpture a cavity, with most repulsive effect.[6]

From the dark opening of the worn insides of the shoes the toilsome tread of the worker stares forth.[7]

Beauty is the form of the purposiveness of an object, so far as this is perceived in it *without any representation of a purpose.* [Footnote:] (It might be objected to this explanation that there are things in which we see a purposive form without cognizing any purpose in them, like the stone implements often gotten from old sepulchral tumuli with a hole in them, as if for a handle. These, although they plainly indicate by their shape a purposiveness of which we do not know the purpose, are nevertheless not described as beautiful. But if we regard a thing as a work of art, that is enough to make us admit that its shape has reference to some design and definite purpose. And hence there is no immediate satisfaction in the contemplation of it. On the other hand a flower, e.g. a tulip, is regarded as beautiful, because in perceiving it we find a certain purposiveness which, in our judgment, is referred to no purpose at all.)[8]

A hole, a cavity, an opening, a void—these are the things an implement allows us to manipulate, and a work of art allows us not to see. The work of art depends on the missing thing, but that thing is not perceived directly. On the contrary, what is perceived is a fullness of design that makes one think that nothing is missing, that purposiveness without purpose is an excess, not a lack. Keats's "Ode on a Grecian Urn" is made up of apostrophes to the inanimate object, not of answers to the questions the speaker asks, or any knowledge that the object might convey. The apostrophes allow for there to be address with no context—a shaping of the void. The shaping of the poem, like that of a pot, circles around and around but is not grounded by a fixed point. The tulip, too, is an urn-like shape: a hollow enclosed within sides and bottom. The tulip is a *cut* flower, however, and Lessing chooses a statue of Laocoön being killed by a serpent to illustrate his aesthetic: in both Kant and Lessing the violence is crucial. The aesthetic object is cut off and detached from the ongoing flow of life. "Hardly anyone but a botanist knows what sort of thing a flower ought to be; and even he, though recognizing in the flower the reproductive organ of the plant. . ."[9] The proximity of the beautiful to annulled reproduction, and hence, to death, is per-

so is food, equip and all things

haps a large part of its attractiveness. After all, the final scene on Keats's
urn is a scene of sacrifice, and the beautiful is "cold"—containing neither
fulfillment nor decay. The "thing," the jug, in its taking in and pouring out
the necessities of life or libation, acts out all the dimensions of the word
"gush": "Middle English *guschen, gosshen*—cf. German *Giss, geissen*—is the
Greek *cheein,* the Indo-European *ghu.* It means to offer in sacrifice."[10] In
Heidegger's text, the thing's outpouring brings together earth and sky, divinities and mortals. His first example of a work of art is a poem about a Roman fountain. Aesthetic authority is immortal—it chooses neither life nor
death.

What happens when Keats's classical urn is brought to the new world?
What does aesthetic authority look like then? Instead of the eternal story of
Greeks and Trojans, what stories does an American urn tell? The first thing
one notices in Wallace Stevens's poem about an urn is that the epic has become an anecdote, and the noble urn, a serviceable "jar."

"ANECDOTE OF THE JAR"
I placed a jar in Tennessee,
And round it was, upon a hill.
It made the slovenly wilderness
Surround that hill.

The wilderness rose up to it,
And sprawled around, no longer wild.
The jar was round upon the ground
And tall and of a port in air.

It took dominion everywhere.
The jar was gray and bare.
It did not give of bird or bush,
Like nothing else in Tennessee.

The "bare" jar is very different from Keats's much-decorated urn. It is,
however, a starker, speeded up, less picturesque, less eloquent version of the
same kind of aesthetic authority. "It took dominion everywhere." The self-
standingness of the made thing is now seen in its effects, not its story. It
shapes the surround. It organizes, from its central place, its environment. It
has the kind of authority that only a thing can possess. The John Wayne,

Handwritten margin notes:
"Gush"
the thing's outpouring connects sacred + profane
Keat's classical urn to Stevens' American Jar

"aw shucks" kind of plainness is what, in the new world, dominates both the "wildness" of the new wilderness and the fanciness of the old world. But the "self-supporting" thing does not achieve self-support on its own. In the first words of the poem, "I placed," the human agency of a first person initiates the process, then disappears. The jar then *seems* to do the rest by itself. Like the "I met a traveler from an antique land, who said. . ." of the beginning of "Ozymandias," this "I placed . . . and . . ." is "placed" at the opening of the poem to indicate the human agency it is necessary to erase in order to achieve the aesthetic effect. The "I placed" occurs on the stage and is quickly hurried off, as Mallarmé says of the witches in the opening scene of *Macbeth:* "Le rideau simplement s'est levé, une minute, trop tôt, trahissant des menées fatidiques."[11]

The word "Tennessee," which is the least European of words, and clearly indicates that we are not in Athens anymore, is very unexpected in the final line of the poem, which we expect to rhyme with something and thus achieve "roundness" in the poem. There have been three rhymes in "-air" before it: "air," "everywhere," and "bare." Another rhyme in -air would bring closure after the totally anomalous "bush" of the next-to-last line. But no—the final line is "Like nothing else in Tennessee." The last line of the poem flouts its failure to rhyme, but it does return to the last word of the first line.

"Tennessee," in fact, has an interesting metrical history. In this poem, it fits into the overall iambic rhythm of the stanzas, and is thus composed of two stressed and one unstressed syllable: TENN-es-SEE. This aligns it with the plain-speaking angularity of the "bare." But in Jon Stallworthy's afterword to the *Norton Anthology of Poetry,* we read the following under "Anapestic": "Two unstressed syllables followed by a stressed syllable, as in 'Tennessee.'"[12] And in expressions like "Tennessee walking horse," it is rather dactylic: a stressed syllable followed by two unstressed ones. The word "Tennessee" thus has a fluctuating meter, floating between a two-syllable foot and a three-syllable one. But in this poem, three-syllable words are what must be mastered. "Slovenly" and "wilderness" represent the unformed excess that perhaps recalls the "fancy" of old-world things. To take "dominion" (another three-syllable word that fits into an iambic pattern), the jar must tame the excess and sprawl of wildness. The erasure of human agency, the dominion of controlled form, and the autonomy of plain things alone constitute an American aesthetic.

Stevens' Jar Poem cont'd

And yet, the word "Tennessee" derives from a Cherokee name, Tanasi.[13] The erasure of agency, far from being innocent, might look more like genocide. The "dominion" taken by the jar can seem more like the U.S. government—killing off the Indians, imposing the Tennessee Valley Authority—than like aesthetic inevitability.

the shape of Stevens' jar

"of a port in air"

hm....

Let us go back to what Heidegger says about the making of a jug. "The potter forms the clay. No—he shapes the void." What is the shape of Stevens's jar? Gray, bare, round, and "tall and of a port in air." What does "of a port" mean? It sounds like an idiom meaning "with a certain stature" and "capable of holding." It gives a certain capaciousness to the jar. But is it actually a known expression? I have not found it outside this poem. "Tall and of a port in air" is taking up room in the line, but says only that the jar is a big container. "Of a port" is a *fake* cliché, a verbal placeholder, itself "of a port" in the line. It is a shaping of the void of signification.

The line "It did not give of bird or bush" refers us to another cliché—this time real rather than fake: "A bird in the hand is worth two in the bush." This saying refers to a "trapping" economy: it is more reliable to count on one bird in a bird-catcher's hand than to be swayed by tales of the numerous birds he hasn't caught yet. A bird in the bush is "wild"; a bird in the hand is dead. But the jar, "like nothing else in Tennessee," belongs to a different economy. Its "dominion" is one of pure form, pure aesthetic authority.

The Ear as a vessel

cannot close or defend

This ever-open receptacle, this *shaped* void, resembles, in the human body, an ear. It, too, seems a hole surrounded by a shape: "The ear is the most tendered and most open organ, the one that, as Freud reminds us, the infant cannot close," writes Derrida.[14] And what is normally poured into the ear? Speech. Address. Words. This externally superfluous, internally empty organ cannot prevent itself from containing speech. It is a container, a receptacle, an always-receptive receptacle. It cannot close, that is, defend itself from being filled with language—or with poison. It is, for example, through

vulnerability of Ear in Hamlet:

the ear that Claudius murders Hamlet's father:

> *Ghost:* . . . Sleeping within my orchard,
>   My custom always of the afternoon,
>   Upon my secure hour thy uncle stole
>   With juice of cursed hebenon in a vial,
>   And in the porches of my ears did pour

> The leprous distillment, whose effect
> Holds such an enmity with the blood of man
> That swift as quicksilver it courses through
> The natural gates and alleys of the body.[15]

[handwritten margin note: The Ear as a vessel ⇊]

Power cannot resist the sense that this open, receptive ear can be dominated. There is something about the flap of skin on the ear's outside that can seem unconnected to the body's working parts: it has no bones, and thus is not part of the muscular system; it can seem mere ornament; the domination has no consequences. Pouring poison into the ear's void is morally quite different from pouring a drink for the gods, but the difference lies in the intentions of the pourer, not in the actions of the vessel. The body's little urns are made to be filled in any case.

This juxtaposition of the aesthetic and the usurping suggests the unsettling possibility that both may be involved in an act of violence. But it is precisely this collusion between beauty and violence that I think Carolyn Forché is getting at in her prose poem "The Colonel":

[handwritten margin note: Carolyne Forché poem "The Colonel" (on beauty + violence) ⇓]

What you have heard is true. I was in his house. His wife carried a tray of coffee and sugar. His daughter filed her nails, his son went out for the night. There were daily papers, pet dogs, a pistol on the cushion beside him. The moon swung bare on its black cord over the house. On the television was a cop show. It was in English. Broken bottles were embedded in the walls around the house to scoop the kneecaps from a man's legs or cut his hands to lace. On the windows there were gratings like those in liquor stores. We had dinner, rack of lamb, good wine, a gold bell was on the table for calling the maid. The maid brought green mangoes, salt, a type of bread. I was asked how I enjoyed the country. There was a brief commercial in Spanish. His wife took everything away. There was some talk then of how difficult it had become to govern. The parrot said hello on the terrace. The colonel told it to shut up, and pushed himself from the table. My friend said to me with his eyes: say nothing. The colonel returned with a sack used to bring groceries home. He spilled many human ears on the table. They were like dried peach halves. There is no other way to say this. He took one of them in his hands, shook it in our faces, dropped it into a water glass. It came alive there. I am tired of fooling around, he said. As for the rights of anyone, tell your people they can go fuck themselves. He swept the ears to the floor with his arm and held the last of his wine in the air. Something for your poetry, no? he said.

"The Colonel" poem
contd
⇓⇓

Some of the ears on the floor caught this scrap of his voice. Some of the ears
on the floor were pressed to the ground.

May 1978[16]

When the colonel says "something for your poetry, no?" what is he referring
to? The bag of ears as a picturesque capsule sketch of his cruelty? The rhetorical deception of the ear's "aliveness" in the glass of water? Poetry's attempt to find perfect metaphors like "dried peach halves" even though it is
morally unseemly to see beauty in horror? We can't know what is in the colonel's head. But the juxtaposition in his mind of poetry and cut-off ears
must be uncomfortable for the writer. There is guilt, or at least embarrassment, when she writes, "There is no other way to say this." The aesthetically
successful metaphor may be morally inappropriate. This prettification—
which is the ultimate end of representation, the making into an aesthetic
object—was what Adorno worried about in poetry after Auschwitz. The
poet is thus right to worry about poetry's collusion with violence.

The ears' "aliveness" is not just the colonel's trick through immersing an
ear in the "gush," however. The poet describes the pathos of the ears' continuing to hear well beyond the colonel's gesture. Some of the ears hear the colonel's voice; some of the ears are pressed to the ground. The poem ends by
describing a form of animation that is not controlled by the colonel.

Politically, animation outside the colonel's control may be what the poet
urges and wishes. But the rhetorical effects are too close for comfort. In order to produce an aesthetic object, the poet, too, may cut and display. What
is unacceptable in the colonel is that he *literalizes* the process of removing
from life, decontextualizing, and displaying that make up the aesthetic act,
not that he does something entirely different from it. No wonder the poet
feels guilty.

II

why the jug?

What is it about a jug—or urn—or jar—that makes it impose itself? Perhaps the same thing that made it one of mankind's first pieces of equipment—at least to judge from many an archeological dig. Perhaps the same
thing that motivates Tupperware and Rubbermaid today: something with
form to contain the formless: leftovers, or, especially, water, or wine, or the

why the jug?

ashes of the dead. Something that can carry a necessity of life as well as death. A container. A vehicle.

Although Heidegger speaks of the jug as if it were an obvious example of a thing, there is really nothing obvious about it. Exemplarity, indeed, is the great unexplained glue that holds together essays that seem to flaunt their arbitrariness. Exemplarity *comes out of* the analysis of the particular; it does not lead to its choice. That said, the choice of example is never as arbitrary as it looks. Take a jug, for instance. What else would bring together earth and sky, gods and mortals, as Heidegger wishes? Through the ability to take in and pour out, through the shaping of something self-standing out of the earth, Heidegger is able to bring together drink and libation, life and worship, mortals and gods. The jug, it seems, is hardly an arbitrary choice if one wishes to do all this. What else is made to carry liquids, or ashes? In other words, life or death?

for Heidegger

This is perhaps what attracts Francis Ponge to the urn as an example of a "thing" whose side he is taking. It is a container of life or of death. If death, it remains hallowed and unchanging. If life, it must go back to the source again and again. According to Lévi-Strauss, tribes exchange women in order to fulfill their marital destiny. And women become the form of communication between tribes—men exchange women as they exchange words. Ponge makes explicit why *containers* should attract so much attention as things: "Couldn't all I have just said about the jug be said equally well of words?" But language as materiality is very different from the empiricism we tend to think of in connection with things. Perhaps that is what a thought about a jug allows one to bring together: the arbitrariness of the sign and the empiricism of things as *both* being a form of materiality with which man has to cope.

Jugs + words

Another form of materiality that may be lurking around the jug is sexual reproduction. Indeed, Ponge makes a point of highlighting the proverb, "The pitcher went to the well once too often"—in French, "La crûche va tellement à l'eau qu'à la fin elle casse." This proverb seems to point to the urn's mortality—its ordinary fragility. But filling and emptying bring up another meaning of the proverb: pregnancy. "If she continues to sleep around, she'll end up pregnant." It is not the woman but her hymen that breaks. Something gently rounded that can be full or empty makes an urn seem to resemble a woman. How feminine is the urn? The Western canon's convention, if not reality, requires that if the pursuing poet is male, the beloved ob-

Jug as sexual/ feminine

ject is female. This convention colors all Western poetry written by men. But it does not hurt that all the words for "urn" that Ponge uses in his poem are feminine in French. The urn's femininity is stressed when Keats calls it "thou still unravished bride of quietness." It can be seen to shape an ideal of female beauty in the visual arts: "Parmigianino's Madonna is the most complete portrayal of his ideal of feminine beauty. . . . The analogy between the form of a beautiful antique vase and the shape of an ideally beautiful woman is one that also fascinated Firenzuola. . . . Firenzuola's . . . views were even illustrated. . . . From right to left are shown two beautiful and two graceless forms."[17]

It is no accident, I think, that "jugs" is slang for "breasts."

Woman as mere container, as vehicle? That is, woman as bearer of something more significant than herself? It is no wonder that abortion continues to be such a vexed issue in the United States. But the aesthetic precisely seems to drive a wedge between sexual reproduction and sexual desire. As we have already seen in Kant's Third Critique, the aesthetic is based on denial: the beauty of the "sexual organs of the plant" is transformed into "the beautiful," which seems to have no function.[18] And a man's attraction to a woman, in the canon, is based on her beauty, not her breeding possibilities. Even Heidegger has something to say about sexual difference vis-à-vis the thing. In the beginning of his essay on the work of art, he writes: "On the whole the word 'thing' . . . designates whatever is not simply nothing. . . . Yet . . . we hesitate to call God a thing. . . . A man is not a thing. It is true that we speak of a young girl who is faced with a task too difficult for her as being a young thing."[19] It is thus not forbidden to treat women as things and to "possess" them as one would a thing. As Wordsworth put it, "A slumber did my spirit seal / duhduhduhduh / She seemed a thing." Women make good things; things make good women. They don't offer the inconvenience of competition.

The framework of the thought about the thing by a man is inflected by the conquest of another "void":

Ham. [lying down at Ophelia's feet] Lady, shall I lie in your lap?
Oph. No, my lord.
Ham. I mean, my head upon your lap.
Oph. Ay, my lord.
Ham. Do you think I meant country matters?

Oph. I think nothing, my lord.
Ham. That's a fair thought to lie between maids' legs.
Oph. What is, my lord?
Ham. Nothing.[20]

a woman's "hole"

Like the ear, a woman's "hole" cannot be closed. From the Renaissance to Freud, female sexuality has been associated with a lack. The appeal of filling a void makes the beautiful or the sublime often seem like a thinly disguised rape. Yeats's poem about Leda and the Swan makes the whole Trojan War come out of Jupiter's rape of Helen's mother. Heidegger may extol the "betrothal" of humans and divinities, earth and sky. But the poet asks the Grecian Urn, "What men or gods are these? What maidens loath? What mad pursuit? What struggle to escape?" The scene is clearly one of aroused male sexuality pursuing reluctant maidens. But there is no perspective in the poem that validates female resistance: immediately after mentioning the maidens struggling to escape, Keats asks, "What wild ecstasy?"

The Street, by Ann Petry, is very explicit about the relation between thinking of a woman as a thing and trying to take power over her. The self-ignorant and chained-dog building superintendent, Jones, says to Lutie Johnson as he attempts to force himself on her, "You little thing. You young little thing."[21] Jones has very little power in the world, but he counts on the power that being male gives him over women. He constantly conflates Lutie with her things: once, scoping out Lutie's apartment while supposedly keeping her son company, he notices a lipstick that had touched her lips and longs to snatch it: "It would be good to hold it in his hands at night before he went to sleep so that the sweet smell would saturate his nostrils. He could carry it in his pocket where he could touch it during the day and take it out and fondle it down in the furnace room" (106). The "would"s and the "could"s in this passage are the mode of fantasy, the tense of imagination, what the text elsewhere calls "the flow of planning" (151). It is the tense of both sexual fantasies and dreams of a better life—but despite the carefully worked-out plots of these fantasies, they never come true because the plotter refuses to see a fundamental given. Jones, for example, refuses to see that Lutie will never be attracted to him. Lutie fails to see the effects of racism and sexism that stack the deck against her. Still on the lookout for possession-by-metonymy, Jones squeezes tightly a blouse he has seen Lutie wear. As he returns home that night, he thinks of Min, the woman he lives with.

Ann Petry's The Street

(male fantasies of women)

Jones' fantasy of Lutie's Lipstick

fantasy as planning

fantasy denying reality

"possesion-by-metonymy"

"He wouldn't be able to stand the sight of her any more after being close to Lutie like this" (109).

The fascination of contiguity—I'm touching the same paper Mallarmé touched—surrounds the beloved or the master with a halo of alluring nearness. But the almost religious reverence in which the fantasizer holds the object that has touched the beloved does not in fact bring her nearer to him, just nearer to his fantasy.

Power that is overdetermined, not individual, is often seen as an image in a mirror. Like many bars, Junto's Bar and Grill, Lutie's neighborhood nightspot, holds out a promise of wishes come true, and expands its virtual reality through a huge mirror.

> There were rows of bottles on the shelves on each side of the big mirror in back of the bar. They were reflected in the mirror, and looking at the reflection Lutie saw that they were magnified in size, shining so that they had the appearance of being filled with liquid, molten gold.
>
> She examined herself and the people standing at the bar to see what changes the mirror wrought in them. There was a pleasant gaiety and charm about all of them. She found that she herself looked young, very young and happy in the mirror.
>
> Her eyes wandered over the whole room. It sparkled in the mirror. The people had a kind of buoyancy about them. All except Old Man Junto, who was sitting alone at the table near the back.
>
> She looked at him again and again, for his reflection in the mirror fascinated her. Somehow even at this distance his squat figure managed to dominate the whole room. . . . For the barest fraction of a second, his eyes met hers in the mirror and then he looked away.

Junto, a white man, with the collaboration of Mrs. Hedges, a huge, scarred black woman he admires, controls most of the area in which Lutie lives. His second-in-command, Boots Smith, a black man, does his bidding, and his word is law. Although Junto doesn't have the usual nervous or condescending attitude of a white man toward blacks, he benefits from the position of unspoken authority his race gives him. He wants to keep Lutie for himself. Because "white superiority" is not a matter of individual psychology but is a more general ideological structure in the United States, Lutie always refers to his effects as emanating from "a figure in a mirror." When Junto has Boots tell Lutie that she will not receive a salary for singing at the bar, she realizes that she will therefore not become independent. "A figure in a mirror lifted a finger, shook his head, and she was right back where she started" (305). When Lutie's son Bub, convinced by Jones to participate in one of his many "plots," is taken to the Children's Shelter, Lutie turns to Boots Smith for the two hundred dollars she thinks she needs to get him out. "A figure in a mirror turned thumbs down and as he gestured, the playground for Bub vanished, the nice new furniture disappeared along with the big airy rooms" (420).

In her own cramped apartment, rage against everything that holds her back begins to boil, and she imagines that she sees Junto on her couch:

> The creeping, silent thing that she had sensed in the theater, in the beauty parlor, was here in her living room. It was sitting on her lumpy studio couch.
>
> Before it had been formless, shapeless, a fluid moving mass—something disembodied that she couldn't see, only sense. Now, as she stared at the couch, the thing took on form, substance. She could see what it was.
>
> It was Junto. (418)

rage + fantasy/imagination

But moments later, the figure whose presence is imaginary in her apartment becomes real in Boots Smith's apartment, where the two men think only about "having" Lutie, and in what order. When Boots does try to kiss Lutie, she strikes out at everything she hates, and kills Boots Smith because he is near at hand. "It was no longer Boots Smith, but a thing on a sofa" (431). <u>Death, in other words, can turn a person into a thing, and a person whose plans are constantly thwarted by racism or sexism into a killer.</u>

objectification through Death and Killing

One can, of course, escape one's pursuer by turning into a thing oneself. The most famous story of a person transformed into a thing is Ovid's tale of the sexual pursuit of Daphne by Apollo.[22] Daphne, who had escaped until then a reproductive destiny, pursued by an infatuated Apollo, flees the amorous god's embrace.

Ovid's tale of Daphne + Apollo

> But he ran the more swiftly, borne on the wings of love, gave her no time to rest, hung over her fleeing shoulders and breathed on the hair that streamed over her neck. Now was her strength all gone, and, pale with fear and utterly overcome by the toil of her swift flight, seeing her father's waters near, she cried: "O father, help! If your waters hold divinity; change and destroy this beauty by which I pleased o'er well." Scarce had she thus prayed when a

down-dragging numbness seized her limbs, and her soft sides were begirt with thin bark. Her hair was changed to leaves, her arms to branches. Her feet, but now so swift, grew fast in sluggish roots, and her head was now but a tree's top. Her gleaming beauty alone remained.

One modern rewriting of this story, by Jorie Graham, situates itself as both male and female, pursuer and pursued, in the poem "Self-Portrait as Apollo and Daphne."[23] While the classical version is based on an opposition between "sides," this poem, like Graham's poem "Orpheus and Euridice," places the tension within the poet; what is being acted out by two characters is what is created by the non-unifiable feelings of one consciousness. Daphne escapes by asking whether Apollo really *knows* what he pursues, but the two of them together collude in making the experience last. Orpheus looks back to discern Euridice among the scores of other women; but he knows he can no longer be married to anyone. These classic stories of males and females portray the poet's familiarity with old scenarios of that opposition, and with what is created—or tiresome—in it.

Because Ovid's tale is a story of successful resistance, and because Apollo contents himself with a poetic prize, not a sexual one, commentators have been even readier than Ovid to get rid of Daphne. Where Ovid mentions that the laurel wreath will crown military leaders and civic guardians, for example, modern commentators who see this story at the dawn of the elegy write:

> The story of Apollo and Daphne itself exemplifies the dramatic relation between loss and figuration. Having insulted Cupid, Apollo is smitten with an unrequited passion for Daphne. He pursues her to the riverbanks of her father, Peneus, whom she begs for deliverance. As Apollo grasps her, Daphne becomes the laurel tree—only her gleaming beauty (*nitor*) remaining unchanged. . .
>
> Instead of becoming the object of a sexual conquest, Daphne is thus eventually transformed into something very much like a consolation prize—a prize that becomes *the* prize and sign of poethood. What Apollo or the poet pursues turns into a sign not only of his lost love but also of his very pursuit—a consoling sign that carries in itself the reminder of the loss on which it has been founded.[24]

Let me open by proposing for our collective meditations the myth relating to the origin of the laurel crown—mark of poetic (and more generally literary) excellence and achievement, and insignia of the god of poetry (as god of much cognate else) himself as well.

It is said that Apollo conceived a violent passion for the wood nymph, Daphne, but that Daphne, cherishing her inviolate virginity, fled his embrace. As a god, of course, Apollo made short work of pursuit: the dark, untried interior withheld from his invasive, luminous probings was in the end to be his. Yet at the very instant in which the god overtook her, Daphne cried out to Gaia, Mother Earth, for help—and Gaia heard, and answered, transforming her on the spot into a bay or laurel tree. Weeping the loss, Apollo consoled himself by plucking a laurel branch, keeping it in remembrance of the nymph. And it is in this way that, as a sign of their divine ancestry and calling, the laurel descended to the poets—a talisman, tribal totem, and prize.[25]

The laurel crown is thus a sign of both "loss" and "achievement"; poetry is born under the sign of failure and consolation. Preferring to tell this story as the origin of poetic signs rather than as a story of two people, critics have tended to see the substitution of laurel tree for nymph as a good thing for poetry. They are happy to sacrifice Daphne for an aesthetic necessity. Raising the level of abstraction, critics thus erase sexual difference: "The story of Apollo and Daphne itself exemplifies the dramatic relation between loss and figuration."

[margin note: modern reading of laurel]

III

But Ovid does not, in Apollo's speech immediately after his sexual "failure," say that the laurel will crown poets, but rather military and civic leaders. Indeed, this whole episode follows an argument between Apollo, fresh from his conquest of a serpent, and Cupid, whose bow and arrows are puny compared with those of great warriors like Apollo. What is at stake is the rivalry between epic and lyric, and what Ovid is doing in this story is making a place within literature for love poetry. If Daphne turns into a laurel tree, Petrarch's Laura is not far behind. But the seriousness and power of desire as opposed to strength still needs to be argued: "Thy dart may pierce all things else, Apollo, but mine shall pierce thee," says Venus's son. It is not surprising if Apollo's first thought about the laurel wreath still concerns military conquerors. The place of lyric achievement was not, in Ovid's day, as secure as it seems now.

[margin note: Ovid's real purpose]

Making a place for love poetry was more possible if it was troped on the story of Apollo and Daphne, male pursuer and female prey, male lover and female object. That is, the seriousness of lyric in comparison with epic was won by making the sexual roles similar to those of conqueror and conquered. The lament of the male lover bewailing his lady's escape installed the heterosexuality and unrequitedness of canonical love.

Interesting things happen when the poet is female, and not—as convention and stereotype would have it—male. In a novel written by a woman, Rachilde, in the late nineteenth century, the female protagonist owns, and embraces before her astonished would-be male lover, an alabaster urn:

Rachilde's (female poet) rendering ⇓

> Among the strange knickknacks of Japanese complication or Chinese tortuousness, there was one admirable objet d'art placed in the middle of the room on a pedestal of old rose velvet, like an altar: an alabaster vase the height of a man, so slim, so slender, so deliciously troubling with its ephebe's hips, with such a human appearance, even though it retained the traditional shape of an amphora, that the viewer remained somewhat speechless.[26]

Female power-reversal ↓

While the female lover, Eliante, begins by obediently reversing the conventional heterosexual scheme, the point of the demonstration, by the end, is to show her male admirer her power and her lack of need of a human sexual partner:

> "Isn't it beautiful! Isn't *he* beautiful. . . You would think, when the light penetrates it obliquely, that it's inhabited by a soul, that a heart burns in this alabaster urn! . . . He will never tell, but he knows. . ."
>
> Leon Reille looked at her with superstitious admiration. He was gaining, for this woman, the respect of a young *savant* already in love with forms, colors, everything that recalled the power of the grace and beauty of his life: art, its transposition into the eternal. . . .
>
> The young woman, her eyes half closed, clung more tightly to the neck of the amphora. She pressed both arms around the collar of the stone flesh, and leaned over the corolla of the opening, kissing the void. . .
>
> She was not offering herself to the man; she was giving herself to the alabaster vase, the one insentient person on the scene. Without a single indecent gesture, arms chastely crossed on this slender form, neither girl nor boy. . . .
>
> Then, the man saw her closed eyelids flutter, her lips half open. . . ; a slight

shudder traversed her body . . . and she gave a small groan of imperceptible joy, the very breath of orgasm.[27]

The male onlooker admires the woman's "artistic sense" in loving a beautiful form; he applauds her appreciation for an inanimate object—until the human lover begins to feel that he is the unsuccessful rival of the insentient one: "'Leave that alone,' he said to her softly. 'You're a wretched fanatic, worshipping yourself in what is, in the end, a base material. Alabaster is a product of the earth which, without the men who sculpt it, would remain . . . earth.'"[28]

The urn is a thing yet somehow it seems animate; Keats's speaker addresses questions to the urn; Eliante makes love to it; Apollo feels Daphne's heart beating under the bark of the tree: "But even in this new form Apollo loved her; and placing his hand upon the trunk, he felt the heart still fluttering beneath the bark." Indeed, it is the voice of a woman trapped in a tree that Anne Sexton imagines as a female reply to the story of Daphne and Apollo. Her poem "Where I Live in This Honorable House of the Laurel Tree" begins:

Anne Sexton's female reply to Ovid's story

> I live in my wooden legs and O
> my green green hands.
> Too late
> to wish I had not run from you, Apollo,
> blood moves still in my bark bound veins.
> I, who ran nymph foot to root in flight,
> have only this late desire to arm the trees
> I lie within.

And ends:

> You gave me honor too soon, Apollo.
> There is no one left who understands
> how I wait
> here in my wooden legs and O
> my green green hands.[29]

Anne Sexton emphasizes two things that the focus on the male pursuer renders invisible: first, "too late" and "too soon" are much more important in female sexuality than in male: female desire, Sexton intimates, is often un-timely, and can often itself be belated with respect to experience; and sec-ond, the "animation" of the tree is an endless immobilization of the woman, as if she gets her wish to become a thing but keeps her human consciousness inside it.

Time, Sexton implies, is a more important factor than essence. Sylvia Plath, too, sees time as the untold dimension in Ovid, but she, unlike Sexton, focuses on the contradictory imperatives women were getting from American society at that time. Her poem "Virgin in a Tree" is one of a series of poems she ostensibly wrote about artworks: here, an early etch-ing by Paul Klee that shows an overripe virgin becoming too heavy for
her tree:

How this tart fable instructs
And mocks! Here's the parody of that moral mousetrap
Set in the proverbs stitched on samplers
Approving chased girls who get them to a tree
And put on bark's nun-black

Habit which deflects
All amorous arrows. For to sheathe the virgin shape
In a scabbard of wood baffles pursuers,
Whether goat-thighed or god-haloed. Ever since that first Daphne
Switched her incomparable back

For a bay-tree hide, respect's
Twined to her hard limbs like ivy: the puritan lip
Cries: "Celebrate Syrinx whose demurs
Won her the frog-colored skin, pale pith and watery
Bed of a reed. Look:

Pine-needle armor protects
Pitys from Pan's assault! And though age drop
Their leafy crowns, their fame soars,
Eclipsing Eva, Cleo, and Helen of Troy:
For which of those would speak

For a fashion that constricts
White bodies in a wooden girdle, root to top
Unfaced, unformed, the nipple-flowers

Shrouded to suckle darkness? Only they
Who keep cool and holy make

A sanctum to attract
Green virgins, consecrating limb and lip
To chastity's service: like prophets, like preachers,
They descant on the serene and seraphic beauty
Of virgins for virginity's sake."

Be certain some such pact's
Been struck to keep all glory in the grip
Of ugly spinsters and barren sirs
As you etch on the inner window of your eye
This virgin on her rack:

She, ripe and unplucked, 's
Lain splayed too long in the tortuous boughs: overripe
Now, dour-faced, her fingers
Stiff as twigs, her body woodenly
Askew, she'll ache and wake

Though doomsday bud. Neglect's
Given her lips that lemon-tasting droop:
Untongued, all that beauty's bright juice sours.
Tree-twist will ape this gross anatomy
Till irony's bough break.[30]

Like many poems by Sylvia Plath, this one has a strict intellectual—but not really musical—design. Each stanza is equivalent in shape (five lines, the shortest being first and last), and each line ends with the same consonant sounds as its fellow in all the other stanzas (instructs—deflects—respect's—protects—constricts—attract—pact's—unplucked, 's—neglect's, and so on). While rhyme traditionally involves echoing *vowel* sounds, Plath's pattern is designed not primarily for the ear but for the mind, and as a difficulty for the poet. Although this seems to be a poem against constriction, the poet enjoys puzzling out the constrictions of form she has set for herself. By equating the consonants, Plath flouts the similarity of sounds on which rhyme is usually based ("Troy," "beauty," "eye," and "anatomy" do not rhyme in the usual sense, nor do "overripe" and "lip.")

To bring together Ovid's three instances of female transformation *maidens saying "no"*

(Daphne, Syrinx, and Pitys) to escape sexual assault, with common advice given to young girls is already disorienting. To play on words ("tart" as "bitter-tasting" and "whore-like"; "chased" as both "pursued" and "chaste") is even more disturbing. But how is one to read Plath's plays on both learned and popular allusions, so that her poem often seems double-voiced?

> "Chased girls who get them to a tree / And put on bark's nun-black / Habit," playing on Hamlet to Ophelia: "Get thee to a nunnery"

> "Switched her incomparable back / For a bay-tree hide," troped on "Tyger's heart wrapped in a Player's hide" (Robert Greene), troped on Shakespeare's *Henry VI, Part 3:* "O tiger's heart wrapped in a woman's hide"

> "Virgins for virginity's sake," troped on "art for art's sake"

> "Tortuous boughs. . . / Till irony's bough break," troped on "Rock-a-bye, baby, in the treetops . . . / When the bough breaks. . ."

The mouth twisted with the taste of sour lemons is, in Plath's poetry, often a sign of old-maid-ness, as in "Two Sisters of Persephone" ("Turned bitter, / And sallow as any lemon, / The other, wry virgin to the last").

transition from hot young maid to ugly old maid

In Plath, also, timing is crucial: up to a certain point, a maid is told to flee sexual advances; after that point, she becomes an *old* maid, someone condemned for not partaking of a sexuality that, earlier, she was warned against. The problem is partly to identify that point, and to transform, utterly, everything repressed into attractiveness. For maximum societal control, a woman should always say "no" to sexuality but "I do" before she loses the sexuality for which she is pursued. Saying yes too soon or no too long condemns a woman to looseness or tightness, to a reputation as "easy" or one as "dried up." She is urged not to be sexual but to be marriageable. The moment that she is of interest to men is very brief. Before it or after it she is childlike or witchlike. The farther she gets from the fleeing Daphne, the more repulsive she grows.

But Plath imagines a world where the worth of chastity never decreases, where Daphne is always applauded for fleeing, where it goes without saying that women should always say no. And indeed, in canonical literature there is little else. Civilization, under the control of "ugly spinsters" and "barren sirs," lets Daphne stay in the tree too long, and thus all women are either desirable and impossible or overripe, glowering, and possible.

Chapter Six

Puppets and Prostheses

Heinrich von Kleist's "Über das Marionettentheater" is known mostly for its statements about puppets, not about mirrors. The head dancer of a well-known troupe astonishes the unnamed narrator of the story by saying that marionettes are much more graceful than human dancers can ever be, and suggests that if one cut off the limbs of humans and replaced them with prostheses, one would get better dancers—the more inanimate, the more reliable.

While cutting off limbs and replacing them with prostheses may seem gruesome, the idea of a dimension that human beings cannot reach is actually a rather common form of aesthetic idealization. "Heard melodies are sweet, but those unheard are sweeter. . ."

> He asked if I had not found certain movements of the puppets, particularly the smaller ones, very graceful when they danced.
>
> I could not deny the fact. . . .
>
> I inquired about the mechanism of these figures and how it was possible, without myriad strings on the fingers, to control the separate members and their tie-points as the rhythm of their movements or dances required.

Kleist on puppets
vs.
humans

He answered that I must not imagine that each member, in the various motions of the dance, had to be placed and pulled individually by the puppeteer.

Each movement, he said, had its center of gravity; it would suffice to control that center, on the inside of the figure; the limbs, which are really nothing but pendulums, follow of themselves, in a mechanical way, without further aid. . . .

"Have you ever heard," he asked, when I silently regarded the floor, "of those mechanical legs that English craftsmen manufacture for hapless accident victims?"

I said no, I had never set eyes on such things.

"I wish you had," he replied, "for if I tell you that these unfortunate people manage to dance with them, I am almost afraid you will not believe me. Nor is it an ordinary dance! The range of their movements is of course limited, but within it they attain to a lightness, a serenity, and a gracefulness that must amaze every thinking person."

I offered, joking, that he had found his man. For the same craftsman who was able to construct those remarkable limbs could doubtless construct a whole puppet to meet his requirements. . . .

"And the advantage of such a puppet over the living dancers?" [I asked.]

"The advantage? First of all, my good friend, a negative one: namely that it would be incapable of affectation. For affectation, as you know, occurs when the soul [*vis motris*] is located at any point other than the center of gravity of a movement. . . . Just observe Madame P——," he continued; "When she plays Daphne . . . pursued by Apollo, [she] looks back over her shoulder: her soul settles in the vertebrae of the small of her back; she bends over as if about to break in two. . . ."[1]

puppets/
humans
and
gravity

Consciousness divides the human being between an idea of self-consciousness and the force of gravity. As a result, consciousness is at war with natural law, and human imperfection is a sign of that war. Puppets, little perfect pendulums hanging and swinging from the fingers, are affected only by gravity, with one important exception: they do not need to *rest* on the ground as humans do—humans fight gravity simply in order to stand up, but in dancing, puppets merely touch it:

"In addition," he said, "these puppets have the advantage of *countergravity*. For they know nothing of the inertia of matter, which of all properties is the most obstructive to the dance: for the force that lifts them into the air is

greater than that which pulls them to the ground. . . . Puppets, like elves, require the ground only to *touch* on, and by that momentary obstruction to reanimate the spring of their limbs; while we require it to *rest* on, and to recover
from the exertions of the dance."[2]

Many writers share Kleist's idealization of puppets—or perhaps his low
estimation of human beings. As the French writer Paul Claudel has written,

> A puppet is the complete animated likeness, not only of the face, but of the
> limbs and the whole body. A living doll, a tiny man in our hands, a concen-
> tration of movement. A puppet is not, like a human actor, held captive by its
> own weight. It has no contact with earth, and moves with equal ease in all di-
> mensions. It floats in an intangible element like a drawing in an empty space.
> Its life is in its center, and its four limbs and head, spread out like rays around
> it, are merely its elements of expression. It is like a talking star, untouchable.[3]

Anatole France, too, compares puppets favorably to human actors: "I am
infinitely thankful to them [puppets] for having replaced living actors. If I
may speak my whole mind, actors spoil comedy for me. I mean good actors.
I might perhaps come to terms with the other sort! But decidedly I cannot
endure excellent actors such as are to be seen at the Comédie-Française.
Their talent is too great; it overwhelms everything. There is nothing but
them. Their personality effaces the work they represent."[4]

It seems that puppets do for some observers resemble divinities in
contrast to fallen, self-aggrandizing human beings. The aura of contact with
a transcendent dimension, in fact, is what often renders puppets eerie.
Sigmund Freud, in his essay "The Uncanny," says that what is uncanny is
the awakening of a system of belief that one thinks one has surmounted: "It
seems as if each of us has been through a phase of individual development
corresponding to [the] animistic stage in primitive men, that none of us has
passed through it without preserving certain residues and traces which are
still capable of manifesting themselves, and that everything that strikes us as
"uncanny" fulfills the condition of touching those residues of animistic
mental activity within us and bringing them to expression."[5]

Victoria Nelson has devoted a whole book—*The Secret Life of Puppets*—
to studying the forgotten or repressed experience of transcendence that puppets, in a seemingly minor way, give access to. The religious frisson of ani-

Nelson's 'Secret
Life of Puppets'

mated God-bodies is tied to the concept of *likeness:* just as God created man in his image, humans, like gods, can create the divine whenever they overcome the prohibition against graven images and carve out animated human-shaped statues of divine beings they can worship:

metamorphosis of:
· spiritualizing the
  material
· materializing the
  spiritual

> This, then, will be a discourse on puppets and idols that explores the meta-morphosis, over a span of two millennia, of two profoundly religious activi-ties of the early history of Western culture: spiritualizing the material by embalming human bodies, and materializing the spiritual by making hu-man simulacra as physical embodiments of the divine. As these two prac-tices of "ensouling" matter move from religion (the realm of belief) to art (the realm of make-believe or imagination), we will see on one hand the Late Antique mummy transformed in secular works of the imagination from a di-vine body within an organized belief system into a kind of organic demon (homunculus, golem, Frankenstein's monster, genetic clone), and on the other hand the moving, talking Late Antique god statue transformed into the automated Neoplatonic daemons of puppet, robot, cyborg, and virtual entity. These invented creatures of our imagination still carry for us, below the level of consciousness, that uncanny aura the unacknowledged "holy" characteristically assumes in a secular context. In the history of puppets and other human simulacra after the decline of religion we can read—in a back-ward image, like a reflection in a mirror—the underground history of the soul excluded from its religious context in Western culture.[6]

Kleist on inanimate
and divine

Kleist indeed concludes his story by equating the absence of conscious-ness to divinity, the inanimate to the divine: "So will grace, having . . . tra-versed the infinite, return to us once more, and so appear most purely in that bodily form that has either no consciousness at all or an infinite one, which is to say, either in a puppet or [in] a god."[7]

A trace of those suppressed religious practices—more deeply embedded in us, even while we deny it, than a completely surmounted primitive stage—comes through in the words of the turn-of-the-century theatrical in-novator Edward Gordon Craig:

> The actor must go, and in his place comes the inanimate figure—the *Übermarionette* we may call him, until he has won for himself a better name. Much has been written about the puppet, or marionette. There are some excellent volumes on him, and he has also inspired some works of art. To-day

in his least happy period many people come to regard him as rather a superior doll—and to think he has developed from the doll. He is a descendant of the stone images of the old temples—he is to-day a rather degenerate form of a god.[8]

And the poet (Rainer Maria Rilke) says directly to the puppet, stressing its substitute nature: "That we did not make you then into an idol, you puppet, and did not succumb to you in fear, was, I want to tell you, because it was not *you* we had in mind. We had in mind something quite different, invisible, that we held over and above ourselves and you, secretly and full of presentiment, and for which we both were only pretexts, so to speak. We had in mind a soul—the puppet soul. . . . Only one could not rightly say *where* you, puppet soul, really were."[9]

Rilke on Puppet soul ⇩

(Kleist,) too, spoke of the puppet's soul, but praised in it its perfect mechanical accord with the law of gravity, whereas humans were always placing their souls, as it were, at odds with it. ✓

Kleist cont'd ⇩

Puppets are surrounded by an aura of otherness—never familiar—and that is what makes them proper stand-ins for the invisible. When the transcendent becomes invisible, all perception of the articulation of those pendulums is lost. (Kleist) likes puppets precisely because they are the perfect mechanisms that humans can never be. The God-Machine is always more god than machine, while Kleist idealizes puppets for being more machine than god. The god-statue does not deny mechanism; it represses it. The human or divine soul is supposed to inhabit a total organic form in which the image does not divide into parts. Instead of the opposition between inanimate and animate, we have the opposition between the organic and the inorganic. God-statues and human beings become similar in that both are indivisible: they are all one thing; this is what makes them appropriate to represent the invisible. The human has a soul to the extent, then, that he or she is imagined as whole, all organic, one. "I answered that, however skillfully he might propose his paradox, he could never make me believe that more charm might inhere in a mechanical doll than in the structure of the human body," says Kleist's narrator.[10] ✓

soul and wholeness?

With his emphasis on mechanism, it is no wonder that Kleist's dancer eventually brings up artificial limbs. In replacing a body part, one has to acknowledge that the body *has* parts. And yet the loss of wholeness an artificial limb represents is so strong that even Kleist's dancer refers to them with

↳ Parts of body: prostheses...

pity: "Have you ever heard . . . of those mechanical legs that English crafts-men manufacture for *hapless accident victims? . . .* These *unfortunate people* manage to dance with them."

The development of prostheses has marked advances in both peacetime and wartime technology: it is possible to survive ever more terrible dismem-berments with ever more life-like prostheses. Breakthroughs in artificial limbs are discoveries involving working joints; rather than making up for a loss, what is possible in the world of replacement parts dictates the form of the operation in the first place.[11]

In his interesting book called *Prosthesis,* David Wills describes his father quoting a line from Virgil and drying the dishes while waiting for a spasm of pain to traverse his stump. Prosody brings to language the mechanical repe-tition that is missing from mere meaning. The mechanical is denied as al-ready a natural part of humanness, but the relations between the living and the mechanical become complicated:

> In this way the wooden leg represents the duality of every prosthesis, its search for a way between emulating the human and superseding the hu-man. . . . [Improved, the prosthesis] takes a big step toward the reproduction of a functioning more strictly analogous to that of the human leg, but that is also a step towards the more strictly mechanical functions of the human, hence toward the nonhuman. . . . They are . . . two competing conceptions of the human. . . . They continue to compete throughout the development of high technology into the domain of robotic operations and into the question of artificial intelligence.[12]

The father's leg was amputated because of a cancer, and the book is punctuated by the paternal artificial limb. But "prosthesis" is also a term for letters added to a word, and it becomes, in Wills's book, a logic that is nei-ther about nor not about its subject, neither autobiography nor not auto-biography.

The mysterious and necessary link joining any artificial limb to a natural body makes the relation between the natural and the artificial the first prob-lem a prosthesis must solve—a first, seemingly insurmountable opposition between the organic and the inorganic: "Prosthesis treats of whatever arises out of that relation, and of the relation itself, of the sense and functioning of

[handwritten margin notes: "development of prostheses"; "David Wills' book 'Prosthesis'"]

articulations between matters of two putatively distinct orders: father/son, flesh/steel, . . . nature/artifice, . . . and so on."[13]

The weight of the bodily wholeness the prosthesis is supposed to restore creates the phenomenon known as the "phantom limb." "It was something between a phantom pain and a rheumatic or arthritic disorder," writes Wills; "Something ethereal, fluid, or mechanical, it mattered little except that it stung like an exposed nerve, like a stump grieving an absent leg."[14] But if the lost member can be felt even when it is gone, who is to say that its presence wasn't always "in the head"? That is, organic form might always have been a fantasy, and the difficulty of getting used to its artificial substitute is the difficulty of living without that fantasy—or is it?

"phantom limb"

> The question raised by prosthesis, naively conceived of as artificial appendage to natural member, is particular, or personal, in two obvious ways. Firstly, in that my father wears a wooden leg; secondly, in that I write criticism. (18)

> As long as the life in the story cannot be recounted without reference to prosthesis one will not be able to find in this a simple appeal to a naturalness of a leg to preempt a supposed artificiality of the rhetorical or academic. (16)

> The use of the first-person pronoun has consistently served as the excuse for arrogating all sorts of privilege to one's discursive position. As a corrective here, the oft-repeated "I" should always be read as a prosthetic "I." (19)

> This exercise is preparatory to a prosthetic leg, a familiar ride on a familiar bicycle suddenly become a difficult apprenticeship, he is suddenly aware of the rank mechanical otherness of the machine he used to climb on without hesitation. . . . As long as there is movement, as long as the body is shifting and turning the wheel he enjoys the illusion of wholeness . . . sailing self-propelled past corporeal and mechanical alike. (22–23)

> But all that functions only because of prosthesis, because the whole never was anywhere . . . because the parts were always already detachable, replaceable. (15)

By the time Wills's father has received the prosthesis he was fitted for, he has become quite adept at doing without what it replaces. The first experience of using the artificial limb is therefore a return to clumsiness, to having an "extra" limb, not to making up for lacking one. Is the limbless body the "organic form," then, and the restored bodily wholeness an artificial encumbrance? If the artificial leg began as a crutch and only later was made to resemble a leg, is it an *addition* or a *replacement*? And does language clarify or obscure the difference?

> The wooden leg is not really wooden. Language has already taken leave of reality, the literal taken leave of itself. . . . By that same logic, it is probably not a leg, either. In any case it is made of steel, or some alloy. It has a vaguely flesh-colored hue to it, very vague, for there is nothing particularly convincing about it as a simulacrum of a human leg. . . . This is your basic two-mode prosthesis: straight or bent. . . . It is a far cry from a peg leg on the one hand, but falls far short of a cyborg's computerized and fully articulated flesh-covered robotic limbs on the other. (26)

The numerous little prostheses of daily life—dental crowns, eyeglasses, hearing aids—seem like *additions,* even if, as with dental crowns, they really do replace a dysfunctional part of nature. What is striking about a prosthesis is its immunity from decay: a sign of life, therefore, is the capacity to die. One of the things that must be gotten used to is the fact that something immortal has taken the place of something mortal.

Human beings also don't seem to be able to define human specificity without some mention of interiority; or, as E. T. A. Hoffmann will put it, "some thinking and feeling." To be human presupposes signs of an inside, in other words, as a source of what appears on the outside. But which is my real interiority—an MRI of my brain or the thinking organ inside my head?

To make things even more complicated, the desire to be human seems to inhere in the very being of a puppet: Pinocchio wants to be a "real boy," little David in the film *AI* competes with a human child for his mother's love, and the puppet in a commercial is in ecstasies over the idea of *wirelessness* (to strains of *Born Free*). The pathos of the story of little David resides in the viewer's identification, not with the human characters in the film but with the artificial protagonist. He becomes the abandoned child in all of us, and the humans, the uncomprehendingly cruel process of growing up.

The principal sign of Pinocchio's "realness" is the disappearance of the signs of his articulation: in a puppet, the joints are marked; in a "real boy," they are erased. Pinocchio becomes a real boy when his body is entirely smooth. Organic form is thus, among other things, an erasure of articulation. This may be why Western cultures are intolerant of any lines on the body—any wrinkles or signs of experience—especially in a love object. "Realness" can be worse or better than humanness, but the results must to some extent project an idealized view of human nature, even with all its faults. Faults just stand as evidence of realness. In E. T. A. Hoffmann's story "The Sand-Man," which Sigmund Freud analyzes in his essay "The Uncanny," people make a show of imperfection in order not to resemble the wooden doll, Olimpia, with whom the hapless and romantic hero falls in love.

> Several lovers, in order to be fully convinced that they were not paying court to a wooden puppet, required that their mistress should sing and dance a little out of time, should embroider or knit or play with her little pug, &c., when being read to, but above all things else that she should do something more than merely listen—that she should frequently speak in such a way as to really show that her words presupposed as a condition some thinking and feeling.[15]

But why wouldn't others seek to resemble human beings, after all? The fantasy of others' desire to resemble oneself is always flattering to one's self-image. What the other is deemed to want is what the subject himself thinks he wants. So the subject and the other supposedly want the same thing, which the subject supposedly has and the other desires. In reality, both lack the same thing, and the flattering nature of this relationship is that if the other wants it, the subject must have it. But both the other's desire and the subject's possession are fantasies of the subject.

Thus, what makes Pinocchio human is his willingness to sacrifice himself for the welfare of others, while his lying and cheating kept him confined to his wooden body. It is at least arguable that lying and cheating are more common among humans than self-sacrifice is, but the ego-ideal of heroism and martyrdom replace the self-interested reality with an other-directed ideal in such a way as to please the consumers (who, after all, are humans) and erase the uncomfortable truth. In the end, Pinocchio has become what we "real people" wish to be.

But, in the Disney version at least, it is *Geppetto's* wish, not Pinocchio's, that the puppet become real. Geppetto wants a son without benefit of woman—woman who becomes not a mother but a good fairy. Pinocchio is subject to the bad sides of people's desire for a boy, as he lies, smokes, drinks, and almost becomes a donkey (an "ass"), but he is saved by a Platonic male lover and paternal stand-in, Jiminy Cricket, his conscience. Walking a tightrope between exploitation and pleasure (rebellious boys go to Pleasure Island), Pinocchio saves Geppetto from the belly of a whale named Monstro. For his pains, the good fairy returns and makes him real. Thus, "realness" is a gift that everyone seeks for Geppetto, and Pinocchio's desire to become a real boy may be nothing more than the desire that Geppetto get his wish. The son, at the end, has surmounted what, according to the film, is specific about male-male love, and can now with impunity fall into Geppetto's embrace.

Three Paradigmatic Prostheses

Then began sixteen years of discomfort, distress, and pain, interrupted only by recurrence of the trouble and further operations. The huge prosthesis, a sort of magnified denture or obturator, designed to shut off the mouth from the nasal cavity, was a horror; it was labeled "the monster." In the first place it was very difficult to take out and replace because it was impossible for him to open his mouth at all widely. On one occasion, for instance, the combined efforts of Freud and his daughter failed to insert it after struggling for half an hour, and the surgeon had to be fetched for the purpose. Then for the instrument to fulfill its purpose of shutting off the yawning cavity above, and so making speaking and eating possible, it had to fit fairly tightly. This, however, produced constant irritation and sore places until its presence was unbearable. But if it were left out for more than a few hours the tissues would shrink, and the denture could no longer be replaced without being altered.[16]

The White Whale swam before him as the monomaniac incarnation of all those malicious agencies which some deep men feel eating in them, till they are left living with half a heart and half a lung. . . .
It is not probable that this monomania in him took its instant rise at the precise time of his bodily dismemberment. Then, in darting at the monster, knife in hand, he had but given loose to a sudden, passionate, corporal animosity; and when he received the stroke that tore him, he probably but felt the agonizing bodily laceration, but nothing more. . . .
    If such a furious trope may stand, his special lunacy stormed his general sanity, and carried it, and turned all its concentrated cannon upon its own mad mark; so that far from having lost his strength, Ahab, to that one end,

did now possess a thousand fold more potency than ever he had sanely brought to bear upon any one reasonable object. . . .

So well did he succeed in that dissembling [concealing his madness], that when with ivory leg he stepped ashore at last, no Nantucketer thought him otherwise than naturally grieved, and that to the quick, with the terrible casualty that had overtaken him.[17]

A man with a wooden leg, who had sat [there] for some years, with his remaining foot in a bucket in cold weather . . . , stumped to the corner.[18]

This unlikely trio—Freud, Ahab, and Wegg—have in common the fact that their prostheses reflect their being to an uncanny extent, and those prostheses seem to bleed all over the rhetoric of the text that supposedly contains them.

With Freud, one catches a glimpse of Freud's daughter Anna, who was the real prosthesis, often taking his place at the lectern to speak for him.

Ahab's ivory leg is made out of whalebone, and Ahab himself, part by part, begins to resemble the white whale he seeks. Scrimshaw carving is a sailor's pastime, and the idea that the object of revenge is *material* means that as the two antagonists confront each other, it is not clear who has dismasted—and who is digesting parts of—whom. The fact that the whale has taken off Ahab's leg indicates that throughout the book the question is one of body parts, not of wholes. After all, even without Ahab's obsessive fixation on one whale, the rest of his crew wants to make a profit on whale parts and whale material. The whale is divided not just into parts but into saleable commodities. Before the whale became an endangered species, it existed as a source of whale-oil futures.

But Charles Dickens really hits the jackpot when he shows how the wooden leg takes over in his text: "Wegg was a knotty man, and a close-grained, with a face carved out of very hard material, that had lost as much play of expression as a watchman's rattle. When he laughed, certain jerks occurred in it, and the rattle sprung. Sooth to say, he was so wooden a man that he seemed to have taken his wooden leg naturally, and rather suggested to the fanciful observer that he might be expected—if his development received no untimely check—to be completely set up with a pair of wooden legs in about six months."[19] Prostheses, then, seem more like reflections of essences and fates than like replacement parts. But perhaps it is language's function to make us think so.

Chapter Seven

Using People

KANT WITH WINNICOTT

Using people, transforming others into a means for obtaining an end for oneself, is generally considered the very antithesis of ethical behavior. And with good reason. Faced with the violence of colonial, sexual, and even epistemological appropriation, ethical theorists have sought to replace domination with respect, knowledge with responsibility. But it often seems as though a thought that begins in intersubjectivity or mutuality ends up sounding like a mere defense of the Other against the potential violence of the Subject. All *too* often, such theorists conclude, as does the following translator of Emmanuel Levinas: "Ontology becomes indebtedness to what is, a quiet listening vigilant against its own interference, cautious of its own interventions, careful not to disturb."[1] But if ethics is defined in relation to the potentially violent excesses of the subject's power, then that power is in reality being presupposed and reinforced in the very attempt to undercut it. What is being denied from the outset is the subject's *lack* of power, its vulnerability and dependence. Respect and distance are certainly better than violence and appropriation, but is ethics only a form of restraint? In this chapter I take for granted the necessity of critiques of the imperial subject, but I would nevertheless like to question the model of intactness on which such critiques usually rely. Might there not, at least on the psychological level, be another way to use people?

The classic formulation of the stricture against using people is given in Kant's Second Critique: "It follows of itself that, in the order of ends, man (and every rational being) is an end-in-himself, i.e., he is never to be used merely as a means for someone (even for God) without at the same time being himself an end. . . . This moral law is founded on the autonomy of his will as a free will, which by its universal laws must necessarily be able to agree with that to which it subjects itself."[2] Kant, of course, warns against treating people as a means *without* also treating them as an end, which is not the same as excluding using people altogether. But using people has nevertheless acquired an entirely negative connotation ("I feel so *used!*").

Using people can be understood simply as exploitation, as when a person with power or resources makes use of the undercompensated labor of others to increase his or her power or resources. Or, interpersonally, using people is commonly associated with a scenario in which one person professes to be interested in another person in order to obtain something for him- or herself. Less instrumentally but just as commonly, people can also use other people in the service of their own narcissistic consolidation, as when, in Heinz Kohut's words, "the expected control over the narcissistically cathected object . . . is closer to the concept which a grownup has of himself and of the control which he expects over his own body and mind than to the grownup's experience of others and of his control over them (which generally leads to the result that the object of such narcissistic 'love' feels oppressed and enslaved by the subject's expectations and demands)."[3] The literary elaboration of this narcissistic enslavement takes the form of idealization and thingification, from Pygmalion's beloved ivory girl to the female bodies turned to milk, cherries, pearls, and gold through the magic of poetry. One of the founding insights of feminist criticism has been to point out that the idealized, beloved woman is often described as an object, a thing, rather than a subject. But perhaps the problem with being used arises from an inequality of power rather than from something inherently unhealthy about *willingly* playing the role of thing. Indeed, what if the capacity to become a subject were something that could best be *learned* from an object? Not an idealized object but rather, say, a smelly blanket with a frayed edge?

That smelly blanket has played a starring role in the theory of transitional objects worked out by D. W. Winnicott. The objectness of the object is fundamental to its function, yet Winnicott is careful to caution against simply equating the transitional object with the blanket, thumb, or teddy bear that may take on this role. Transitional objects, he explains, are the first "not-me" possessions, objects that are neither "internal" to the baby (that is, hallucinatory, like, at first, the mother's breast) nor "external," like reality, of which at first the baby has no knowledge, but something in between. The transitional object is not a narcissistic object—it does not offer an image of body wholeness like the image in Lacan's mirror. It is not an image but a thing.[4] The most valuable property of the transitional object is probably its lack of perfection, its irrelevance to the question of perfection.

As its name implies, the transitional object is a "between." It is often associated with the blanket or teddy bear to which the child grows attached, but Winnicott tries to keep opening a different space between—between, for example, the thumb and the teddy bear. Winnicott's task is to put something into words that is hard to put into words. In the introduction to *Playing and Reality*, he explains that what he is trying to keep hold of is not an object but a paradox:

> It is now generally recognized, I believe, that what I am referring to in this part of my work is not the cloth or the teddy bear that the baby uses—not so much the object used as the use of the object. I am drawing attention to the paradox involved in the use by the infant of what I have called the transitional object. My contribution is to ask for a paradox to be accepted and tolerated and respected, and for it not to be resolved. By flight to split-off intellectual functioning it is possible to resolve the paradox, but the price of this is the loss of the value of the paradox itself. This paradox, once accepted and tolerated, has value for every human individual who is not only alive and living in this world but who is also capable of being infinitely enriched by exploitation of the cultural link with the past and with the future.[5]

This is a typical move in Winnicott's text: going within a sentence or two from establishing the finest possible distinction to making the broadest possible cultural claims. This is indeed a huge claim, that accepting and tolerating the still-not-really-explained paradox opens the way for all of cultural life. The paradox of the transitional object functions like the transitional object itself, as a domain of play and illusion that allows an interpreter, like an infant, to accept and tolerate frustration and reality. To intellectualize too soon is here to think of the transitional object as an object rather than a paradox.

Winnicott's theory of transitional phenomena is itself a transitional phenomenon in theory. He describes development as having a beginning, a middle, and an end, and says that theorists have not said enough about the middle. Much of his writing involves making the right space for itself ("prepare the ground for my own positive contribution")—situating exactly what he is saying between two things he is not saying. This expanded middle is where Winnicott's unparalleled subtlety is located, between two crudenesses—the crudeness of the way in which he describes the mother's task of being perfectly available and then optimally frustrating as a task that is only seen from the infant's point of view, and the way he privileges heterosexual reproductivity as a sign of adult health (the blightedness, for example, of those whom he pronounces "not married"). Winnicott's beginning and end shed no new analytical light on normative stereotypes of the good mother and the healthy adult (happily married with children). But in his own domain—somewhere between where the good mother becomes the good enough mother and where the healthy adult can play—he rises to the occasion to "put into words" something that ordinary language has to stretch to render.

"I hope it will be understood that I am not referring exactly to the little child's teddy bear or to the infant's first use of the fist (thumb, fingers). I am not specifically studying the first object of object-relationships. I am concerned with the first possession, and with the intermediate area between the subjective and that which is objectively perceived" (3). Winnicott says he is "reluctant to give examples." The naming and exemplifying functions of language are the ones to hold in abeyance, to make room for something not-to-be-formulated. "Of the transitional object it can be said that it is a matter of agreement between us and the baby that we will never ask the question: 'Did you conceive of this or was it presented to you from without?' The important point is that no decision on this point is expected. The question is not to be formulated" (12). This, then, is the paradox, which he explains in a later essay in similar terms: "The baby creates the object, but the object was there waiting to be created and to become a cathected object" (89). Winnicott explicitly envisions the transitional object as a kind of navel of the arts: he includes not only objects but also words, patterns, tunes, and mannerisms in his lists of things that can function as transitional objects.

This paradox of unlocatability is also, in fact, similar to the paradox of the moral law in Kant, as stated in a footnote to the *Foundation of the Metaphysics of Morals*: "The only object of respect is the law, and indeed only the law which we impose on ourselves and yet recognize as necessary in itself."[6] This is not to say that the moral law *is* the transitional object, but only to suggest that it manifests the same kind of paradox.

The function of the transitional object in Winnicott, then, is to open a space for experience: the transitional object is that through which the baby gains experience of a state between the illusion of the mother's total adaptation to needs and reality's total indifference to them. The object helps the baby learn to tolerate frustration, loss of omnipotence, separation.

The transitional object is not only something that cannot be understood in terms of a dichotomy between subject and object, since it helps bring that dichotomy into being, but is also something about which there is agreement as to what will not be asked. A space is made for the object within language. The transitional object is part of a contract of nonformulation. The apparent one-on-one relation between baby and thing is set in a social, almost legal, dimension agreed to by adults. In one of Winnicott's many lists, this one called a "Summary of Special Qualities in the Relationship," the first special quality is a question of rights: "The infant assumes rights over the object." I'd like to look closely at this list of qualities. Listen for the grammatical roles of the infant, the object, and "us," and for the relations between active and passive verbs.[7]

1. The infant assumes rights over the object, and we agree to this assumption. Nevertheless, some abrogation of omnipotence is a feature from the start.

In this first point, the infant is the subject, and the object an object. The word "assumption" plays a complicated role here: do we agree to the infant's assumption of rights, or do we agree to the assumption that the infant has rights? Are we agreeing to the rights, or to the idea? In the second sentence, "infant," "object," and "us" have all grammatically dropped out. Instead, we find a description of a feature: abrogation of omnipotence. Who is abrogating omnipotence? The infant whose rights are not absolute? Or "us," whose agreement is not entirely the law here. An obvious reading would have it that although the infant is allowed power over the object, the nature of this power is from the start a falling away from the kind of power an infant experiences over an internal object. Nevertheless, the sentence describes the abrogation of omnipotence as if it had a separate existence, as if it were functioning as a transitional object in its own right.

2. The object is affectionately cuddled as well as excitedly loved and mutilated.

In this second point, and in all five remaining points, the object is the subject of the sentence. Here, the infant is the implicit agent of verbs in the passive voice. Why is the infant not mentioned? It is as though the sentence has to be written from the point of view of the object, as though the actions of cuddling, loving, and mutilating had to be experienced by the object rather than enacted by the infant. As though the infant cannot be allowed to have so much agency without violating the nature of the transitional phenomenon.

3. It must never change, unless changed by the infant.

This is a law, but whose? Is it a warning to the parents not to wash the blanket? Is it a condition of the object's being considered a transitional object by the infant? Is it a rule the object must obey, or the adults? Or an apprenticeship in agency that must be practiced by the infant?

4. It must survive instinctual loving, and also hating and, if it be a feature, pure aggression.

Is this a law or a test? The difference between this point and the second one is this emphasis on survival, about which we will say more in a moment.

5. Yet it must seem to the infant to give warmth, or to move, or to have texture, or to do something that seems to show it has vitality or reality of its own.

Why does this "it must" begin with "yet"? This feature has a logical relation of contrast to the preceding one, but what is the contrast? It must survive . . . yet it must seem to live. Is survival not an appearance of life? Perhaps the object's survival in point four is a sign of its inanimateness; its thingliness resists destruction as a living thing could not. And yet it does have vitality to the extent that it has reality.

6. It comes from without from our point of view, but not so from the point of view of the baby. Neither does it come from within; it is not a hallucination.

This point in many ways returns to the first point. Baby and adult points of view are both mentioned, this time with more contrast. It is a question of inside and outside in two ways: where is the object (inside or outside the baby); where is the point of view (inside or outside the baby). The second sentence is a return to the abrogation of omnipotence: the object is not a hallucination. Thus the baby's point of view is not described: only what it is not (the object comes neither from without nor from within—this was the question not to be formulated, and it is still, in a sense, not formulated here).

The seventh feature begins like the others, but the voice of the theorist soon takes over, with a celebration of culture that reads like an epitaph to the object:

7. Its fate is to be gradually allowed to be decathected, so that in the course of years it becomes not so much forgotten as relegated to limbo. By this I mean that in health the transitional object does not "go inside" nor does the feeling about it necessarily undergo repression. It is not forgotten and it is not mourned. It loses meaning, and this is because the transitional phenomena have become diffused, have become spread out over the whole intermediate territory between "inner psychic reality" and "the external world as perceived by two persons in common," that is to say, over the whole cultural field.

"Its fate is to be gradually allowed to be decathected." What is the point of view of this sentence? It begins from the point of view of the object, facing its fate. Winnicott's capacity to capture the pathos of the object as it loses meaning, and to do so without overt personification, is somehow very moving. Yet the sentence is not entirely from the object's point of view: its fate is to be *gradually allowed to be* decathected. Temporality belongs to the infant, not to the object. Unless of course the object always wanted to be decathected, and is gradually freed from the infant's interest. The infant's role in the object's experience of fate is to let the object go. But Winnicott does not say: "The infant gradually outgrows the object." The change in the infant is experienced as a change in the object, yet it is experienced only *by* the object, since it is a change that involves losing the object's capacity to have a point of view.

After these seven points, Winnicott concludes, "At this point my subject widens out into that of play, and of artistic creativity and appreciation, and of religious feeling, and of dreaming, and also of fetishism, lying and stealing, the origin and loss of affectionate feeling, drug addiction, the talisman of obsessional rituals, etc." (5). Winnicott, in his description of these manifestations of play, does not play so freely as to fail to distinguish, by adding the word "also," between good play and bad play.

But what about the question of using people? Doesn't "using people" still sound like something unethical? Let us return to Winnicott, this time to an essay entitled, "The Use of an Object and Relating through Identifications" (86–94). In this essay, Winnicott distinguishes between object relating and object use. Some patients, it seems, are unable to "use" the analyst. Instead, they "relate to" the analyst by constructing a false self capable of finishing the analysis and expressing gratitude. But the real work has not been done. What is that real work? In comparing the analyst to the transitional object, Winnicott suggests that the subject's problem is an inability to "use people." This, then, is the notion of "using people" that we wish to explore through Winnicott.

Winnicott's analysis shows that, in some patients, the inability to use people leaves them trapped in a narcissistic lock in which nothing but approval and validation, or disapproval and invalidation, can be experienced. The whole scenario of destruction and excited love, which the transitional object must survive, cannot happen. The properly used object is one that survives destruction. The survival of the object demonstrates that the baby is not omnipotent, that the object is not destroyed by destruction, that the object will not retaliate in kind if the baby attacks, that the object will not leave if the baby leaves. Separation is possible only if the baby believes the object will still be there to come back to. The baby cannot *use* the object for growth if the baby cannot separate from it for fear of destroying it or losing it—object relating is contrasted with object use in that object use involves trust that separation can occur without damage, while object relating means that attention to the object must be constantly maintained and damage repaired, otherwise the object will be destroyed or will leave. At stake is the place of reality: "If all goes well; the infant can actually come to gain from the experience of frustration, since incomplete adaptation to need makes objects real, that is to say, hated as well as loved" (11)—that is, ambivalence is a sign that the object is real.

Analytic patients who are unable to "use" the analyst are stuck in a fantasy of omnipotence (the analyst will not survive my rage), which is based on a denied dependency (I cannot survive if the analyst does not survive). Thus, the relation implies a power inequality that is both exaggerated and denied. Such people think the analyst cannot survive use, which might involve "excitedly loving and mutilating." But if the patient does learn to use people, Winnicott writes, "In psychoanalytic practice the positive changes that come about in this area can be profound. They do not depend on interpretive work. They depend on the analyst's survival of the attacks, which involves and includes the idea of the absence of a quality change to retaliation. These attacks may be very difficult for the analyst to stand" (92). At this point, Winnicott drops in a footnote: "When the analyst knows that the pa-

object use
vs.
object relation

tient carries a revolver, then, it seems to me, this work cannot be done." The patient must experience the infantile magnitude of his destructiveness without making it real. Which means that the analyst must remain in the power position—but not truly in danger—in order to exercise therapeutic inertness. Using the analyst means experiencing all the infantile feelings of omnipotence and dependency so as to learn to tolerate and integrate them rather than shut them out through a false system of premature respect and concern. The ethical position of the analyst is to refrain from retaliating *and* to refrain from interpreting. In this, the analyst is in the classic ethical position of the powerful one exercising restraint. It is in the less powerful position that, paradoxically, restraint has become the problem. By allowing the patient the space and the time to try out both the feelings—of omnipotence and powerlessness—and their meanings, the patient comes into a more realistic and creative relation to his true strengths and limits. The object becomes real because it survives, because it is outside the subject's area of omnipotent control. The narcissistic lock of reparation and retaliation is opened to let in the world.

As is usual with Winnicott, something other than a mere description of these psychic processes happens in his text *in language*. Let me quote an extended passage from the middle of the essay. "This change (from relating to usage) means that the subject destroys the object. From here it could be argued by an armchair philosopher that there is therefore no such thing in practice as the use of an object: if the object is external, then the object is destroyed by the subject" (90). The armchair philosopher is here playing the role of the intellectualizer away of the paradox: the object is either inside or outside, destroyed or not destroyed. But look at what happens to the armchair philosopher in the next sentence: "Should the philosopher come out of his chair and sit on the floor with his patient, however, he will find that there is an intermediate position." The dead metaphor of the chair comes alive in order to propel the philosopher onto the floor, where what he will find is an intermediate position. Something about that intermediate position is enacted by this passage from metaphor to literality. The intermediate position is not in space but in what it is possible to say. "In other words, he will find that after 'subject relates to object' comes 'subject destroys object' (as it becomes external); and then may come '*object survives* destruction by the subject.'" The intermediate position is the between as beyond. "But there may or may not be survival." The realness of the object requires that the possibility exists for it to really be destroyed.

> A new feature thus arrives in the theory of object-relating. The subject says to the object: "I destroyed you," and the object is there to receive the communication. From now on the subject says: "Hullo object!" "I destroyed you." "I love you." "You have value for me because of your survival of my destruction of you." "While I am loving you I am all the time destroying you in (unconscious) *fantasy.*" (90)

[handwritten margin note: Address to object ⇓]

The object is there to receive the communication. The structure of address animates the object as a "you," a destroyed "you," a loved because destroyed "you." The object's survival of destruction is what makes it real. The reality of others depends on their survival, yes, but also on their destruction (in fantasy).

Winnicott's dramatized direct address to the object seems excessive with respect to what is required by the description. That is, the language of address adds something. What does it add?

As a way of approaching this question, let me return for a moment to Kant. This point in Winnicott recalls a strange moment in Kant's *Critique of Practical Reason,* in which he suddenly, and without warning, directly addresses duty in one long sentence:

[handwritten margin note: Kant's address to 'Duty' ⇓]

> Duty! Thou sublime and mighty name that dost embrace nothing charming or insinuating but requirest submission and yet seekest not to move the will by threatening aught that would arouse natural aversion or terror, but only holdest forth a law which of itself finds entrance into the mind and yet gains reluctant reverence (though not always obedience)—a law before which all inclinations are dumb even though they secretly work against it: what origin is there worthy of thee, and where is to be found the root of thy noble descent which proudly rejects all kinship with the inclinations and from which to be descended is the indispensable condition of the only worth which men can give themselves?[8]

Isn't this a version of the question not to be formulated about the transitional object—did you create that or did you find it? Could there be a relation between duty and the teddy bear, not because the teddy bear teaches concern for others but because in neither case is it possible to say whether the object is inside or outside the subject? And does direct address to an abstract or inanimate object somehow act out the paradox that must be tolerated if there is to be a full range of cultural life?

The ludic side of Kant is usually quite well concealed. Yet here, in the middle of a discussion of "the incentives of pure practical reason," after scornful comments about fanaticism and sentimentalism, Kant suddenly feels an impulse to play. In a long-drawn single breath, he utters an apostrophe, playing at animating Duty, sublime and mighty name. In the midst of describing duty as that which "elevates man above himself as a part of the world of sense," that which gives "personality, i.e., the freedom and independence from the mechanism of nature," Kant's language suddenly generates a personality beyond the world of reference, a personification to receive the communication.[9]

In Winnicott, as we have seen, the subtle animation of the object, or at least the object's point of view, is a constant feature. That Winnicott's language is often out in a space of play ahead of him, or encrypted in a space within him, is something of which he himself occasionally takes note. Beginning an essay entitled "The Location of Cultural Experience" with an epigraph from Tagore, he writes, "The quotation from Tagore has always intrigued me. In my adolescence I had no idea what it could mean, but it found a place in me, and its imprint has not faded" (95). His ability to describe language as having a place rather than a meaning is already a structure of object use. In another essay, Winnicott finds himself quoting a Shakespeare sonnet, and lets it lead him where he wasn't necessarily planning to go:

> The object is repudiated, re-accepted, and perceived objectively. This process is highly dependent on there being a mother or mother figure prepared to participate and to give back what is handed out.
>
> This means that the mother (or part of mother) is in a "to and fro" between being that which the baby has a capacity to find and (alternatively) being herself waiting to be found.
>
> If the mother can play this part over a length of time without *admitting impediment (so to speak)* then the baby has some experience of magical control. . . .
>
> In the state of confidence that grows up when a mother can do this difficult thing well (not if she is unable to do it), the baby begins to enjoy experiences based on a "*marriage*" of the omnipotence of intrapsychic processes with the baby's controlling of the actual. (47, emphasis added)

Marriage follows upon not admitting impediments, not because all roads in Winnicott should lead to marriage (although they do) but because

Winnicott is capable of *using* language in just the way he speaks of *using* objects—using language to play fort-da with, and letting language play him. His actual interpretations often draw his material back into a frustratingly familiar ideology, but his descriptions of language acting in him or on him somehow escape that closure. (Even his anti-birth-control essay, "The Pill and the Moon," involves his involuntary composition of a poem.)[10]

Winnicott ends the paragraph of dialogue between infant and object, and by implication between patient and therapist, by concluding, "In these ways the object develops its own autonomy and life, and (if it survives) contributes-in to the subject, according to its own properties" (90). The object's own properties operate like a third in the relation between baby and object—a third that makes it possible to experience the world, a third composed of the interaction itself. Winnicott ends his article on the use of an object by saying: "Study of this problem involves a statement of the positive value of destructiveness. The destructiveness, plus the object's survival of the destruction, places the object outside the area of objects set up by the subject's projective mental mechanisms. In this way a world of shared reality is created which the subject can use and which can feed back other-than-me substance into the subject" (94).

Perhaps a synonym for "using people" would be, paradoxically, "trusting people," creating a space of play and risk that does not depend on maintaining intactness and separation. It is not that destructiveness is always or in itself good—far from it. The unleashed destructiveness of exaggerated vulnerability or of grandiosity without empathy is amply documented. But *excessive* empathy is simply counterphobic. What goes unrecognized is a danger arising not just from infantile destructiveness but from the infantile *terror* of destructiveness—its exaggerated and paralyzing repression. Winnicott describes the process of learning to overcome *that* terror, which allows one to trust, to play, and to experience the reality of both the other *and* the self. And this, it seems to me, suggests the ethical importance of "using people."

The Personhood of Things

Chapter Eight

Romancing the Stone

Two Symptomatic Stories

I

Sometime in 1820 on Milos, a Greek island, a classical statue of Venus was disinterred in a farmer's field. She lacked her lower arms but was otherwise intact. Around her waist was a seam where two marble blocks were joined, and there was evidence of another join between the upper and lower arms. Further excavation unearthed a hand holding an apple and two statues of Hermes. A part of a plinth that contained a partial inscription accompanied the statue for a while, then was lost. The statue's ownership was at first divided between the two ships that had come to take it away: an Ottoman ship destined for a Turkish dignitary, and a French ship destined for Louis XVIII. After it was loaded on the ship bound for France, the statue, purchased in 1821 by the Marquis de Rivière, was first given to Louis XVIII and then installed in the Louvre, formerly a royal palace but now democratized into the Musée Napoléon, full of imperial booty belonging to the nation. A decision was made to display her alone, and not to restore her. Quatremère de Quincy, one of the nineteenth century's foremost archeologists, explained: "L'imagination, suppléant ce qui manque, ajoute à la beauté qui reste, une mesure . . . de beauté, qu'elle suppose. Quand l'objet est intègre, il offre à l'esprit une image terminée. Il y a plus rien au-delà."[1]

II

From 1799 to 1803, Thomas Bruce, seventh earl of Elgin, was appointed British ambassador to the Ottoman Empire. A lover of art and antiquities, Lord Elgin directed his hired team of artists to make drawings and casts of Greek works. He was worried that the weather and Turkish indifference would destroy the Parthenon, and was given authority by the Sublime Porte, the seat of the Ottoman government, to remove anything he wanted. After detaching walls, bas-reliefs, columns, and architectural detail from the Parthenon and shipping them to London, Elgin and his men unpacked and somewhat haphazardly reassembled the artifacts in his "shed" in Park Lane. In 1816 the British government purchased Elgin's collection for roughly half of what it had cost him, and installed the "Marbles" in the British Museum. Those who came to see the Marbles there were often moved, but some, like Byron, were outraged at the removal of Greek artifacts from Greece. In the 1980s, the Greek culture minister, Melina Mercouri, was still trying, unsuccessfully, to get them back. That was at the height of the repatriation movements affecting many museums. When a member of the British Parliament, for example, demanded the return of A. A. Milne's original stuffed animals from their climate-controlled case in the New York Public Library, the idea was dismissed. On the one hand, a museum is a display of objects out of context: one could not return everything to its rightful place without destroying the very idea of a museum. On the other hand, taking something from another place and cavalierly displaying it as testimony to the power of one's own nation is an imperialist gesture par excellence.

For total repatriation to be possible, two conditions would have to obtain that have never been met: everything would have to *have* a rightful place; and the militarily weaker would have to be respected by the stronger. To restore everything to its place, besides being impossible, implies that something aesthetic doesn't precisely inhere in displacement: art is perhaps, in fact (as Mary Douglas says of dirt), "matter out of place." The exhibit in the British Museum was formerly known as the Elgin Marbles. Now it is called the Parthenon Frieze. Lord Byron, it will be remembered, fought and died in the Greek war of independence, the attempt to restore Greek control of Greece. He died in 1823.[2]

These two stories, perhaps, explain why the fate of Greek sculpture was so different in France and in England, which were, after all, at war with each other when the artifacts were "found." In England, when Keats writes about Greek artifacts they always tell a story, possess a kind of group immortality, speak of a whole culture. In France, the figure of the female beloved was easy to see in the single stone individual. In the second half of the nineteenth century there arose in France what was called Parnassian poetry, a cult of form and scorn for usefulness that often consisted of impassioned apostrophes addressed to an unfeeling statue. According to the earlier Romantic aesthetic, Alphonse de Lamartine had boasted in introducing a new edition of his *Meditations poétiques,* one of the central texts of French Romanticism, that he had brought poetry down from Parnassus, and replaced the lyre with the very fibers of the human heart. But the Romantic cult of sincerity and exposure of those (equally conventional) "fibers of the human heart" had led to such displays of emotion that poetry again took refuge on the mountain of the classical muses. Venus de Milo's stony unresponsiveness allowed for the unrestrained development (and absence of context) of the poet's addresses to an isolated female figure, while the frenzy of his passion turned to poetry rather than to masochism. Leconte de Lisle, for instance, a learned classicist and leading Parnassian poet, throws his voice into the void of address and the perfection of form in order to end with an imperative to the statue of Venus de Milo to inspire him, and in order to pray to the statue for his own well-formed verses:

"VÉNUS DE MILO"
Marbre sacré, vêtu de force et de génie,
Déesse irrésistible au port victorieux,
Pure comme un éclair et comme une harmonie,
O Vénus, ô beauté, blanche mère des Dieux!

Tu n'es pas Aphrodite, au bercement de l'onde,
Sur ta conque d'azur posant un pied neigeux,
Tandis qu'autour de toi, vision rose et blonde,
Volent les Rires d'or avec l'essaim des Jeux.

Tu n'es pas Kythérée, en ta pose assouplie,
Parfumant de baisers l'Adonis bienheureux,
Et n'ayant pour témoins sur le rameau qui plie
Que colombes d'albâtre et ramiers amoureux.

Et tu n'es pas la Muse aux lèvres éloquentes,
La pudique Vénus, ni la molle Astarté
Qui, le front couronné de roses et d'acanthes,
Sur un lit de lotos se meurt de volupté.

Non! Les Rires, les Jeux, les Grâces enlacées,
Rougissantes d'amour, ne t'accompagnent pas.
Ton cortège est formé d'étoiles cadencées,
Et les globes en choeur s'enchaînent sur tes pas.

Du bonheur impassible ô symbole adorable,
Calme comme la Mer en sa sérénité,
Nul sanglot n'a brisé ton sein inaltérable,
Jamais les pleurs humains n'ont terni ta beauté.

Salut! A ton aspect le coeur se précipite,
Un flot marmoréen inonde tes pieds blancs;
Tu marches, fière et nue, et le monde palpate,
Et le monde est à toi, Déesse aux larges flancs!

Iles, séjour des Dieux! Hellas, mère sacrée!
Oh! que ne suis-je né dans le saint Archipel,
Aux siècles glorieux où la Terre inspirée
Voyait le Ciel descendre à son premier appel!

Si mon berceau, flottant sur la Thétis antique,
Ne fut point caressé de son tiède crystal;
Si je n'ai point prié sous le fronton attique,
Beauté victorieuse, à ton autel natal;

Allume dans mon sein la sublime étincelle,
N'enferme point ma gloire au tombeau soucieux;
Et fais que ma pensée en rythmes d'or ruisselle,
Comme un divin métal au moule harmonieux.

*   *   *

Sacred marble, clothed in force and genius,
Irresistible Goddess, of victorious port,

Pure as lightning and as harmony,
O Venus, o beauty, white mother of the Gods!

You are not Aphrodite, rocked by the waves,
Resting your snowy foot upon your azure shell,
While all about you, a vision pink and blond,
Golden laughter dances with a swarm of Games.

You are not Kythera, lolling at ease,
Perfuming happy Adonis with your kisses,
With no one watching from the bending branch
But alabaster doves and love birds.

And you are nor the Muse with eloquent lips
Or modest Venus, or soft Astarte
Who, her brow crowned with roses and acanthus,
Swoons with pleasure on a lotus bed.

No! Laughter, Games, and Graces intertwined,
Blushing with love, do not accompany you.
Your train is made of cadenced stars,
The chorus of the spheres follows your steps.

Adored symbol of impassive happiness,
Calm as the Sea in its serenity,
No sob has racked your inalterable breast,
Never have human tears tarnished your beauty.

Hail! The heart leaps at your sight!
A marmoreal flood covers your white feet;
You stride, proud and naked, and the world trembles,
And the world is yours, Goddess of the capacious flanks!

Islands! Home of the Greeks! Hellas, sacred mother!
Oh! why wasn't I born in the sacred Archipelago
At the glorious time when the inspired Earth
Saw the Sky descend at its first call!

Though my cradle, floating on the ancient Thetis,
Was not caressed by her warm crystal;
Though I did not pray beneath the Attic pediment,
Victorious beauty, at your native altar,

Strike in my breast the sublime spark,
Don't close my fame in a careworn tomb;

Cause my thought to flow in golden rhymes
Like a divine metal into a harmonious mold.

(Translation mine.)

The golden age of Greece as represented by the statue was, according to this poem, a time when apostrophe ruled the world: "la Terre inspirée / Voyait le Ciel descendre à son premier appel." The poetic power of apostrophe that demonstrates to de Lisle that Romanticism has been successfully escaped, and all signs of pleasure or even feeling eliminated ("Tu n'es pas Kythérée . . . parfumant de baisers l'Adonis . . . ni la molle Astarté / Qui . . . se meurt de volupté"), make the goddess an even more reliable guardian of form. The statue is barely more alive than the poet, but nevertheless, a live poet asks an inanimate addressee to answer his prayers. The exchange of the characteristics of life and death is one of the dangers—or pleasures—of loving a statue. As Théophile Gautier, an early proponent of Parnassianism, put it in his preface to *Mademoiselle de Maupin:* "[If] there is something noble and fine about loving a statue, it is that your love is quite disinterested, that you need not feel the satiety or weariness of victory, and that you cannot reasonably hope for a second wonder like the history of Pygmalion."[3]

The locus classicus of the story of loving a statue is indeed Ovid's tale of Pygmalion. Dissatisfied with the imperfections of real women, Pygmalion, a sculptor, carves himself his ideal woman out of ivory: "Pygmalion looks in admiration and is inflamed with love for this semblance of a body" ("miratur et haurit pectore Pygmalion simulati corporis ignes").[4] Pygmalion kisses the statue, dresses it, brings it gifts, lays it on his bed, and prays to Venus on her feast day, "If ye, O gods, can give all things, I pray to have as wife"—he does not dare add "my ivory maid" but says "one like my ivory maid." But Venus knows what he means, and when he returns home, he kisses the statue and finds her warm. The text marks the metamorphosis by changing its pronoun: the "it" becomes a "she." "She seemed warm to his touch. Again he kissed her, and with his hands also he touched her breast. The ivory grew soft to his touch and, its hardness vanishing, gave and yielded beneath his fingers, as Hymettian wax grows soft under the sun and, moulded by the thumb, is easily shaped to many forms and becomes usable through use itself."[5] In other words, he is continuing to sculpt her, to be in love with the work of his own hands. As the text has made explicit from the beginning, "And with his own work he falls in love" ("operisque sui concepit amorem").

Pygmalion's story is one of the few happy stories of loving a statue. Usually there is some trade-off or downside or punishment for the realization of this fantasy. As Paul de Man writes about a similar apostrophe to Shakespeare by John Milton (in a poem containing the lines: "Then thou, our fancy of itself bereaving, / Dost make us marble with too much conceiving"): "'Doth make us marble' . . . cannot fail to evoke the latent threat . . . that by making the death [dead?] speak, the symmetrical structure of the trope implies, by the same token, that the living are struck dumb, frozen in their own death."[6] Parnassian poetry often holds out the hope—or the horror—that one will be as good as dead.

Théodore de Banville, one of the foremost theorists of Parnassianism, writes a light-hearted poem to Venus testifying to this same exchange of properties:

"À VÉNUS DE MILO"

O Vénus de Milo, guerrière au flanc nerveux,
Dont le front irrité sous vos divins cheveux
Songe, et dont une flamme embrase la paupière,
Rêve aux plis arrêtés, grand poème de pierre,
Débordement de vie avec art compensé,
Vous qui depuis mille ans avez toujours pensé,
J'adore votre bouche où le courroux flamboie
Et vos seins frémissants d'une tranquille joie.

    Et vous savez si bien ces amours éperdus
Que si vous retrouviez un jour vos bras perdus
Et qu'à vos pieds tombât votre tunique,
Nos froideurs pâmeraient dans un combat unique,
Et vous m'étaleriez votre ventre indompté,
Pour y dormir un soir comme un amant sculpté!

*   *   *

O Venus de Milo, warrior with eager flanks,
You whose well-proportioned brow beneath your divine hair
Muses, and whose lids are smoldering with a flame,
Still, frozen-folded dream, great poem of stone,
Overflow of life by art repaid,
You who have been pensive for a thousand years,
I adore your mouth where anger burns
And your breasts that quiver with a tranquil joy.

And you know so well those uncontainable loves
That if one day you got back your lost arms
And your tunic slipped down over your broken feet,
Our coldnesses would swoon in unique combat,
And you would spread out your unconquered body
For me to lie on all night like a sculpted lover!

(Translation mine.)

It is interesting that one of the signs of imminent animation is the finding of lost body parts. One of the things that characterizes statues, paradoxically, is that they break. The fact that Madame Donalger in *The Juggler* was married to a man who had lost his nose makes him a statue, not just a castrato. In this poem, no sooner has Venus de Milo become whole and animate than her living lover turns to stone.

Le Parnasse contemporain was the somewhat self-contradictory title chosen by a group of young poets for what began as a little poetry magazine, launched through the combined efforts of Catulle Mendès and Louis-Xavier de Ricard, and ended as a series of three collective volumes published by Alphonse Lemerre, above whose bookstore the young poets held rowdy poetry readings, and featuring such poets as Théodore de Banville, Charles Baudelaire, Théophile Gautier, Leconte de Lisle, Stéphane Mallarmé, and Paul Verlaine.

The first and best-known volume, published in 1866, gives a good idea of the impassivity, impersonality, and "cult of form" favored by Parnassian poetry. In his 1872 *Petit traité de poésie française,* Banville went so far as to declare that all of poetry could be summed up in the notion of rhyme. If poetry were simply equated with the overflow of emotions, with the search for truth, or with moral or political vision, it would lose its specificity. As Baudelaire put it in 1859, "The poetic principal is strictly and simply the human aspiration toward superior Beauty . . . independent of passion, which is the intoxication of the heart, and of truth, which is the nourishment of reason. Passion is a *natural* thing, too natural even, not to introduce a discordant, wounding tone into the domain of pure Beauty."[7] Echoing Kant's definition of beauty as a form of purposiveness without purpose, Baudelaire often defined poetry as an end in itself: "Poetry cannot, on pain of death or decay, be assimilated into science or morality. Truth is not its object; its only object is itself."[8]

Gautier, to whom Baudelaire had dedicated his *Fleurs du Mal,* was the acknowledged progenitor of the group. Although he had once been totally identified with Romanticism, he resisted the role of social visionary it often led to. He bemoaned relevance and utilitarianism in art, whether socialist or bourgeois. The function of art was to be beautiful—and useless. As he had already written in his 1835 preface to *Mademoiselle de Maupin*, "Nothing is really beautiful unless it's useless: everything useful is ugly, for it expresses a need, and the needs of man are ignoble and disgusting, like his poor weak nature. The most useful place in a house is the latrine. For myself . . . I am among those to whom the superfluous is necessary. . . . I prefer to a certain useful pot a Chinese pot which is sprinkled with mandarins and dragons."[9]

In his poems for the first volume of *Le Parnasse contemporain,* the young Mallarmé showed himself to be a faithful disciple of Gautier, depicting himself giving money to a beggar on condition that he *not* spend it on bread ("A un pauvre"), turning his back on "life" ("Les fenêtres"), and attempting to leave behind "voracious art" in order to paint fine designs on a Chinese cup ("Epilogue," later entitled "Las de l'amer repos. . ."). Parnassian poetry seems to bear out the Lacanian distinction between desire and need; in his essay "The Signification of the Phallus," Lacan writes, in effect, that desire is what is left of the demand for love when the satisfaction of all possible needs is subtracted from it. Desire, in other words, is both indestructible and unsatisfiable. What could stand for this better than love for a statue?

This "cult of form" or "art for art's sake" is often represented in Parnassian poetry as love for a statue. The Parnassian equation of Art with sculpture has several sources: the rise of studies of ancient Greece (the same philhellenism that led Byron to fight for Greece's independence from Turkey); the serene, durable, and visible intricacies of form; and the aesthetics of desirable difficulty. Although Parnassian poets wrote in many verse forms, the place of honor went to the sonnet, with its block-like solidity and slight asymmetry. The 1866 volume of *Parnasse contemporain* indeed ended with a series of sonnets by diverse hands.

In Gautier's poem "L'Art" (included in the 1858 edition of his *Emaux et camées*) the poet eschews soft, yielding, malleable media like wax and displays his art by sculpting the hardest and most resistant material possible:

Oui, l'oeuvre sort plus belle
D'une forme au travail
   Rebelle,
Vers, marbre, onyx, émail. . . .

Statuaire, repousse
L'argile que pétrit
   Le pouce,
Quand flotte ailleurs l'esprit;

Lutte avec le carrare,
Avec le paros dur
   Et rare,
Gardiens du contour pur; . . .

Sculpte, lime, cisèle;
Que ton rêve flottant
   Se scelle
Dans le bloc résistant!

*   *   *

More beautiful, the work that
From rebellious form
   Emerges:
Verse, marble, onyx, enamel. . . .

Sculptor, put aside
The clay shaped by
   The thumb
When elsewhere floats the mind.

Fight with the carrara
And rare, hard,
   Parian marble,
Keepers of the pure contour; . . .

Sculpt, file, chisel,
Let your floating dream
   Be sealed
In the resistant block!

               (Translation mine.)

The ideal self, which Lacan calls "the statue in which man projects himself," and the self in front of a mirror—Ovid calls the fascinated Narcissus "like a statue carved from Parian marble," while Kleist has his youth and observer see the well-known sculpture the *Spinario* in the mirror of a locker room—

suggest that what is desired in a beloved or self of stone is precisely the hardness, the coldness, the inanimateness, of a statue. It is in the material's resistance to art that its artistic value lies. The sculptor is often, as in Thomas Hardy's *The Well-Beloved,* the son of a stonemason: the unwieldiness of the material lies behind the artist as an ancestor.

The turn-of-the-century movement called Decadence was often a form of Parnassianism run riot. Thus, while Banville entitled one of his volumes of poetry *Les Caryatides,* Rachilde has her hero follow a dark woman among three Caryatids holding electric lanterns. The woman at first seems hard to distinguish from the statues.

A characteristic associated with both statues and resistance in the minds of the Parnassian poets was whiteness. Gautier's "Symphonie en blanc majeur" is a monochromatic tour de force in which a woman's pure, white body is compared to snow, satin, marble, frost, silver, opal, ivory, ermine, alabaster, dove down, swans, hawthorn flowers, and other white substances. Yet this celebration of whiteness ends:

> Beneath the ice where calmly it resides
> Oh! who can ever melt this heart!
> Oh! who might induce a blush
> On this implacable whiteness!

Whiteness may be loved as a refusal to submit, but the fantasy of conquest looms all the more large. This resistance is enough to equate statues with chastity rather than with death. One cannot help seeing in this a connection to the nineteenth-century concern with racial purity, as empires stretched around the globe. It was in the mid-1850s that Joseph-Arthur de Gobineau's *Essai sur l'inégalité des races humaines* appeared, and set the terms of racist discourse for many years. Non-white women were seen as sensual and lascivious, while white women represented chastity and untouchableness, whether or not this difference had any basis in fact. The paean to whiteness also allowed for many sexualized fantasies about writing on the white page. Of course, nineteenth-century poets would have been very surprised to learn that those chaste Greek statues were once painted.

Sylvia Plath often represents a Parnassianism taking root in a twentieth-century woman poet, hardly afraid of seeing death as poetry's ultimate aim. As she writes in "Edge," which her husband put last in her *Collected Poems,*

The woman is perfected.
Her dead

Body wears the smile of accomplishment,
The illusion of a Greek necessity

Flows in the scrolls of her toga,
Her bare

Feet seem to be saying:
We have come so far, it is over.[10]

As a sign of a racial connection—often just below consciousness—in Parnassian poetry, among the many poems to alabaster and marble women, there is in fact one sonnet in *Parnasse contemporain* in which Baudelaire addresses a black woman:

"TO A MALABAR WOMAN"
Your feet are as delicate as your hands, and your full hips
Would be the envy of the most beautiful white woman:
To the pensive artist your body is sweet sand precious:
Your velvet eyes are blacker than your flesh. . . .

(Translation mine.)

In Rachilde's *Juggler* and in Jensen's *Gradiva* (to which we will turn shortly), a deep concern and perhaps a repressed wish is expressed by the hero about whether a lady he thinks is white is really black. "Prove to me that you are not a negress!" cries Leon Reille to the woman he is pursuing; archeologist Norbert Hanold, headed for Pompeii, overhears two German tourists, a man and a woman, talking of the strength of the sun in Italy when the woman exclaims, "What if you should suddenly have a negress for a wife?"[11] The whiteness and purity of Greek statues could be used to support the most genocidal movements we have known: in Leni Riefenstahl's film of the 1936 Berlin Olympics (held in part to glorify Nazism), Greek statues turn into competing athletes. The Olympics themselves were like a revival of ancient Greece, and, by implication, Nazism its direct descendant.

The idea that classical Greece is the origin and unfallen childhood of European culture led Mikhail Bakhtin, for example, to see the epic as unified and the novel, that "baggy monster," as heteroglossic, heterogeneous, dialogic. This makes those pure, white, unfeeling statues into signs of origin, and every narrative of maturation into a fall. The pleas of modern man fall on deaf ears, and not just because a statue is inanimate. Baudelaire does not directly contest the notion of Greek purity, but he is more interested in modern man's predicament vis-à-vis that origin than in arguing about the origin per se:

"LE FOU ET LA VÉNUS"

. . . Cependant, dans cette jouisssance universelle, j'ai aperçu un être affligé.

Aux pieds d'une colossale Vénus, un de ces foux artificiels . . . tout ramassé contre le piédestal, lève les yeux pleins de larmes verra l'immortelle Déesse.

Et ces yeux dissent:—"Je suis le dernier et le plus solitaire des humains. . . . Cependant, je suis fait, moi aussi, pour comprendre et sentir l'immortelle Beauté! Ah! Déesse! ayez pitié de ma tristesse et de mon délire!"

Mais l'implacable Vénus regarde au loin je ne sais quoi avec ses yeux de marbre.

*   *   *

"THE FOOL AND THE VENUS"

. . . However, amidst this universal rapture, I noticed an afflicted creature.

At the feet of a colossal Venus, one of those artificial fools . . . all heaped against the pedestal, raises his tear-filled eyes toward the immortal Goddess.

And his eyes say, "I am the lowest and the most lonely of humans. . . However, I am made, I as well, to understand and to feel immortal Beauty! Oh Goddess! Take pity on my sorrow and my madness!"

But the implacable Venus looks into the distance at something or other with her eyes of marble.[12]

Are those marble eyes that look at the unknown animate or inanimate? Does the statue of Venus not take pity on the fool because she is a thing, or because she is looking away from him? Is the object of desire here alive or not?

In Lacan's "Mirror Stage," the subject is infatuated with his ideal self as a *form.* In other words, the ideal self pursued by the subject is *aesthetic,* and this "cult of form" may be related to the human capacity to love an image. The question of whether the image is animate or inanimate, or compatible with "life," is unsettlingly answered when Hardy's sculptor, feeling the love of a woman for the only time in his life, loses his aesthetic ability. But, then, perhaps there is something in human "life" that is incompatible with life.

Baudelaire was both fascinated and repelled by this aesthetic. According to therapist Marsha Abrams, the fantasy most closely linked to the impassive sculpture is the fantasy or memory of the "mother's back": a mother walking away from the needy child, turning her back on him.[13] Orientalist and classicist references combined to produce a large number of Parnassian poems about sphinxes and Venuses, often quite explicitly about mothers who do not nourish. Like this one by Théophile Gautier:

"LE SPHINX"
Dans le Jardin Royal où l'on voit les statues
Une Chimère antique entre toutes me plaît:
Elle pousse en avant deux mamelles pointues,
Dont le marbre veiné semble gonflé de lait.

Son visage de femme est le plus beau du monde;
Son col est si charnu que vous l'embrassseriez;
Mais, quand on fait le tour, on voit sa croupe ronde,
On s'aperçoit qu'elle a des griffes à ses pieds.

Les jeunes nourissons qui passent devant elle
Tendent leurs petits bras et veulent avec cris
Coller leur bouche ronde à sa dure mamelle;
Mais, quand ils l'ont touchée, ils reculent surpris.

C'est ainsi qu'il en est de toutes nos chimères:
La face en est charmante et le revers bien laid.
Nous leur pressons le sein, mais ces mauvaises mères
N'ont pas pour notre lèvre une goutte de lait.

*   *   *

In the Royal Garden where the statues are
My favorite is an ancient Chimera;
She thrusts forward her two pointed breasts
Whose veined marble seems to burst with milk.

Her woman's face is loveliest of all;
Her neck so fleshy it invites your kiss:
But, if you circle to her rounded haunch
You'll see her feet are tipped with claws

The little toddlers playing at her feet
Lift up their arms and try to press
Their whimpering mouths against her stony breasts;
But, on touching her, they draw back in surprise.

And thus it is with all our chimeras:
Their face is charming and their back grotesque.
We reach for their breast, but those bad mothers
Don't give our lips a single drop of milk.

> (Translation mine.)

This deception caused by a front that lures and a back that wounds is explained at length by the poet in the last stanza. "I'm talking about imaginary hopes," he says; "First they attract you and later you find yourself disappointed and unnourished."

This combination of walking around a statue and finding, with shock, that the beautiful front is not borne out by a view of the back, becomes, for Baudelaire, an example of "spleen" rather than "ideal" in the poem "Le Masque: Statue allégorique dans le gout de la Renaissance." His narrating voice is shocked when he sees a beautiful statue terminate, he thinks, in two heads. When he sees that the radiant face is a mask, behind which the true face is crying, "he" (it is difficult to say who is speaking here) answers the question, "Why is she crying?" by saying the following:

—Elle pleure, insensé, parce qu'elle a vécu!
Et parce qu'elle vit! Mais ce qu'elle déplore
Surtout, ce qui la fait frémir jusqu'aux genoux,
C'est que demain, hélas! il faudra vivre encore!
Demain, après-demain et toujours!—comme nous!

*   *   *

She's crying, numbskull, because she has lived!
And because she's alive! But what really gets her down,

What makes her tremble to her toes,
Is that she'll have to go on living
Tomorrow and the next day and forever!—like us!

(Translation mine.)

But, precisely, she's not alive and she doesn't resemble us. It is only in allegory that she can *represent* the duality of being alive. And it is only by making her *speak* that Baudelaire can really embody that doubleness. The most famous but also the most understatedly ambivalent treatment of a beloved statue is also by Baudelaire, a sonnet consisting entirely of a prosopopeia from beauty's own mouth, suggesting that her unfeelingness is intentional:

"LA BEAUTÉ"

Je suis belle, ô mortels! comme un rêve de pierre,
Et mon sein, où chacun s'est meurtri tour à tour,
Est fait pour inspirer au poète un amour
Eternel et muet ainsi que la matière.

Je trône dans l'azur comme un sphinx incompris;
J'unis un coeur de neige à la blancheur des cygnes;
Je hais le movement qui déplace les lignes,
Et jamais je ne pleure et jamais je ne ris.

Les poètes, devant mes grandes attitudes,
Que j'ai l'air d'emprunter aux plus fiers monuments,
Consumeront leurs jours en d'austères études;

Car j'ai, pour fasciner ces dociles amants,
De purs miroirs qui font toutes choses plus belles:
Mes yeux, mes larges yeux aux clartés éternelles!

*   *   *

I am beautiful, mortals, like a dream of stone,
And my breast, where each is wounded in his turn,
Is made to inspire in poets such a love
Eternal and mute, like matter itself.

I sit enthroned mysterious like a sphinx
I join my snowy heart to the whiteness of swans;

I hate the motion that disturbs the lines
And never do I cry and never laugh.

The poets, facing my grand attitudes
Which I borrowed from proud monuments,
Will consume away their days in austere study

For I, to fascinate those docile lovers,
Possess pure mirrors that beautify all things:
My eyes, my wide eyes, charged with eternal light.

(Translation mine.)

Note that in this poem, those who are fascinated and wounded by Beauty are explicitly called poets. The hardness of many of these statues, although there are fascinating leads to follow in poets' lives, belongs to the realm of Art, not Life. The mirror in which Narcissus died for love of an image, the mirror in which the dreamer first sees the rose, the mirror in which an ephebe loses his grace trying to equal a statue, are effects of Beauty's eyes. Everything thus transformed into an image is in the poet's virtual reality.

Would classical Greece stand for an idealized unity if its artifacts were not scattered all over Europe? Is the function of their dismemberment merely to radiate wholeness? Is the story told by the image at odds with the story told by the substance? I will turn to the functions of the strange severed hands that remain behind when the main action has been completed in three otherwise very different nineteenth-century works: Henry James's "The Last of the Valerii," Nathaniel Hawthorne's *Marble Faun,* and Auguste Villiers de l'Isle-Adam's *L'Eve future.* In each case, the main character seems to point to another time, either the past or the future. In Henry James's story, a statue of Juno unearthed on his estate brings out the pagan worshiper in the Italian count. In Hawthorne's novel, the title character, supposed to resemble the statue of a faun by Praxiteles, may be the last member of the hybrid races, if he, like the faun in the statue, has furry ears. In Villiers's novel, the inventor Thomas Edison fabricates an artificial woman to replace in his European count's affections the vulgar American woman who looks, but does not behave, like the Venus de Milo. It is no accident that two of these texts are written by Americans in Europe, and one by a European about America (set in exotic Menlo Park, New Jersey, where Edison did indeed establish the first industrial research park). If Greece stands in the nineteenth century as

Europe's pure, lost origin, America represents the all-too-real future, the place of greatest distance from that origin, a westernmost place of both progress and loss.

Henry James's "The Last of the Valerii" tells the story of an American heiress who marries an Italian count. She is as much in love with his villa as she is with him, until one day first a hand, then the rest of a statue of Juno is unearthed on his land. The count, smitten by the goddess, installs her in a temple-like outbuilding and seems to withdraw into a pagan adulterous affair with the statue. The meddling American godfather of the American wife finally coaxes the count part way back into the modern world; the count, after offering the Juno a blood sacrifice, withdraws while his wife has the Juno reburied, but he keeps the detached hand. The story ends as follows:

> He never became, if you will, a thoroughly modern man; but one day, years after, when a visitor to whom he was showing his cabinet became inquisitive as to a marble hand, suspended in one of its inner recesses, he looked grave and turned the lock on it. "It is the hand of a beautiful creature," he said, "whom I once greatly admired."
>
> "Ah—a Roman?" said the Gentleman with a smirk.
>
> "A Greek," said the count, with a frown.[14]

The visitor, with his knowing smirk, has understood what might be called adultery in space, but not the count's adultery, as it were, in time. Perhaps that is what a statue offers—unfaithfulness to the contemporary.

Unfaithful to the contemporary Lord Ewald certainly is, in Villiers de l'Isle-Adam's novel *L'Eve future,* or *Eve of the Future Eden.* Ewald, who is on the point of committing suicide, comes to the laboratory of the American inventor Thomas Edison, whose life he had once saved. He tells Edison that his despair is caused by the fact that the woman he loves, Alicia Clary, resembles the Venus de Milo on the outside, but is nothing but a vulgar modern shopgirl on the inside. Ewald worships Alicia's form but cannot bear her reality:

> "Miss Alicia is barely twenty. . . . Her body presents an ensemble of lines that would awe the greatest sculptors. . . . She is, really and truly, the splendor of a humanized *Venus Victrix*. . . ." Now, between Miss Alicia's body and soul,

there was not a disproportion . . . there was a disparity. . . . Her intimate being stood out as if in contradiction with her form. . . . "The sole misfortune
afflicting Miss Alicia is reason. . . . This sense which the statue of Venus
Victrix expresses with its lines, Miss Alicia . . . could inspire as well as her pro-
totype—if she kept quiet and closed her eyes. . . . To contemplate Miss Alicia
dead would be my desire."[15]

The deadly competition between two women, which was present but less
explicit in many of the texts we have examined, pits an idealized "eternal
feminine" (figured by the statue) against a real but therefore imperfect
woman. There is an unsettling bond between idealization and death.

Lord Ewald is so fascinated by the discrepancy between Alicia's form and
Alicia's life that he takes her to the Louvre, where he wants to observe her reaction to her marble double:

Once in Paris, something extraordinary happened [says Ewald to Edison].
Doubting my eyes and my reason, I had a mad sacrilegious idea, I admit it,
which took hold of me when I confronted this dreary creature with the great
stone which is, I assure you, her very image, the Venus Victrix. Yes, I wanted
to see how this tiresome woman would respond to that presence. So one day,
I took her on a tour of the Louvre, saying jokingly, "My dear Alicia, I think
I'm going to give you a surprise." We crossed the galleries and I put her
brusquely vis-à-vis the eternal marble.

This time, she pulled back her veil. She looked at the statue with a certain
astonishment. Then stupefied, she exclaimed naively, "She looks like me!"
["tiens; MOI!"]

A moment later she added, "Yes, but, of course, I have my arms, and I
have a more distinguished bearing!"

Then she had a kind of shiver. Her hand, which had left my arm to grasp
the balustrade, took my arm again. She said to me in a low voice, "These
stones . . . The statues . . . it's cold here. Let's leave."

Once outside, since she had remained silent, I had some vague hope of a
miraculous word. Nor was I to be disappointed! Miss Alicia, who was pursuing her own thoughts, pressed closely against me, then said, "But if they have
gone to so much expense for that statue, then won't I be a success?"

Alicia Clary is an opera singer and actress, and she recognizes the commercial value of her appearance. What Ewald holds against her, at bottom, is her

immediate translation of the worth of things into their exchangeability. When she sleeps with her fiancé who then abandons her, what she regrets in her "error" is "certainly not honor itself (a superannuated abstraction) but the benefit which such an asset brings when prudently preserved" (17). Whereas Ewald believes that beauty is sublime, almost religious, and virginity, for example, priceless. (It is now, of course, the credit card companies that enlarge their domain of equivalents by citing the "priceless." It is precisely the merchants of exchange value for whom pricelessness sells.) Villiers, in this novel, is chewing over this process of the commodification of artistic forms. The realization that writing had entered the marketplace and had to be bought and sold like other commodities was not an easy one for most nineteenth-century poets.

Ewald, who has already called this moment sacrilegious, believes that beauty, like divinity, is beyond price, is that which escapes commodification, that which inspires only awe and worship. Living is truly what Alicia does wrong: a live person can never be an *object* as well as a dead person—or a stone person. Behaving like a *subject* is often a beautiful woman's mistake.

"I confess that remark gave me vertigo," says Ewald. "Stupidity pushed to such extremes seemed like damnation." He takes Alicia back to her hotel and returns to the Louvre. "I re-entered the sacred room. And after looking upon the goddess whose form contains the starry night, for the only time in my life, I felt my heart swell with one of the most mysterious sobs which ever suffocated a living man." Ewald, like Henry James's count, experiences a moment of sublime *jouissance* with his goddess.

Yet this worship of sublime pricelessness does not prevent Ewald from entering into a contract to, in effect, buy an ideal woman for himself. Edison promises Ewald that he, the master inventor, can construct a perfect android, exactly resembling Alicia in physical appearance but with a demure, always suitable personality built on literary recordings and the sensitive echoing of her interlocutor. To give Ewald a sample of the android's quality, Edison points to what looks like a human female arm lying alone on a silk cushion. Ewald clasps the hand, finds that it is warm, that it responds to his touch. It makes his flesh crawl to feel the artificial flesh grasp him. He is a reluctant Pygmalion, unable to believe that the thing will ever really become a "she." But the obstacle to such a miracle is *his doubt,* not her artificiality, and so he *does* fall in love with the android when he converses with her without knowing it is she.

In the end, both the real and the artificial woman go down in a ship-wreck, Ewald mourns the android, and Edison, after reading about the ship-wreck in the newspaper, meditates in his laboratory. His glance distractedly falls on "the charming arm, the white hand with its enchanted rings." This is how the novel ends.

The hand in Hawthorne's novel does not belong to the faun but rather to a young woman painter, Hilda, the whitest and most virginal character in the novel (as opposed to the "dark lady" of the novel, the woman with a past, Miriam Schaffer, also a painter). A sculptor, Kenyon, who loves Hilda without her being aware of it, has secretly modeled her hand in marble. In the passage in which the hand is displayed, Kenyon shows Miriam an elabo-rate box that looks like a jewel case: "Lifting the lid, however, no blaze of di-amonds was disclosed, but only, lapt in fleecy cotton, a small, beautifully shaped hand, most delicately sculptured in marble. Such loving care and nicest art had been lavished here, that the palm really seemed to have a ten-derness in its very substance. Touching those lovely fingers—had the jealous sculptor allowed you to touch—you could hardly believe that a virgin warmth would not steal from them to your heart."[16] Again, the severed hand seems to have a life, a warmth, a responsiveness to the touch. When Miriam asks Kenyon how he has persuaded the shy maiden to let him "take her hand in marble," he replies that she was not aware that he had done so, that he has stolen it. And Miriam murmurs, "May you win the original one day." To win a maiden's hand is to marry her, not keep her hand in a box. The cliché becomes ghoulish as it is literalized.

In all of these romances of stone, attraction to a statue combines with a high degree of violence: severed hands, sacrifices, shipwrecks, and, in *The Marble Faun,* a murder, suggest that love affairs with statues can be hazard-ous to one's health. While the aesthetic process involves the cutting out of life, each of the detached arms is kept like a relic. The preciousness of a piece of the body and the removal of context and function obscurely preserve the memory of human simulacra as embodiments of the divine.

A recent popular film directed by Jennifer Lynch strangely sums up what is at stake in the relations between violence and the statue. In the film *Boxing Helena* (1993), a surgeon named Nick Cavanaugh, who specializes in reattaching severed limbs, sequesters a woman named Helena, on whom he has an obsessional crush. Unlike Alicia Clary, she doesn't have the misfor-tune of resembling the Venus de Milo, but there is one sequence in which, mesmerized by one of the numerous reproductions of the statue around Nick's house, she timidly places her hand on the goddess of love's haunches. In flashbacks, we see (mostly from the back) sequences of Nick's promiscuous, rejecting mother, who has just died (been boxed). When Helena is struck by a car, Nick, instead of repairing her legs, removes them as well as her arms, and sets her up in a throne-like box, attending to all her needs. The film reveals Nick's rageful idealization as revenge against his castrating and possibly incestuous mother. Once he has abducted Helena (like his Trojan predecessor), he ignores his long-suffering fiancée, Ann. He both reduces Helena to the state of impotence and dependency he suffered under his mother, and becomes the good mother himself as he cares for her. In one fantasy sequence, her arms grow back to caress and hold him, as he caresses and holds her. As in Banville's poem about Venus de Milo, the restoration of the arms is a restoration of total embrace. The film indeed begins and ends with a plaster reproduction of Venus de Milo in the surgeon's family home. When the entire dismemberment sequence is revealed to have been a dream (the filmmaker doesn't quite dare not to take everything back), the surgeon nevertheless wanders over to the statue and, caressing it, murmurs, "I'm still haunted by my love for her." Who is the "her" here? Helena? The mother? The statue?

Boxing Helena literalizes something about the aesthetic process. It is a process that detaches its object from "life," places it in a frame, box, or on a pedestal, and attributes to it a form of autonomy or self-standingness that is actually a form of absolute dependency. Cut up and boxed, Helena can neither move nor feed herself without help, yet her state resembles the kind of autonomy sought for the work of art and obtainable only if the artwork is not living. A living subject, however, must say "I placed" before effacing itself and letting the art object do its thing. The violent transition between person and thing is demonstrated by all the severed (and indeed boxed?) hands we have just seen: detached and displayed, cut and posted.

Chapter Nine

Surmounted Beliefs

The possible psychological ramifications of the impassive statues of women were suggested by the film *Boxing Helena* and by Marsha Abrams's theory of the statue as the mother's back. But what if the rejected child grows to like his torture? What if his desire becomes masochistic? What if he misses his vampire? One would say there is evidence galore in Baudelaire's work of such a conclusion, excluding for the moment the aesthetic uses he might have found for his displays of masochism:

> Toi qui, comme un coup de couteau,
> Dans mon coeur plaintif es entrée;
> Toi qui, forte comme un troupeau
> De démons, vins, folle et parée,
>
> De mon esprit humilié
> Faire ton lit et ton domaine;
> —Infame à qui je suis lié
> Comme le forçat à la chaîne,

Comme au jeu le joueur têtu,
Comme à la bouteille l'ivrogne,
Comme aux vermines la charogne,
—Maudite, maudite sois-tu!

J'ai prié le glaive rapide
De conquérir ma liberté,
Et j'ai dit au poison perfide
De secourir ma lâcheté.

Hélas! Le poison et le glaive
M'ont pris en dédain et m'ont dit:
"Tu n'es pas digne qu'on t'enlève
A ton esclavage maudit,

Imbécile!—de son empire
Si nos efforts te délivraient,
Tes baisers ressusciteraient
Le cadavre de ton vampire!"

*   *   *

You invaded my sorrowful heart
Like the sudden stroke of a blade;
Bold as a lunatic troupe
Of demons in drunken parade,

You mortified my soul
Made your bed and your domain;
—Abhorrence, to whom I am bound
As the convict is to the chain,

As the drunkard is to the jug,
As the gambler to the game,
As to the vermin the corpse,
I damn, you out of my shame!

And I prayed to the eager sword
To win my deliverance,
And have asked the perfidious vial
To redeem my cowardice.

Alas! the vial and the sword
Disdainfully said to me;

"You are not worthy to lift
From your wretched slavery,

You fool!—if from her command
Our effort delivered you forth,
Your kisses would waken again
Your vampire lover's corpse!"[1]

In this poem, the speaker, like the classic masochist, wants to be free of, but remains attached to, the hurtful object. In the poem "L'Héautontimorouménos" (The Self-Torturer), one can watch, through the grammar, the external object become internal:

Je te frapperai sans colère
Et sans haine, comme un boucher,
Comme Moïse le rocher!
Et je ferai de ta paupière,

Pour abreuver mon Sahara,
Jaillir les eaux de la souffrance.
Mon désir gonflé d'espérance
Sur tes pleurs salés nagera

Comme un vaisseau qui prend le large,
Et dans mon coeur qu'ils soûleront
Tes chers sanglots retentiront
Comme un tambour qui bat la charge

Ne suis-je pas un faux accord
Dans la divine symphonie,
Grâce à la vorace Ironie
Qui me secoue et qui me mord?

Elle est dans ma voix, la criarde!
C'est tout mon sang, ce poison noir!
Je suis le sinistre miroir
Où la mégère se regarde!

Je suis la plaie et le couteau!
Je suis le soufflet et la joue!
Je suis les membres et la roue,
Et la victime et le bourreau!

Je suis de mon coeur le vampire,
—Un de ces grands abandonnés
Au rire eternel condamnés,
Et qui ne peuvent plus sourire!

*   *   *

I'll strike you without rage or hate
The way a butcher strikes his block,
The way Moses smote the rock!
So that your eyes may irrigate

My dry Sahara, I'll allow
The tears to flow of your distress.
Desire, that hope embellishes,
Will swim along the overflow

As ships set out for voyaging,
And like a drum that beats the charge
In my infatuated heart
The echoes of your sobs will ring!

But am I not a false record
Within the holy symphony,
Thanks to voracious Irony
Who gnaws on me and shakes me hard?

She's in my voice, in all I do!
Her poison flows in all my veins!
I am the looking-glass of pain
Where she regards herself, the shrew!

I am the wound, and rapier!
I am the cheek, I am the slap!
I am the limbs, I am the rack,
The prisoner, the torturer!

I am my own blood's epicure
—One of those great abandoned men
Who are eternally condemned
To laugh, but who can smile no more![2]

The speaker becomes both torturer and victim, both addict and substance.
The second poem shows how interchangeable the positions of sadist and

masochist are. But a new force of torture has entered the poem: irony. The poet, in other words, is torn now not just by opposing forces but by the inability to tell whether either side should be taken seriously. Occupying both sides of a violent uncertainty, the poet still doesn't know how to "take" what he feels. Baudelaire as a poet is no longer prey to the torture he is addicted to; he *knows* it, and makes his poetry out of it—what he elsewhere calls "La conscience dans le Mal."

It is difficult to find in Baudelaire a non-self-consuming position. It is therefore interesting to find that the classic of masochism, Leopold von Sacher-Masoch's *Venus in Furs,* is loaded with stone statues. Severin, the model masochist, shows his early self-recognition by falling at the feet of a statue of Venus, saying all the Christian prayers he knows, and then being unable to resist kissing the statue on her ice-cold lips. Indeed, the text's narrator begins by sitting by the fire with a stone statue of the goddess of love wrapped in furs, who expatiates on the differences between paganism and Christianity: "You modern men, you children of reason, cannot begin to appreciate love as pure bliss and divine serenity; . . . as soon as you try to become natural you become vulgar. To you Nature is an enemy. You have made devils of the smiling gods of Greece and you have turned me into a creature of evil. . . . Stay in your northern mists and Christian incense and leave our pagan world to rest under the lava and the rubble. Do not dig us up; Pompeii was not built for you."[3] Like Victor Hugo in the preface to his play *Cromwell,* the goddess equates Christianity with self-opposition: anything one desires is for that reason sinful; any "natural" impulse must be opposed. When the narrator makes the acquaintance of Wanda, whose slave he will become, she shares that attitude toward what has been lost with paganism: "It was Christianity, whose cruel emblem, the cross, has always seemed to me somewhat horrific, that first brought an alien and hostile element into nature and its innocent instincts. The struggle of the spirit against the senses is the gospel of modern man. I do not wish to have any part in it" (159). The narrator, painting her portrait, notes, "There is little of the Roman in her features, but much of the Greek" (163–164).

Christianity, of course, was merciless in its condemnation of competing beliefs, whether paganism, animism, fetishism, or other so-called superstitions. It is interesting how often these differences are underpinned by the status of *things.* Masochism and fetishism were separated from the range of sexual possibilities, and consigned to the category of abnormalities. Animism concerns the belief in the possible aliveness of the inanimate. But the closest and therefore the most likely danger was *idolatry*. In the second commandment, prohibiting graven images, the word "image" is emphasized by "or any likeness of anything" (Exodus 20:4). When Moses disappears for a long while to get God's law, the crowd gets restless waiting for him, and Aaron makes them the Golden Calf to worship. In the second set of tables, made because Moses was so angry that he broke the first, the biblical text says, "thou shalt make thee no graven image" (Exodus 34:17). What the monotheistic god wants to forbid, therefore, is the making of likenesses that risk becoming gods; the danger of polytheism lies in the potential animation of a statue. Instead of eliminating competition from polytheism directly, Yahweh prohibits the making of images. Therefore the possibility of coming alive must be very present in a statue; and its divinity uncannily near. The possibility of making and animating god-bodies, which Victoria Nelson sees behind the appeal of puppets, can exist in all religions. Otherwise, why would the Taliban have been so eager to blow up the ancient Buddhas?

The making of images is both a religious crime and an artistic necessity. It is therefore no surprise to find art expressing negative feelings toward the images it creates. Mérimée's story "La Vénus d'Ille" makes its bronze statue of Venus into a murderer, and constantly refers to her as "l'idole." When the son of the family is found dead on the morning after his wedding, a tale of the statue's not letting go of a ring he intended to give his bride, and the sound of the heavy steps of the statue to and from the room where he is found dead, point to the statue as rightful bride and killer. The testimony of the bridegroom's widow fills the house with a "terreur superstitieuse." The statue of Venus has already caused mischief by falling on, and breaking, the leg of one of the workmen who dug her up. The antiquary who took possession of the statue, and who was the father of the dead man, soon dies himself, and his widow has the statue melted down to make a bell for her church.

The magic powers of an object, pointing as they do to some archaic religion, must be thoroughly disavowed by Christians. Former slave Frederick Douglass, both in his original *Narrative* (1848) and in his subsequent rewriting of his autobiography, *My Bondage and My Freedom* (1855), is in a typical bind as he accepts a gift from an African and disavows it for his reader at the same time. It is no accident that the object in question, which will protect him from the cruel overseer, is a *root:*

I found Sandy to be an old adviser. He was not only a religious man, he professed to believe in a system for which I have no name. He was a genuine African, and had inherited some of the so-called magical powers, said to be possessed by African and eastern nations. He told me that he could help me; that, in those very woods, there was an herb, which in the morning might be found, possessing all the powers required for my protection, (I put his thoughts in my own language;) and that, if I would take his advice, he would procure me the root of the herb of which he spoke. He told me further, that if I would take that root and wear it on my right side, it would be impossible for Covey to strike me a blow; that with this root about my person, no white man could whip me. . . .

Now all this talk about the root, was, to me, very absurd and ridiculous, if not positively sinful. I at first rejected the idea that the simple carrying [of] a root on my right side (a root, by the way, over which I had walked every time I went into the woods), could possess any such magic power as he ascribed to it, and I was, therefore, not disposed to cumber my pocket with it. I had a positive aversion to all pretenders to "*divination.*" It was beneath one of my intelligence to countenance such dealings with the devil, as this power implied. But, with all my book-learning—it was really precious little—Sandy was more than a match for me. "My book-learning," he said, "had not kept Covey off me" (a powerful argument just then), and he entreated me, with flashing eyes, to try this. If it did me no good, it could do me no harm, and it would cost me nothing, anyway. Sandy was so earnest, and so confident of the good qualities of this weed, that, to please him, rather than from any conviction of its excellence, I was induced to take it.[4]

Frederick Douglass has learned his Christian lessons well: superstitions about magic powers could be "positively sinful." On the other hand, since he is arguing against slavery, it just could not be that nothing from Africa, nothing repressed by the white man, has value. Yet he knows the name of the primitive belief system that Christianity condemns in Africans (pagans and primitives), "divination," and doesn't want to do anything to undermine the credibility of his text. He professes to know nothing about what Sandy gives him, to take it just to make Sandy feel good, and then to have no idea why, in fact, he does beat the overseer. But does his new power come from the root itself, or from its significance: "You are not alone"? He manages to have it both ways, to benefit from the presence of the root and disavow it at the same time.

Baudelaire, in his earliest art criticism, sees sculpture as a step beyond fetishism:

POURQUOI LA SCULPTURE EST ENNUYEUSE

L'origine de la sculpture se perd dans la nuit des temps: c'est donc un art de Caraïbes.

En effet, nous voyons tous les peuples tailler fort adroitement des fétiches longtemps avant d'aborder la peinture. . . .

La sculpture se rapproche bien plus de la nature. . . .

La sculpture a plusieurs inconvénients qui sont la conséquence nécessaire de ses moyens. Brutale et positive comme la nature, elle est en même temps vague et insaisissable, parce qu'elle montre trop de faces à la fois. C'est en vain que le sculpteur s'efforce de se mettre à un point de vue unique; le spectateur, qui tourne autour de la figure, peut choisir cent points de vue différents.[5]

*   *   *

WHY SCULPTURE IS BORING

Sculpture's origins are lost in the mists of time: it is thus an art of Caribs.

Indeed, we see all peoples skillfully carve fetishes long before attempting painting. . . .

Sculpture is close to nature. . . .

Sculpture has some disadvantages which are the necessary consequences of its means. Abrupt and positive like nature, it is at the same time vague and ungraspable, because it displays too many sides at once. The sculptor tries in vain to put himself in a unique position; the spectator, who goes around the figure, can choose a hundred different points of view.

(Translation mine.)

At nearly the same time, Karl Marx, whose theory of the fetishism of the commodity will later have such a large impact, writes:

The nations which are still dazzled by the sensuous splendor of precious metals, and are therefore still fetish-worshippers of metal money, are not yet fully developed money-nations. . . . The sensuous consciousness of the fetish-worshipper is different from that of the Greek, because his sensuous existence is still different. The abstract enmity between sense and spirit is necessary so long as the human feeling for nature, the human sense of nature, and therefore also the *natural* sense of *man,* are not yet produced by man's own labour.[6]

Freud, too, at the beginning of his career, just after he published his book on dreams, said, in his three essays on sexuality: "There are some cases . . . in which the normal sexual object is replaced by another which bears some relation to it, but is entirely unsuited to serve the normal sexual aim. . . . Such substitutes are with some justice likened to the fetishes in which savages believe that their gods are embodied."[7]

Baudelaire, Marx, and Freud, as typical men of the nineteenth century, were sure they knew that men more primitive than themselves were fetish-worshippers, and found in the sensual enjoyment of the material something divine. A figure that is a thing in the world, and not just a representation of one, can itself contain the heightened aliveness it gives access to, and can be an object of adoration. In Freud's later essay on fetishism, the sentence about savages drops out, and in Marx's diatribes against the fetishism of the commodity, fetishism seems to inhere in capitalism. In other words, for both Marx and Freud, the fetishism they analyze is a fully contemporary phenomenon. And no longer merely a primitive system of belief.

Does this mean that something in modern man still longs to worship and enjoy sensual experience—or has never stopped? Or does it mean that questions of belief and animation still make their presence felt despite their apparent dismissal by modern science? I'm not sure how to answer these queries, but doubtless they are among the questions that have encouraged me to explore this topic.

Because the nineteenth century was the golden age of imperialism, and because Baudelaire, Marx, and Freud had such similar notions of what primitives believe, one would think there was a misunderstood cultural form that would explain what, originally, constituted the proper meaning of the fetish. But at least one anthropologist, William Pietz, has argued that to search for the origins of the fetish would be fruitless. "My thesis is that the fetish, as an idea and a problem, and as a novel object not proper to any prior discrete society, originated in the cross-cultural spaces of the coast of West Africa during the sixteenth and seventeenth centuries."[8] It is precisely the failure to define the fetish's proper meaning that has called the fetish into being in the first place.

Why do Marx and Freud both have recourse to the same term, "fetishism," to designate a contemporary blindness? The sexual sense of being aroused by the presence of particular objects or qualities was common enough when Freud adopted it for his purposes not to need particular explanation, but Marx, in the section of *Capital* titled "The Fetishism of Commodities and the Secret Thereof," connects it to the world of religion: "In order, therefore, to find an analogy, we must have recourse to the mist-enveloped regions of the religious world. In that world the productions of the human brain appear as independent beings endowed with life, and entering into relation both with one another and the human race. So it is in the world of commodities with the products of men's hands. This I call the Fetishism which attaches itself to the products of labour, so soon as they are produced as commodities."[9] As commodities, the products of labor have, most particularly, exchange value. "There it is a definite social relation between men, that assumes, in their eyes, the fantastic form of a relation between things" (72). The delusion that man is laboring under, in other words, is twofold: first, he doesn't see the human labor (and thus, the human community) behind commodities, and second, he has a *false* belief in animation, as if the things on store shelves had wills of their own and entered into relations with each other.

Animation, for Marx, is always a delusion, drawing as it does on a metaphysical realm where the beings supposedly endowed with "life" end up having power over those who dreamed them up in the first place. The role of humans in this structure is doubly falsified: they are not seen as laborers and not seen as creators. But the truly infuriating thing for this consummate literalist is that it is *humans* who misvalue humans in this way, not taking their work into consideration, and erring whenever they raise their eyes to the sky. There is thus in the fetishism of the commodity an illegitimate exchange of properties: the necessary human acts are invisible, and the commodities seem to have a life of their own. *Persons* are thus robbed of volition, which is given to *things* instead.

For someone so intent on stamping out false animation, Marx is hyperaware of its rhetorical effects. Soon after condemning the illusion of animation, Marx writes: "Could commodities themselves speak, they would say: Our use-value may be a thing that interests men. It is no part of us as objects. What, however, does belong to us as objects, is our value. Our natural intercourse as commodities proves it. In the eyes of each other, we are nothing but exchange-values" (83). Commodities have eyes, then, and natural intercourse? By animating the commodities by means of prosopopeia, Marx makes them the spokesthings for the delusions of volition he is denouncing.

If it is false to consider commodities alive, it is equally false to base one's evidence on their point of view. Unless they are animate, they don't have a point of view. If their animation covered over the social relations of human labor, then perhaps there is a human social process behind their "natural intercourse" as well. To benefit from the properties of an item (use-value) may be either individual or collective. But what fixes a price (exchange-value), however mysterious it may be, is a social process that belongs to men and not to commodities. Like that of the arbitrary sign, their value is determined only by social agreement. And therefore the opposition is not man versus thing, but man the corporeal individual versus an abstract social process. Wanting to bring the working individual into view, Marx sees price not as arbitrary and fixed by convention, but as directly corresponding to the amount of labor-power required for the thing's production. The appeal of the thing on the market can be dispelled by a sober and literal correspondence between work and exchange. Therefore it is surprising to find that the following fantasmagoria open his discussion of the fetishism of the commodity:

> A commodity appears, at first sight, a very trivial thing, and easily understood. Its analysis shows that it is, in reality, a very queer thing, abounding in metaphysical subtleties and theological niceties. . . . It is as clear as noon-day, that man, by his industry, changes the forms of the materials furnished by Nature, in such a way as to make them useful to him. The form of wood, for instance, is altered, by making a table out of it. Yet, for all that, the table continues to be that common, every-day thing, wood. But, so soon as it steps forth as a commodity, it is changed into something transcendent. It not only stands with its feet on the ground, but, in relation to all other commodities, it stands on its head, and evolves out of its wooden brain grotesque ideas, far more wonderful than "table-turning" ever was. (71)

"Standing on one's head" is something that all readers of Marx associate with Hegel's position in Marx's project as a whole: "The mystification which dialectic suffers in Hegel's hands, by no means prevents him from being the first to present its general form of working in a comprehensive and conscious manner. With him it is standing on its head. It must be turned right side up again, if you would discover the rational kernel within the mystical shell" (20). It is thus thinking in the wrong direction which turns things upside down, and religion's function is to envelope the delusion in the mists of unclarity and irrationalism. Marx's aim is to demystify by turning things in the opposite direction.

Why wood? Why a table? "Wood" evokes fairy tales from ancient times: lost in the woods, woodsmen, and so on. "Wood" is also one of those terms that easily migrate into human life or description: "wooden leg," "wooden face." But while "wood" is migrating into human life, a table cannot even be described without seeming anthropomorphic: it has "legs," a "head," a "foot." These are metaphors drawn from the human body, but they are the only literal terms that exist for the parts of a table. A table is thus anthropomorphic from the start. Marx has only to play around with an existing figurative structure: the table "steps forth" on legs that one cannot not attribute to it. In other words, one *cannot* eliminate from language all trace of anthropomorphism: sometimes it is built into the naming structure itself. The demystification will never be complete.

There is one additional reason why tables are perfect for Marx's description of metaphysical delusion: in the second half of the nineteenth century the craze for séances spread across Europe and America. "Table-turning" was often the first sign of being contacted by the dead. Table-turning parties were all the rage. Tables shook when rapped by a ghost: table-turning was thus a transcendence of the usual laws of nature, and if the ideas of a table are even more wonderful than table-turning, they are wonderful in the same way. The "metaphysical subtleties" so elaborately summoned in occult practices surround that everyday thing, closer to home, the commodity.

For Marx's analysis of the fetishism of the commodity, then, there is an illegitimate exchange of properties between persons and things: things take volition from humans, and the work of humans is invisible. It is commodities that seem to have a social life; the social relations among humans are not seen. Thus, humans deludedly lust after the magic of things, instead of bonding with other humans on the basis of their common laboring condition.

Marx's aim to strip away every trace of illusion and stay with the hard literal fact, already belied, as we have seen, by habits of language and social life that don't fit neatly into either side, does not allow for two human drives that aren't satisfied with literality: desire and worship. Freud's analysis, although it says nothing about worship, promises to elucidate the mysteries of desire.

Freud begins his extensive 1927 analysis of fetishism with an example from one of his patients: the patient's fetishistic precondition for sexual interest was a "shine on the nose" (in German, "Glanz auf der Nase"). It later turned out that his fetish should be understood in English ("Glance at their nose") rather than German, English being the forgotten language of the patient's nursery. The fetish was thus the nose itself, not the shine.

Going back to Marx for a moment, however, one should not be so quick to eliminate that shine. A commodity is often enhanced by gleaming packaging, which surrounds the object on the store shelves with an aura of desirability. Commodities are often surrounded by superfluous boxes, whose job is to arouse the buying desire, not to enclose the product, whether or not the box turns out to be necessary to the product (if we recall "boxing Barbie," the more necessary the box, the more fantasy inheres in the object—"doll cannot stand alone without box"). Shopping, in other words, is a desire structure, not just an economic structure.

Time after time, Freud comes to the unsurprising conclusion that a fetish is a substitute for the penis, "but . . . not a substitute for any chance penis, but for a . . . penis that had been extremely important in early childhood . . . [and] . . . should have been given up . . . the woman's (the mother's) penis the little boy once believed in."[10] The fetish is thus a substitute for a penis that does not exist.

A fetish, in Freud's account, does not derive from a general state but from a traumatic scene: the boy's discovery of sexual difference. "A fetish is a story masquerading as an object," wrote the psychoanalyst Robert Stoller. The fetish allows the little boy to go on denying sexual difference.

The fetish covers over what the mother does not have by parading very visibly in front of the lack, allowing the boy to maintain the belief that all bodies are like his, and that he need not fear for any of his parts. The boy both perceives the mother's lack and denies it at the same time. The fetish offers the man another advantage over the ordinary heterosexual, writes Freud: "It is easily accessible and he can readily obtain the sexual satisfaction attached to it. What other men have to woo and make exertions for can be had by the fetishist with no trouble at all" (154). Often the fetish is associated with the last sight before the traumatic absence: shoe, foot, underwear, or fur and velvet (pubic hair).

In the film *Blue Velvet,* the fetishist Frank does indeed clutch a piece of blue velvet in order to achieve sexual satisfaction. But "Blue Velvet" is also a song sung by his object of desire, Dorothy, and the signifier "blue" occurs in all of her songs, as well as in the name of Frank's favorite beer, Pabst Blue Ribbon. The role of the first, forgotten language (in Freud's patient), and the role of the migrating signifier (in the film) indicate that the importance of language itself to the fetishistic structure is minimized if one sees the fetish as substituting for an organ. Yet there is something intuitively right about seeing sexuality spread by language.

The film begins not with Frank but with a cut-off ear. The camera zooms in on the ear both early and late in the film (made by David Lynch, the father of the maker of *Boxing Helena*). It is as though the ear were a *bouche d'ombre,* an oracle, through which the film's secret would arise. This body part out of place gives access to the violence and the mystery, which is perhaps the mystery of what a sexual body is. "Are you a detective or a pervert?" Sandy asks Jeffrey early in his investigations. But she is the one with her ear to the floor over her father's office, starting the quest off by saying, "I hear things."

In the film *Blue Velvet,* the human body becomes a manipulated thing, covered with makeup, lit and darkened, twisted with drugs and inhalers, cut into parts, dressed in wig and velvet, feeling and trying not to feel. The monstrous singer Ben even usurps Hoffmann's title from Freud's essay on the uncanny:

> A candy-colored clown they call the sandman
> Tiptoes to my room every night
> Just to sprinkle stardust and to whisper
> Go to sleep, everything is all right.

If all hearing in this film is overhearing, no investigation can stay unaffected by what it discovers. Sandy's question, "Are you a detective or a pervert?" is based on a false opposition between "mere" looking and sexual looking. What Jeffrey learns in all the scenes in which he observes without being seen is that there is no innocent form of looking: the more the observer is affected, the more he "knows." The more the observer finds out, the more different from himself he becomes. Looking, in other words, is itself sexual, and the boy in Freud's scenario couldn't be traumatized unless he had already looked with desire.

What about women? In Freud's scenario there seems to be no place for an observer who doesn't see—who scotomizes—sexual difference. But the discovery that the mother is not "phallic" may traumatize the girl as well as the boy. As Jacques Lacan puts it, the girl "finds the signifier of her own desire in the body of him to whom she addresses her demand for love. Perhaps it should not be forgotten that the organ that assumes this signifying function takes on the value of a fetish."[11] If the sight of the female body is traumatic for both sexes because of what the mother *does not have,* then anything a man *has* is a substitute for the mother's phallus as well. The little girl is as invested in the reality of the substitute for the nonexistent as the little boy.

Walter Benjamin, trying to merge the Marxist sense of the fetish with the development of displays of goods in department stores—the development of desire as a necessity of capitalism—says the following about the fetishism of the commodity in his book on Baudelaire:

> If the soul of the commodity which Marx occasionally mentions in jest existed, it would be the most empathetic ever encountered in the realm of souls, for it would have to see in everyone the buyer in whose hand and house it wants to nestle. Empathy is the nature of the intoxication to which the *flâneur* abandons himself in the crowd. "The poet enjoys the incomparable privilege of being himself and someone else as he sees fit. Like a roving soul in search of a body, he enters another person whenever he wishes. For him alone, all is open; if certain places seem closed to him, it is because in his view they are not worth inspecting" ("Les Foules"). The commodity itself is the speaker here. Yes, the last words give a rather accurate idea of what the commodity whispers to a poor wretch who passes a shop-window containing beautiful and expensive things. These objects are not interested in this person; they do not empathize with him. In the sentences of the significant prose poem "Les Foules" there speaks, with other words, the fetish itself with which Baudelaire's sensitive nature resonated so powerfully; that empathy with inorganic things which was one of his sources of inspiration.[12]

Baudelaire could make anything into a speaker: "je suis un vieux boudoir" (I am an old boudoir), "je suis un cimetière" (I am a cemetery), "je suis la pipe d'un auteur" (I am an author's pipe), "moi, mon âme est fêlée" (my soul is cracked). But his most comfortable structure for expressing emotion is direct address: "Viens-tu du ciel profond ou sors-tu de l'âbime, O Beauté" (Do you come from the deep sky, or from the abyss, O Beauty); "O toison!" (O fleece!); "je t'adore à l'égal de la voûte nocturne" (I adore you like the night sky); "verse-moi moins de flamme!" (pour me less fire!);

"J'implore ta pitié, Toi, l'unique que j'aime" (I implore your pity, You, the only one I love); "O Lune de ma vie! Emmitoufle-toi d'ombre" (O moon of my life, muffle yourself in shadow); "Andromaque, je pense à vous!" (Andromaque, I am thinking of you!). Except for this last example, these poems are not addressed to specific individuals but rather describe the subject himself. This is even more true when he addresses the poems to part of himself: "Sois sage, o ma Douleur, et tiens-toi plus tranquille" (Be good, my Sorrow, and hold still); "Que diras-tu, mon coeur, coeur autrefois flétri" (What do you say, my heart, heart that was formerly wilted). The fact of address, in French or English at least, makes it easy to step into the role of the speaker. The shifters "I" and "you" fit anyone who utters them. But there also seems to be about speech an aura of allegory: one of the first full-length allegories was, after all, *Psychomachia*. Feelings are treated like another person, and other people give the poet access to himself: "N'es-tu pas . . . la gourde / Où je hume . . . le vin du souvenir?" (Are you not the gourde / Where I drink the wine of recollection?). The dialogue structure makes articulate the poet's self-estrangement: the poems not only describe his inner debate but also detail his attachment to his own abjection. As Walter Benjamin wrote to Max Horkheimer: "Baudelaire's unique importance consists in having been the first . . . to have apprehended . . . the productive energy of the individual alienated from himself."[13]

Attempting to think with both Marx and Freud, Benjamin could combine the eroticism of the prosthesis (the prosthesis of the mother's phallus) with the mystic attraction of the commodity. It is precisely the false gleam of the commodity that Marx wants to combat. But Benjamin knows that literality does not sell commodities.

While Freud's scenario for fetishism seems to call out for a removal of the blinders preventing "correct" sight, Benjamin seems to intuit something far less natural. In his unfinished *Arcades* project, Benjamin analyzes the Parisian glass-roofed galleries (arcades) that were already disappearing in Paris (but gave rise to department stores and malls) in order to understand how commodity capitalism mobilized desire and display in the service of a new pleasure: shopping.[14]

> Each generation experiences the fashions of the one immediately preceding it as the most radical antiaphrodisiac imaginable. In this judgment it is not so far off the mark as might be supposed. Every fashion is to some extent a bitter

satire on love: in every fashion, perversities are suggested by the most ruthless means. Every fashion stands in opposition to the organic. Every fashion couples the living body to the inorganic world. To the living, fashion defends the rights of the corpse. The fetishism that succumbs to the sex appeal of the inorganic is its vital nerve. (79)

Hallmark of the period's fashions: to intimate a body that never knows full nudity. (68)

Empathy with the commodity is fundamentally empathy with exchange value itself. The flâneur is the virtuoso of this empathy. He takes the concept of marketability itself for a stroll. Just as his final ambit is the department store, his last incarnation is the sandwich-man. (448)

If the flâneur is the last remainder of aristocracy, he now combines idler, rapist, burglar, homeless person, and prostitute, in a world in which everything is for sale: "Moreover, he is no buyer. He is merchandise" (42).

In a world of fig leaves and piano skirts, the confusion of the animate with the inanimate is perfectly natural. The trick is to channel the easily excited desire toward commodities. The fetishism of the commodity draws on the appeal of sexual reproduction to, in fact, defend the rights of the corpse: the substitute for full nudity is sexier than the body. If there is no end to the elaborations of the inorganic, the organic becomes a poor thing indeed. The secret of capitalism is to enlist the *rhetoric* of nature in the service of the limitless sex appeal of the inorganic.

Freud, however, sticks by his opinion of the natural as healthy, the unnatural as unhealthy, and the perverse as a symptom. But fetishism, according to Freud, belongs to the terminology of an older psychology. Speaking about "Gradiva," the tale by Wilhelm Jensen to which he devoted a long analysis early in his career, and a reproduction of the classical bas-relief that he kept in his own consulting room, he writes:

> The psychiatrist would perhaps assign Norbert Hanold's delusion to the great group of paranoia and designate it as a "fetichistic erotomania," because falling in love with the bas-relief would be the most striking thing to him and because, to his conception, which coarsens everything, the interest of the young archaeologist in the feet and foot-position of women must seem suspiciously like fetishism. All such names and divisions of the different kinds of delusion are, however, substantially useless and awkward.[15]

Freud, in contrast to "old-school psychiatrists," sees Hanold's interest in women's feet not as a desire in itself but as a memory-trace for his forgotten childhood love. "In the fancies of Norbert Hanold about Gradiva [the bas-relief], we thought we recognized already the remnants of his childhood friendship with Zoe Bertgang." "Zoe," which means "life" in Greek, and "Bertgang," which in German means "lively gait," just as "Gradiva" does in Greek, redoubles the fact that the childhood friend had a distinctly lively step, which Hanold recognized on the bas-relief he saw in Rome. "We had already believed, of course, that the Greek ancestry of the mythical Gradiva was an after-effect of the Greek name, Zoe, but with the name, Gradiva, we had ventured nothing. . . . [T]his very name now shows itself to be a rem-nant, really a translation of the repressed family name of the supposedly for-gotten beloved of his youth."[16]

We will return to this work of translation later, but for now let us start with the role of Hanold's profession. His devotion to women of stone and brass rather than flesh is a necessity of his profession as an archeologist. The father of Zoe, Hanold's neighbor, is a zoologist, and thus studies "life" as in-tently as Hanold studies death.

Freud seems to have set up a simple logic: love of statue = sick = re-pressed, love of real woman = healthy = free from repression. The only strange element in this structure is the animal Jensen uses to represent life: the housefly. Life is that which annoys; it occurs just where it is not wanted. "Hunger or thirst for blood did not impel them, but solely the diabolical de-sire to torture; it was the 'Ding an sich' in which absolute evil had found its incarnation," says Jensen's text.[17] Coming out of repression, like coming out of a freeze, might be torture, but why does this unappealing creature repre-sent life?

Another source of ambivalence is the role of science in Jensen's text—and in Freud's. "Science, which he [Hanold] serves, has taken this interest [in living women] from him and transferred it to women of stone or bronze," writes Freud, as if science were the bad mistress who had caused the delu-sion.[18] Deciding to undertake a journey to Italy, Hanold finds himself sur-rounded by empty-headed couples on their honeymoons. He, of course, has archeology as his traveling companion. But somehow she is less satisfying than usual: "For his traveling companion, science, had, most decidedly, much of an old Trappist about her," writes Jensen; she "did not open her mouth when she was not spoken to, and it seemed to him that he was almost forgetting in what language he had communed with her" (35). When Hanold finds himself in Pompeii, she becomes even more unsatisfying.

> Not only had all his science left him, but it left him without the least desire to regain it; he remembered it as from a great distance, and he felt that it had been an old, dried-up, boresome aunt, dullest and most superfluous creature in the world. What she uttered with puckered lips and sapient mien, and presented as wisdom, was all vain, empty pompousness, and merely gnawed at the dry rind of the fruit of knowledge without revealing anything of its content, the germ of life, or bringing anything to the point of inner, intelligent enjoyment. What it taught was a lifeless, archeological view and what came from its mouth was a dead, philological language. (44–45)

Jensen thus works within a simple opposition: dissatisfaction with archeology = desire for life; choosing the lifelessness of academic knowledge = choosing death. Science collaborated with Hanold's turn away from life; it was in service of a symptom. To make the opposition more piquant, Jensen not only animates science but figures the opposition as a contest between two women: Hanold's female traveling companion becomes more and more unattractive as life gains the upper hand. Science goes from "having much of an old Trappist about her" to being "an old, dried up, boresome aunt" as the honeymoon couples surrounding Hanold become more appealing. The rhetoric of domination—science is first the lady he serves, then an old Trappist, then an old aunt—becomes more and more ridiculous and repressive. Nothing mitigates the reader's desire for her defeat. She becomes just the opposite of an object of desire, and desiring itself becomes a good.

Freud's interpretation of Jensen's charming stereotypes is more crude, but his attitude toward science is altogether different from Jensen's. "He is enraged even at his mistress, science," writes Freud about Hanold, and then quotes the passage about the aunt.[19] Never does Jensen describe science explicitly as Hanold's mistress. Freud thus takes for granted a sexual dynamic more lightly drawn in the tale.

Yet Freud reveals that he himself has been fighting with science for a long time, that science to him is more masculine than feminine, more of an authority than a mistress; that he is far from content to leave science behind, but would like nothing better than to be considered part of it. For Freud, science itself is at once the object of desire and the adversary. He wants to defeat—but also be blessed by—the most prestigious knowledge of his time. The question of Freud's "scientificness" continues to rage even today. Thus, while Jensen thus tells a light-hearted tale of romance and delusion and Freud bows to a masculine authority, neither of them takes femininity very seriously. Jensen, as a creative writer, is not divided about the lifelessness of academic knowledge, but Freud, as a neurological researcher, does not set up biological "life" as an unquestioned value. If Freud's research on dreams changes science, that is much more significant than one more honeymoon.

Freud's ambivalence toward science, strangely, translates at first into a much more dynamic form of animation. Freud often refers to himself in the third person as "the present writer," as if to make his conclusions more scientific; as if to diminish his *own* animation. Three years after the publication of *The Interpretation of Dreams,* "orthodox science," however, was not convinced that the "present writer" had really solved the mystery of dreams. "The first question," writes Freud, "is whether the dream has any meaning at all, whether one should grant it the value of a psychic process. Science answers, *No.*"[20] Science and the present writer not only disagree; what they say to each other is quoted. Science has not only the power of life but also the power of speech.

It was to bolster his theories of dream interpretation without being classed among the "superstitious" that Freud decided to look at the made-up dreams of a fictional character. "Story-tellers are valuable allies, and their testimony is to be rated high, for they usually know many things between heaven and earth that our academic wisdom does not even dream of. In psychic knowledge, indeed, they are far ahead of us, ordinary people, because they draw from sources that we have not yet made accessible for science."[21] Jensen's story came accidentally to hand, and confirmed to a remarkable degree everything Freud had said about dreams. "How did the author come upon the same knowledge as the physician, at least upon a procedure which would suggest that he possessed it?" asks Freud (187). It must be because it is true. "Science does not yet recognize the significance of repression nor the fact that it needs the unconscious for explanation to the world of psychopathological phenomena; it does not seek the basis of delusion in psychic conflict, and does not regard its symptoms as a compromise-formation. Then our author stands alone against all science? No, not that—*if the present writer may reckon his works as science*" (185).

"The present writer," Freud, is more scientific than orthodox science; his dream interpretation, confirmed by the fictional dream of a creative writer, is not the theory of some superstitious madman but should belong to science itself. Science, for Freud, is not a malign mistress or an anti-life force from which life must be liberated but an ego-ideal that is very much part of life. Only old-fashioned, unmodernized science is animate: here there is no trace of animation. While Jensen can foster our belief that life = good and death = bad, Freud cannot always accept that scheme. Or rather, maybe he does *consciously* but his unconscious knows better.

Much is made of the name of the remote place where Zoe and her father are staying: the Albergo del Sole—the Sun Hotel. Zoe plays with the Italian word and its translation, especially on learning that Hanold has purchased there an antique brooch said to have belonged to a Pompeiian girl who perished in the eruption of 79. The fact that in French the sun is masculine while in German it is feminine has often been cited as evidence that there is nothing natural about gender in language, but that gender difference does determine what myths the sun can and cannot fit into. In addition, as Saussure reminds us, there are some languages in which it is impossible to say "sit in the sun." The noonday sun in Pompeii is sweltering, but as the "ghostly hour," it is the time when Hanold seeks to encounter Gradiva, who may be a ghost or may have come back to life. Each translation of the "sun" may in fact bring additional linguistic connections with it: in English, the word "sole" is the part of the foot that is very visible in Gradiva's gait. This pun does not exist in the German original, but one begins to suspect that uncanny linguistic connections lie all about, just waiting, like statues, to be unearthed in some farmer's field.

Jensen tells a love story in which Norbert Hanold and Zoe Bertgang recognize their love for each other. Freud reads it as a successful psychoanalysis. Both of them see Hanold "cured" of his deluded attraction to a bas-relief, as he replaces it with its proper object, a living woman. Old-fashioned psychiatry would call Hanold a foot fetishist, but Freud, seeing Hanold's peeping under women's skirts as an attempt to answer the question of whether the bas-relief was drawn from life, considers Hanold a scientist. Science seeks not pleasure but rather knowledge. Hanold is hardly a foot fetishist; his interest in feet is merely a means to an end.

Why, then, does Jensen's text end the love story in the following way? "Norbert Hanold stopped before them and said in a peculiar tone, 'Please go ahead here.' A merry, comprehending, laughing expression lurked around his companion's mouth, and, raising her dress slightly with her left hand, Gradiva *rediviva* Zoe Bertgang, viewed by him with dreamily observing eyes, crossed with her calmly buoyant walk, through the sunlight, over the stepping-stones, to the other side of the street."[22] Does Hanold love the bas-relief or the living woman? Is he able to get excited by the real girl when she *doesn't* resemble the sculpture? When he instructs the living woman to demonstrate the beloved walk, is it totally *un*true that Hanold is a foot fetishist?

Freud's text, of course, ends differently, but is perhaps equally entwined in the mysteries of desire. Hanold's initial dream makes him contemporary with the living Gradiva, and present at her death when Vesuvius erupted in 79 A.D. His desire to see the living Gradiva lie down combines with an archeologist's fantasy: "This was the wish, comprehensible to every archaeologist, to have been an eye-witness of that catastrophe of 79," writes Freud. This is the first time anyone has mentioned this wish. It draws genuine longing out of Freud, though. "What sacrifice would be too great, for an antiquarian, to realize this wish otherwise than through dreams!"[23] The desire for knowledge can be as intense as the desire for flesh.

Chapter Ten

Artificial Life

Alan Turing (1912–1954), who worked on the first computers and is widely credited with doing the research at the foundation of the field of artificial intelligence, developed a test (the Turing test) to differentiate computers from human beings. If a person takes a thing, sight unseen, for a person, the thing is said to have passed the Turing test. The reports of the chess match between champion Gary Kasparov and IBM's Deep Blue in 1996 took the form of a classic face-off between natural and artificial intelligence: a classic dramatization of the Turing test.

Deep Blue uses sophisticated parallel processing, with 256 specially configured chips analyzing 200 million possible chess positions a second. As impressive as that sounds, however, it is the same "brute force" computing that has dominated the computer world for 50 years. . . .

Joerg [Christopher F. Joerg, the mastermind behind MIT's "brute force" computer, "* Socrates"] doesn't think AI [artificial intelligence] will do well in computer chess or any other application until computer speed and memory hits a plateau. AI guru [Marvin] Minsky's view is that AI's real jump will come when it uses human-like variety in problem solving.[1]

The *New York Times* carried the following opinion piece the next day:

> Human worth hung in the balance this weekend. . . . Humanity's collective self-esteem was once more on the line.
>
> The latest blow to our chauvinism began in the first round of the six-game match when Deep Blue bested our best after only 36 moves. . . . Suddenly, we once again needed to explain ourselves to ourselves.
>
> We have a habit of perpetually redefining "creativity" as that which humans do and "brute force" as the stuff of machines. In each age, we have redrawn the borders of the inviolably human. . . .
>
> From Copernicus pushing us from the center of the universe to Darwin tying us to the lowliest of life forms, man has routed himself from his place of relative importance in the cosmos.
>
> But why should our self-esteem be more threatened by losing a game of self-projection than it is flattered by building a device capable of out-projecting us? That we can assemble an artifact capable of beating us at our own game is a stunning triumph for human ingenuity. . . .
>
> Highest and hardest of all is the challenge of accurate self-description. When a computer can produce a more intriguing rationalization than Mr. Kasparov's, a more moving lament in the face of checks to its own bruised ego, then humans will indeed have something to worry about.[2]

It seems as though people are reassured when the human is something *more* than the computer: if a computer can do x, a person, even while doing x less well, is always said to do $x + n$. The ability $x + n$ is usually the human's ability to produce art: "What gives art significance and value," says Yale art historian David Gelernter (best known as a victim of the Unabomber), "is that a person has something to say."[3] "I think that chess is cerebral and intellectual," says Douglas Hofstadter, author of *Gödel, Escher, Bach,* "but it doesn't have deep emotional qualities to it, mortality, resignation, joy, all the things that music deals with."[4] This quotation offers one clue to the emotional superiority of humans: something inanimate isn't concerned with mortality.

The uniqueness of humans is often tied to some quality humans possess that machines can't duplicate. But this ignores the instances where the human being functions like a machine. The rhythms of assembly-line production, spoofed in Charlie Chaplin's *Modern Times,* require that the human operator function like the automated equipment that surrounds him. The relentless speed of the machine has made cyborgs of us all.

Another suggestive use of a machine involves a computer program called ELIZA made to function like a therapist. To the comment "It's hot today," for example, ELIZA responds, "Why do you tell me it's hot today?" Here is an account by Sherry Turkle, professor of the sociology of science, of a conversation she had with ELIZA's designer, Joseph Weizenbaum, on the day Turkle first arrived at MIT: "Weizenbaum thought that ELIZA's easily identifiable limitations would discourage people from wanting to engage with it. But he was wrong. Even people who knew and understood that ELIZA could not know or understand wanted to confide in the program. Some even wanted to be alone with it."[5] ELIZA's limitations might produce exactly the therapeutic effect the users are looking for. In other words, training in mirroring, repeating, and refraining from interpreting indicate that a therapist must learn to cease to exist, must *un*learn human behavior, to be effective. Knowing that ELIZA doesn't understand might reassure rather than discourage those patients who will trust a machine more than a person.

The prospect of death may be what human beings have in common, and the particular consciousness of death may have effects on human art. One of the essays in a volume titled *Artificial Life* indeed ends with a section called "AL and Art": "Let us end this brief review with the relationship between AL and art. As we already advocated, art inheres in the very foundations of AL. Synthesis, which is the central method in the AL toolbox, becomes artistic creation when the Artificial Lifer . . . is free from any constraint (especially the unpleasant constraints imposed by reality) and is only limited by the power of his or her imagination."[6] Mortality may infuse all human speaking with a kind of pathos that something that can neither live nor die cannot have. So that if a person "has something to say," it is first and foremost "I am alive" but in the face of death. This is perhaps why the poetic canon starts with elegies; why laments over someone's—someone else's—death are often the first steps in a poetic career. The speaker finds voice in the fact that someone (not the speaker) has died. The speaker feels the shadow of mortality, but also feels that it has spared him for the moment.

While research on artificial intelligence asks the thorny question, "What is thinking?" research on artificial life asks the even thornier question,

"What is life?" There are many attempts to answer the latter question, as we shall see in a moment, but very few focus on mortality. Indeed, as one specialist puts it, "In synthetic life systems implemented by computers, death is not likely to be a process that would occur spontaneously, and it must generally be introduced artificially by the designer."[7] Mortality is still the privilege of the humans designing the system. And feeling and saying meaningful things seem to accompany it.

So what are the criteria for life that A-life researchers use?

- It is made by humans rather than by nature
- It is autonomous
- It is adaptive; it can learn from experience; it evolves
- It reproduces
- It has a sense of self-representation
- It has some kind of metabolism
- It interacts with its environment
- It is a functional whole, a pattern in space and time[8]

A good example of the types of things that fit these criteria is the computer virus. Carbon-based biological life, the saying goes, is only one form that life could have taken.

Of course, many people still believe that true life incorporates some magic essence or spark: "Modern biochemistry and molecular biology are often considered to be the ultimate defeat of vitalism. Vitalism is here considered a quasireligious belief that living organisms contain a unique vital principle, a mystical life-force or something similar, that cannot be explained within the framework of natural science."[9] It is no wonder that Frankenstein is the precursor here: Mary Shelley manages to have it both ways. Her protagonist, not knowing any better, reads avidly the works of the alchemists Cornelius Agrippa, Paracelsus, and Albertus Magnus before being corrected and set on the track of modern chemistry by his professors at the University of Ingolstadt, Professors Kempe and Waldman. "Two years passed in this manner, during which I paid no visit to Geneva [his home], but was engaged, heart and soul, in the pursuit of some discoveries, which I hoped to make. None but those who have experienced them can conceive of the enticements of science."[10]

Frankenstein assures us several times that his discovery of the secrets of animation was entirely scientific—that is, that no trace of vitalism remained in it—but somehow his labors seem uncanny and magical despite him.

> Unless I had been animated by an almost supernatural enthusiasm, my application to this study would have been irksome, and almost intolerable. To examine the causes of life, we must first have recourse to death. I became acquainted with the science of anatomy: but this was not sufficient; I must also observe the natural decay and corruption of the human body. In my education my father had taken the greatest precautions that my mind should be impressed by no supernatural horrors. . . . [A] church-yard was to me merely the receptacle of bodies deprived of life. (30)

The inquiry might have been entirely scientific, but the description of the discovery, and the fact that he will not share it with Walton, give it an aura of magic: "[A] sudden light broke in upon me. . . . What had been the study and desire of the wisest men since the creation of the world, was now within my grasp" (30–31). The origin of Mary Shelley's novel, according to her 1831 preface, was in the desire to emulate German ghost stories, along with a conversation she overheard about Dr. Darwin's experiments and galvanism. The appeal of scientific discovery in a context of supernatural dread even surrounds the origins of the story itself.

What is foundational, then, in *Frankenstein*, is not the divergence of the scientific from the supernatural but the fact that the path of science itself can lead to the taboo. Knowledge itself is uncanny; one can never be sure whether or not the knowledge one finds is forbidden. The more avidly science pursues its enigmas, the more likely it is that the searcher seeks forbidden fruit. By stealing something that belongs to the gods, the scientist magnifies himself, becomes god-like himself. By comparing his fate with that of Prometheus, punished for bringing a benefit to mankind, he shows himself to be both grandiose and guilty.

One result, which is also an aim, of research on artificial life is the blurring of the boundary between life and non-life. "Connectionism opened the way for new ideas of nature as a computer and of the computer as part of nature," writes Sherry Turkle. "And it thus suggested that traditional distinctions between the natural and artificial, the real and the simulated, might dissolve."[11]

The toy market has indeed benefited from this blurring of boundaries.

Witness the appeal of toys that behave like pets. Tamagotchis, which were invented in Japan, are little egg-shaped toys made to function as virtual pets: they need to be fed, cared for, and trained, or they will die. Mortality does play a large role in adopting one, therefore, but first and foremost it is a sign of neglect on the part of the human caretaker. But Tamagotchis do die, and that necessitates a Tamagotchi graveyard. I found a Web site for one that announced, "This is a Tamagotchi Cemetary [*sic*]. Feel free to mourn your Tamagotchi by sending a memory, or simply read the epitaphs of others who have lost their Tamagotchi in this struggle for life. We are all in this struggle together, and after you sign, read all the other stories. It might make you feel a lot better." Some of the mourners' comments follow:

Tamagotchi name: Ducky. Age: 8. He was very greedy, but that was my fault really. I forgot about him for one day. . . . But he was so cute with his big beak! I never expected him to live long anyway.

Tamagotchi name: Beatie Bow. Age: 12. She was so sweet! Even when I forgot to do something for her, she battled on until the end. . .

Tamagotchi name: Fi Fi. Age: 7. She was good in her days. I'm sorry I let you get washed. . . .

Tamagotchi name: Saturn. Age: 12. My baby died in his sleep. I will forever weep. Then his batteries went dead. Now he lives in my head.

Tamagotchi name: Calvin V. Age: 24. Poor Calvin V. He committed suicide.

Tamagotchi name: Dr. Malcom X. Age: 64. Dr. Malcom X was a good Tamagotchi. During the middle of his life, though, I got lazy. During about 30 years of his life, he was on for about 15 minutes a day. I ended up re-starting him because I felt that he never got the attention he truly deserved.

Those who think that one more thing to worry about doesn't sound like fun would be appalled at the improvements that have been brought to bear on these virtual pets. The Furby, for instance, speaks "Furbish" until taught by his owner to speak English, and in 1998 the toys had twenty-four names, three different pitches of voice, six fur patterns, and four eye colors. In 2005 Hasbro introduced a new Furby, driven by "Emoto-tronics," with a wide range of emotions and motions, advanced voice recognition, and enhanced communications. Features included:

- Flexible beak
- Moving eyes
- Patented eyelid technology
- Moving eyebrows
- Moving plumage
- Moving and curving ears
- Voice recognition
- Touch sensors
- Speaks Furbish and learns English

A Furby gives us a theory of education as complex as that of Frankenstein's monster reading *Plutarch's Lives, Paradise Lost,* and *The Sorrows of Young Werther*—all in French. Reading and being shaped by what one reads can happen in solitude, but Furbies require interaction. For a Furby owner, therefore, language pedagogy becomes fundamental to intimacy.

Of course, not all forms of mechanical life are made to simulate natural life as a whole. Giant arms and round vacuum cleaners simply do their jobs and that is all. In tasks too hazardous or too undesirable or impossible for human workers, it is common to supplement humans with machines. This is the origin of robots (from a Czech word, *robota,* meaning "the term of labor a serf owes his master"; first introduced in a 1920 play by Karel Capek, *R.U.R.*) A robot, in other words, is the fantasy of the perfect slave.

There is a robot aesthetic that complicates things still further. Techno, a toy dog who could be trained like a real dog, was made to simulate not biological life but a machine: he was a metallic silver color equipped with non-working, machine-like joints. While Darth Vader in the *Star Wars* movies is a human and R2D2 a robot, Darth's shiny metallic black suit is more spiffily and futuristically robotic than R2D2's appearance. The "false Maria" in Fritz Lang's *Metropolis* looks much more like something constructed by humans than Edison's android Hadaly does in Villiers's novel *Eve of the Future Eden.* There is often something sinister and self-willed about robots, in fact. Like the multiplying brooms in *The Sorcerer's Apprentice,* robots can turn against their masters, either because they don't know when to stop, or through outright rebellion. X. X. Miller, in his study of robots, calls this the "fear of children growing up to become rivals." In fact, for Miller, there is always something uncannily Oedipal about robots. That is perhaps why the research on "emotional" robots is so concerned to make them look and act like babies. Rodney Brooks, director of MIT's artificial intelligence lab, discusses what led to the creation of the lab's robot, Kismet: "Our radical belief is that interaction with the world is the key to intelligence."[12]

In what is doubtless the most famous artificial life film of all time, director Ridley Scott's *Blade Runner* (1982), the prefatory events that lead to the film's action are described as follows:

> Early in the twenty-first century, the Tyrell Corporation advanced robot evolution into the NEXUS phase—a being virtually identical to a human—known as a *Replicant*.
>
> The NEXUS 6 Replicants were superior in strength and agility, and at least equal in intelligence, to the genetic engineers who created them.
>
> Replicants were used off-world as slave labor, in the hazardous exploration and colonization of other planets.
>
> After a bloody mutiny by a NEXUS 6 combat team in an off-world colony, Replicants were declared illegal on Earth—under penalty of death.
>
> Special police squads—Blade Runner Units—had orders to shoot to kill, upon detection, any trespassing Replicant.
>
> This was not called execution.
>
> It was called retirement.

Colonization and slavery go together here—as they once did in the United States. Chattel slavery permitted people to be treated like things: owned, traded, and worked as if they had no feelings. The original subtitle for Harriet Beecher Stowe's *Uncle Tom's Cabin* was in fact "The Man Who Was a Thing."[13] Slave rebellions were constantly feared by the masters, and the deeds of escaped rebels, as in *Blade Runner,* were unpredictable. Those rebel slaves, too, were usually shot on sight. But look at the vocabulary used in the film. If the mutiny was "bloody," the casualties probably numbered some humans, but "penalty of death," "shoot to kill," and "execute" suggest that replicants can die a violent death, and hence are alive. Although "retire" in an intransitive sense is a common human activity, "to retire something" is usually said with reference to products being withdrawn from the market. Thus, instead of confronting the violent death that the blade runner's act would accomplish for living creatures, the replicants face the no-man's-land of no-longer-used machines. The blade runner's fatal round-up of illegals is made into merely a clean-up of disused things.

The replicants are made to copy human beings exactly, except for their emotions. Out of concern that the replicants might develop their own emotions over time, they are given a built-in four-year life span. The stage is set for their confrontation with mortality, then, and for the moral comparison of replicants with human beings. The similarities between humans and replicants are reinforced by the juxtaposition of old technologies for making artificial humans: one of the replicants is shot near a row of department-store mannequins; the character J. R. Sebastian, whose body is wracked with premature aging, makes intricate mechanical toys ("I make friends," he says). Sebastian and Eldin Tyrell are in the midst of a game of chess when Roy Baty (one of the replicants) walks in. Tyrell wonders why he hasn't come before. Roy says to the head of the corporation, "It's not easy to meet your maker." Roy says that his problem is death and that he wants his maker to give him "more life." But Tyrell says he can't. Roy kisses Tyrell on the lips as he simultaneously puts out the old man's eyes.

The Oedipal scenario, so obvious here, is nowhere in the story on which the movie is said to be based, Philip K. Dick's "Do Androids Dream of Electric Sheep?" Only the artificial owl and snake in the film recall the story, which is set in San Francisco (not LA, like the film) and shows signs of belonging to the Vietnam era (the looming corporate presence and manufacturer of replicants in the story is the Rand Corporation, a highly incorporeal member of the military-industrial complex): its crux lies in knowing what is real and what simulated.

Blade Runner, on the other hand (and I refer to the "Hollywood version," not the "director's cut"), is firmly set in Reagan-era LA—it advertises incessantly in neon, the rainy city is traversed by futuristic hovercraft, and the miserable, retrograde city dwellers speak a mixture of Japanese, Spanish, German, and what have you, understood by every good street cop. The world of the film noir voice-over prepares the viewer to identify with the blade runner Deckard: will he have to shoot the female replicant he loves, or will they live happily ever after? Although the huge buildings in the city are modern, the police station in which Deckard meets his boss is old-fashioned. The voice-over tells us that his job is to kill the four "skin jobs" (replicants) that are walking the streets. Holden, the man who tried to administer the Voight-Kampff empathy test to one of them, was shot when asking about the replicant's mother; the replicant fired the shot while saying, "Let me tell you about my mother!" Replicants, of course, are not of woman born. Their memories of the past are implants, and their family photos, fictions.

The Voight-Kampff test is designed to detect the involuntary human responses to empathy. It is thus a sophisticated version of the Turing test, used to differentiate humans from machines. It is interesting to note that the telltale sign of humanness is detected when the body is functioning most like a machine.

Roy Baty, the leader of the replicant rebels, not only searches for and kills his "father" but also quotes canonical poetry (Blake's *America*) and saves Deckard's life. The passage from Blake that Baty quotes concerns angels and thunder, and makes this drama seem like *Paradise Lost*. The pathos of his impending death is raised to mythic status through its metaphysical context, and his salvation of Deckard, whom just a moment before he had been chasing across the improbably gothic roof of what is identified as the Bradbury building, makes him into a Christ figure in the end (it does not hurt that, to stay alive, he drives a nail through his hand). "I don't know why he saved my life," meditates Deckard in a voice-over. "Maybe in those last moments he loved life more than he ever had before—not just *his* life."

As Deckard flies away with Rachael, he opines, "I didn't know how long we would have together—who does?" The mystery of mortality strikes him anew; both Rachael and Deckard may in fact be replicants, but not knowing their termination dates makes them similar to humans. As was the case for Edison in *Eve of the Future Eden,* the idea of artificial life does not function as the key to difference but makes the mystifications of vitalism more apparent. Faced with the implication of a human essence, the human inventor can only shrug and ask rhetorical questions. And both create life as a commodity. "More human than human," said Tyrell earlier; "that's our motto."

Chapter Eleven

Real Dolls

In a text otherwise uninterested in female patients as representative humans, Freud cites the relation between women and their dolls:

> We remember that in their early games children do not distinguish at all sharply between living and inanimate objects, and that they are especially fond of treating their dolls like live people. In fact, I have occasionally heard a woman patient declare that even at the age of eight she had still been convinced that her dolls were certain to come to life if she looked at them in a particular, extremely concentrated, way. . . . But, curiously enough, while the Sand-Man story deals with the arousing of an early childhood fear, the idea of a "living doll" excites no fear at all; children have no fear of their dolls coming to life, they may even desire it.[1]

Dolls are thus things the coming alive of which excites infantile desire rather than fear. Freud is looking for instances where intellectual uncertainty about something's aliveness (the theory he is refuting) is not uncanny. "The resuscitation of the dead in accounts of miracles, as in the New Testament, elicits

feelings quite unrelated to the uncanny. . . . And we should hardly call it uncanny when Pygmalion's beautiful statue comes to life" (246). The coming
to life of the dead or inanimate is thus, on the one hand, central to Christianity, and, on the other, a model for the work of art. The replacement of
death by eternal life and the desirability of the artwork are two of the struc-
turing forces of European civilization. Nothing has repressed or surmounted
them; that is why they are not uncanny. On the contrary, the life they involve is entirely legitimate and desired. A remainder of the uncanniness of
unwanted life, however, occurs when one wishes a being dead and it exhibits
more life: the unsettling persistence of the doll Chucky in the *Child's Play*
movies, for example, or the recovery of the intruder in *Wait until Dark,*
when the blind victim thinks she has knocked out her attacker. What is uncanny is what goes against one's waking wishes or beliefs. It is not uncertainty over something's aliveness that Freud says is uncanny, it is its contradiction of our wishes.

Indeed, scholar Terry Castle sees the invention of the uncanny going
hand in hand with the Age of Reason. "At numerous points," she writes,
"it is difficult to avoid the conclusion that it was during the eighteenth century, with its confident rejection of transcendental explanations, compulsive
quest of systematic knowledge, and self-conscious valorization of 'reason'
over 'superstition,' that human beings first experienced that encompassing
sense of strangeness and unease Freud finds so characteristic of modern
life."[2] It is no accident that Freud chooses a story by Hoffmann to illustrate
his theory: Hoffmann was fascinated by new inventions, and even wrote
a story called "The Automaton." In "The Sand-Man," the protagonist,
Nathanael, falls in love with a wooden doll. This gives Hoffmann the
chance to satirize both the new sciences and German romanticism, in which
Nathanael is a would-be participant. Romanticism gravitates, according to
Hoffmann, toward a none too closely examined ideal—which is why a Romantic can be duped by a doll.[3] He also implies, in Olimpia's invariable "Ah!
Ah!" that a Romantic author wants from the other only a mirror image,
only a response that ratifies his brilliance.

The sexual idealization of an inert but beautiful woman, in which male
narcissism finds no other will to hamper him, has been analyzed many
times,[4] and is the driving force in Villiers's *L'Eve future.* Indeed, the phenomenon of life-size, inflatable sex toys puts inanimate women at the service of confidence-deficient men. For men, playing with dolls, a sign of

sissy-hood at a young age, becomes masculinity-enhancing when the doll is too big to function as a baby and becomes a "babe" to be treated with the insensitivity expected of adult males in Western culture. A number of years ago, for example, columnist Bella English wrote against the grossness of some male Red Sox fans who, when the game lost their interest, passed around an inflatable woman. "The message of the doll-fondling is that the violation of women is OK, a sport even."[5] Clearly the "sex appeal of the inorganic" is here an apprenticeship in treating persons like things.

But let us look again at a real doll who, for many, perniciously keeps the dream of idealized and inert femininity alive in the United States. Barbie, the doll so many people love to hate, was the brainchild of Ruth and Elliot Handler, inspired by a German doll made of a cartoon prostitute, Lilli. Like Miss America, the beauty queen first associated with prostitution rings in Atlantic City, the working girl soon became the American ideal of femininity: beautiful, independent but deferential, pizza-eating and movie-going, totally involved in the rhythms of the dating scene, compliant but ambitious, not saddled with either parents or children. Or nipples. The body of the foot-high, pink plastic fashion model, curvaceous yet pruned of its erogenous zones, became for little girls both role model and toy. For the first time, a doll was made not as a baby but as a woman; not as someone to cuddle and shape but as someone to emulate. Barbie (named after Ruth and Elliot's daughter) possessed the secrets of adult femininity seemingly without any of the awkwardness, messiness, or embarrassment experienced by her human owners. The flavor of her past as a sex toy for men doesn't damage her appeal; on the contrary, it seems to guarantee her heterosexuality. In 1999, many flesh-and-blood celebrities gathered to celebrate her fortieth birthday. The *Boston Globe,* in an article about this event, couldn't resist an almost inevitable tendency to treat the doll as animate. Headlined "A $2 Billion Doll Celebrates Her 40th without a Wrinkle," the article ends with: "But, heck, she can't be too upset. After all, the girl's got a billion pairs of shoes."[6]

Over the years, Barbie and her *entourage* have undergone many transformations. The Talking Barbie that first worked with a button and a tape has become an interactive computer. The arched feet capable of wearing only special Barbie high heels were briefly, during the Birkenstock era, jointed so that they could stand flat—until the Mattel Corporation found that little girls missed those improbable feet. According to M. G. Lord, it is those prong feet that help maintain the link between Barbie and fertility god-desses: with them, she digs into the earth.[7] Then there is the whole vexed question of Barbie and ethnicity, analyzed brilliantly by Ann Ducille in her article "Dyes and Dolls: Multicultural Barbie and the Merchandizing of Difference."[8] It should not be forgotten that the experiments of Kenneth and Mamie Clark that underlie the landmark desegregation ruling in *Brown v. Board of Education* (1954) involved black and white dolls.

Many writings by African American women include a scene of sadism, curiosity, or violence against dolls who represent "everybody's dream of what was right with the world": white, blue-eyed girls.[9] Texts from early in the century are about Shirley Temple dolls, but later texts concern Barbie. In ei-ther case, the little black girls in the stories must learn to cherish in their dolls a white, even Aryan, ideal of femininity. "Good" hair and "good" noses are the unsubtle ways the white ideal has already impinged on their lives, but the dolls prepare them for loving white people themselves. "Frieda brought her four graham crackers on a saucer and some milk in a blue-and-white Shirley Temple cup. . . . What I felt at that time was unsullied hatred. But before that I had felt a stranger, more frightening thing than hatred for all the Shirley Temples of the world," writes Toni Morrison in her novel *The Bluest Eye*.

> It had begun with Christmas and the gift of dolls. The big, the special, the loving gift was always a big, blue-eyed Baby Doll. From the clucking sounds of adults I knew that the doll represented my fondest wish. I was bemused by the thing itself, and the way it looked. What was I supposed to do with it? Pretend I was its mother? . . . When I took it to bed, its hard unyielding limbs resisted my flesh—the tapered fingertips on those dimpled hands scratched. If, in my sleep, I turned, the bone-cold head collided with my own. It was a most uncomfortable, patently aggressive sleeping companion. . . . I had only one desire: to dismember it. To see of what it was made, to discover the dear-ness, to find the beauty, the desirability that had escaped me, but apparently only me. Adults, older girls, shops, magazines, newspapers, window signs—all the world had agreed that a blue-eyed, yellow-haired, pink-skinned doll was what every girl child treasured.[10]

A similar story is told in the first volume of Maya Angelou's autobiogra-phy: "My gift from Mother was a tea set—a teapot, four cups and saucers and tiny spoons—and a doll with blue eyes and rosy cheeks and yellow hair painted on her head. . . . Bailey and I tore the stuffing out of the doll the day after Christmas, but he warned me that I had to keep the tea set in good condition because any day or night she might come riding up."[11] But the ideology of desirable white femininity the doll both represents and conveys has already infected the young Maya's real-life image of herself: "Wouldn't they be surprised when one day I woke out of my black ugly dream, and my real hair, which was long and blond, would take the place of the kinky mass that Momma wouldn't let me straighten? My light-blue eyes were going to hypnotize them."[12]

Hence the imperative to create "Black Barbie," which Ann Ducille writes of so powerfully. She analyzes the commercial failure of "colored Francie" in 1967 and the ninety or so Barbie dye jobs that currently mark the world's diversity, and the fashion reasons for producing "black" dolls that only *seem* to have higher buttocks or fuller hips but are actually close enough to the original "icon of true white womanhood and femininity" to be able to exchange clothes with all the others. After documenting the ups and downs of black Barbie and the ideological effects of an ideal of femininity, Ann Ducille raises a troubling issue: "I am not so sure that most of us would want to buy a doll that 'looked like us.' . . . Cultural critics like me can throw theoretical stones at her all we want, but part of Barbie's infinite appeal is her very perfection."[13] Barbie didn't invent the ideal of femininity that dominates her society, but she incarnates it. The damaging messages she conveys to women do not come from the pink plastic creature alone; they would have no effect if those messages weren't also coming from elsewhere. Something stronger than a doll keeps women worrying about their defects, which, until they are overcome, prevent them from blaming anything outside themselves.

Chapter Twelve

Animation

The ending of Ann Ducille's article on multicultural Barbie dolls goes as follows: "Is Barbie bad? Barbie is just a piece of plastic, but what she says about the economic base of our society—what she suggests about gender and race in our world—ain't good."[1]

After ten closely argued pages in which the doll is as silent as a thing, Barbie finally speaks. Although what something "says" about society is often figurative, the feminine pronoun ("she says") and the colloquial "ain't" suggest that we hear the literal speaking voice of the doll. And the miracle of her animation allows her to pronounce upon gender, race, and the economic base of our society. It is *because* she is normally silent that her words have so much authority.

Why *is* it that speaking things are so ubiquitous today, from dreaming dentures to heroic Maalox bottles? It is almost as if the "fetishism of the commodity" against which Marx inveighs were not a false transfer of life from the producers to the products but the secret of commercial success. How else can one make denture adhesives or antacid remedies appealing?

Animation, indeed, was at the root of the Disney empire, and Japanese anime films are all the rage. The difference between movies and animation was once the difference between painting and photography—except that animators discovered their freedom from natural law more quickly than painters did. Where once the animated cel was a work of human making, computers now do the work of the human hand. The animated film is still "made" rather than "found," but so is the photograph likely to be. Indeed, it always already was: Nadar himself speaks of posing dummies in his scenes because human beings found it difficult not to move during the long photographic sessions.[2]

Which was why, in the 1980s, "vintage" animation art brought such high prices. Even production art from the 1988 movie *Who Framed Roger Rabbit?* was sold at Sotheby's, and, when that sale showed that collectors wouldn't balk at modern animation, cels from Disney's *The Little Mermaid* were auctioned off. But when 250 items from the film *Beauty and the Beast* were put up for auction, purists questioned their status as "originals." That film, the only full-length animated feature to be nominated for the Best Picture Oscar, was the first to make extensive use of computer animation: the backgrounds were indeed watercolors painted by humans, but the animated characters in the film were not. To make cels for the sale, artists had to copy the colors and forms of the animation actually used in the film. These "originals" were thus produced after the fact, the hand imitating the computer.[3]

Barely six months later, the *New York Times* reported another attempt by an animated character to challenge the boundary between "made" and "found." Glen Keane, chief animator for Disney, emboldened by the success of *Aladdin,* had told *Premiere* magazine that he would "love to see an animated character nominated for Best Actor."[4] This statement caused Peter Watson, the author of the *New York Times* article, to protest in defense of the honor of human beings: "Aladdin is not an actor," which became the title of his piece. Watson, it seemed, saw this idea as another encroachment of popular culture into the domain of "serious" art, "as if the iconography of cartoons is on a par with higher art forms—Pinocchio a match for Pontormo. . . . [T]his crowd of pushy puppeteers will soon be comparing Disneyland to Rome."[5] The boundary crossing that outraged Watson was not the one between life and death but rather the one between "high" and "low" art. Conflating "a TV advertisement featuring talking phones" with "a Shakespeare play or a Whitman poem" annuls the very meaning of taste, he wrote. Shakespeare and Whitman may be full of prosopopeia, but talking phones (which multiply the figure of voice) are not canonical, and the canon still differentiates the "real thing" from trash. While animation is an age-old rhetorical trick, animated characters are not real actors. It would be interesting to know which side Watson would put Oscars on.

Computer animation brought the toys in the nursery to life in Disney-Pixar's *Toy Story.* This is the perfect combination of the fantasy of childhood animism with the animation done by machines. A primitive belief is surmounted, but then the human hand is surmounted, too. It is as though everything humans create could be tainted with animism, as if animation by human hands participates in a quaint world of old-fashioned magic, dispelled only by the intervention of nonhuman creators. The "virtual reality" of toys among themselves (Barbie, one should note, was in the original scenario, but Mattel wanted to leave the fantasies of consumers free, and found that the film's depiction of her voice and actions was too definite; they wouldn't give permission to use her image) is the basis of a story drawn by computers: something comes to life on one side, and becomes inanimate on the other. Representations from fantasizing humans are no longer left in the hands of humans.

This combination of ancient magic with modern science often pervades the fantasies of scientific invention, especially when the inventor himself fosters his showmanship. In Villiers de l'Isle-Adam's novel about Ewald and Edison, for example, Villiers takes "the wizard of Menlo Park" further in the direction Edison was already going in. The inventor of the phonograph regrets not having been there to record: "'*Il n'est pas bon que l'homme soit seul!*'—puis *l'Eritis sicut dii! Le Croissez et multipliez!* . . . enfin le sombre quolibet d'Elohim: *Voici Adam devenu comme l'un de nous;*—etc.!" ("'*It's not good that man should be alone!*—*Ye shall be as gods! Be fruitful and multiply!* . . . finally the dark saying of Elohim: *See Adam has become like one of us;*—etc.!")[6] And, instead of calling the phonograph a mere toy, and making jokes at his expense, "J'eusse blamé, par exemple, le Phonographe de son impuissance à reproduire, en tant que *bruits,* le bruit . . . de la Chute de l'Empire romain . . . les bruits qui courent . . . les silences *éloquents* . . . et, en fait de *voix,* de ce qu'il ne peut clicher ni la voix de la conscience." ("I would have reproached the Phonograph, for example, its inability to reproduce, as sound, the sound of the Fall of the Roman Empire, . . . rumors, . . . eloquent silences, . . . and speaking of voices, its inability to capture the voice of conscience.")[7] While his critics have engaged in wordplay at his expense, Edison discovers a much more serious problem for the phonograph: the difficulty, through language, of telling the difference between sound-images used literally and sound-images used figuratively, to name everyday things having nothing to do with sound. In other words, it is impossible to record all the sounds in the world because language makes empiricism impossible. The sounds that matter most to mankind may not be sounds at all.

In fact, in Villiers's novel, Edison spends most of his time questioning what we think we know about persons and things. When Ewald expresses doubts that Edison's android will successfully replace his disappointing girlfriend, Edison replies by examining the question.

"But such a creature would never be more than an insensible doll, with no intelligence!"

"My Lord," Edison replied gravely, "I swear to you. Take care that when you juxtapose the copy with the model and listen to both of them, you don't mistake the living creature for the doll."

"Let's leave it at that, he [Ewald] said. "The conception is overwhelming. The piecework will always betray the machine. . . . You can reproduce the identity of a woman? You, of woman born?"

"A thousand times more identical to herself than she herself! Yes, indeed. Since not a day goes by without modifying some of the lines of a human body and since biological science proves to us that the body entirely renews its atoms approximately every seven years. Can a body really be said to exist? Can it ever resemble itself? Do you, I, that woman, have this evening the body we had at 1:20 this afternoon! Resemble oneself! What kind of a prehistoric Troglodite prejudice is that?" . . .

"One loves only an animate creature, someone with a soul," Lord Ewald said.

"So?"

"The soul is the unknown. Will you animate your Hadaly?"

"We animate also a projectile with the speed of X. Now X is an unknown too."

"Will she know who she is, I mean what she is?"

"Do we ourselves really know who we are? And what we are? Would you demand more of the copy than God thought himself obligated to grant to the model?" . . .

"However, Mr. Wizard, if one could never improvise, simply and naturally!" [said Lord Ewald.]

"Improvise!" Edison cried. "Do you believe that one ever improvises anything? Don't you know that you just recite? . . . [A]ren't all worldly conversations like the complimentary close of a letter?" (73)

The real Edison did attempt to market a "talking" doll equipped with a tiny phonograph, but *after* Villiers's novel was published in 1886. Villiers is supposed to have composed the bulk of his novel in the mid-1870s, and he anticipates many later technological developments: cinema, computer modeling (here called "photosculpture"), fax machines, and so on. But Villiers must have revised his novel after the big Edison show in Paris at the international Electrical Exhibition in 1881 (there was also a World's Fair in Paris ten years later, where the historical Edison met Gustave Eiffel). Edison, who began as a telegraph operator, was famous for taking credit for other people's (or collective) inventions; he both fostered and debunked the myth of the solitary genius; he really did build the first "industrial research park," in Menlo Park, New Jersey; and he often researched very industrial subjects, like separating ores, storage batteries, and giant rollers. He also developed strategies for publicizing his inventions that won him the nickname "the wizard of Menlo Park." When he pulled a switch, said "Let there be light!" and illuminated his Menlo Park compound, one would never have guessed what a tight race to the patent office had precipitated his work on the light bulb. Edison prepared a large shipment of talking dolls for Christmas in 1889, but withdrew them from the market because of continuing problems with the small phonograph. In any case, the fictional Edison is motivated partly by chivalry toward his friend Edward Anderson's wife, who was abandoned for an actress, which means all that he says in the novel about artifice has a double edge. He has been waiting for someone to come along with convincing reasons to give the doll final form, and Lord Ewald's desire to possess Alicia Clary's form but not her content fills the bill perfectly.

Much of the novel is taken up with explanations of how Hadaly is made, and how she will become Alicia Clary's replacement. Inside her chest are two gold cylinders, which make her appear to breathe, sigh, move like a well-brought-up young woman, and speak thoughts composed by the greatest writers of the century. Edison claims that anything can mean anything, and everyone plays a part. The difference will be that, instead of being in discord with Ewald, the new Alicia will echo him perfectly. During an eclipse, Ewald is suddenly so enchanted with Alicia that he cries out to stop the experiment. It is at this point that his beloved says, "Don't you recognize me? I am Hadaly."

The artificial woman in Villiers's novel is always called "l'Andréid"—the Android. And the "False Maria" in Fritz Lang's *Metropolis*—loosely based on Villiers's Eve—really does look like a machine. But the people actually working in the field of "artificial life" look back not to an android but to re-animated body parts—which they call "wetware"—in *Frankenstein* for their origin. It is Mary Shelley's novel—started in 1816, the same year as "The Sand-Man," from which Villiers takes several epigraphs—that seems to begin the tradition of "science horror." "We are on the verge of duplicating Dr. Frankenstein's feat and, therefore, of duplicating the consequences that lead to his ultimate ruin," says Christopher Langton in his "Editor's Introduction" to an important collective volume on artificial life.[8] Before we tackle the topic of artificial life, then, it is perhaps helpful to look at Mary Shelley's novel.

The novel goes to great lengths to establish itself as an epistolary novel, to establish paired relationships as its mode: Walton and his sister, Frankenstein and Walton, creator and creature. Only the first is an actual epistolary relation, though—a real correspondence, which is probably because its participants *don't* correspond. The other relations, while often long and intense *narrative* relations, are spoken, not written. "I had determined, once," says the recently rescued Frankenstein to Walton; "that the memory of these evils would die with me; but you have won me to alter my determination. You seek for knowledge and wisdom, as I once did; and I ardently hope that the gratification of your wishes may not be a serpent to sting you, as mine has been. I do not know that the relation of my misfortunes will be useful to you, yet, if you are inclined, listen to my tale."[9] The long narrative that follows is thus meant for a specific listener; it is a cautionary tale based on a resemblance between the narrator and the hearer. Within the tale is embedded another tale between doubles: the tale told to his maker by the creature created by Frankenstein. But this tale is told in order to persuade Frankenstein to make a female monster with whom his male monster can disappear. Both tales, in other words, count on their rhetorical strength for their didactic effect. In Frankenstein's case, he knows he has whetted Walton's appetite for the secret of life, and purposely frustrates it:

I see by your eagerness, and the wonder and hope which your eyes express, my friend, that you expect to be informed of the secret with which I am acquainted; that cannot be: listen patiently until the end of my story, and you will easily perceive why I am reserved upon that subject. I will not lead you on, unguarded and ardent as I then was, to your destruction and infallible misery. Learn from me, if not by my precepts, at least by my example, how dangerous is the acquirement of knowledge. (31)

The monster, on the other hand, knows from experience that he can persuade only if he is *not* seen: "'Thus I relieve thee, my creator,' he said, and placed his hated hands before my eyes, which I flung from me with violence; 'thus I take from thee a sight which you abhor. Still thou canst listen to me, and grant me thy compassion. . . . Hear my tale. . . . On you it rests, whether I quit for ever the neighborhood of man, and lead a harmless life, or become the scourge of your fellow-creatures, and the author of your own speedy ruin'" (67).

The exchange of burning looks between Walton and Frankenstein is the recognition or projection of their similarity; the blindness the creature tries to bring about makes his tale more like writing than like speech. The narrative relation between Walton and Frankenstein is like that of a mirror; the relation between creator and creature refuses to mirror—or perhaps mirrors too well. The monster narrates his solitude, his abandonment by his creator and his abuse by all other human beings who see him. He requests only that Frankenstein make him a female of his species whom he might love and who might love him, to disappear with forever. Frankenstein has mixed feelings: "His words had a strange effect upon me. I compassionated him, and sometimes felt a wish to console him; but when I looked upon him, when I saw the filthy mass that moved and talked, my heart sickened, and my feelings were altered to those of horror and hatred" (99). Frankenstein nevertheless agrees to his creature's request, saying, "I consent to your demand, on your solemn oath to quit Europe for ever, and every other place in the neighborhood of man" (100). But Frankenstein goes back on his promise and destroys the half-completed female monster, and the male monster, enraged, wreaks havoc on everything Frankenstein holds dear.

Describing his thoughts as he proceeded toward his first creation, Frankenstein outlines the appeal of becoming God:

No one can conceive the variety of feelings which bore me onwards like a hurricane, in the first enthusiasm of success. Life and death appeared to me ideal bounds, which I should first break through, and pour a torrent of light into our dark world. A new species would bless me as its creator and source;

many happy and excellent natures world owe their being to me. No father
could claim the gratitude of his child so completely as I should deserve their's.
Pursuing these reflections, I thought, that if I could bestow animation on lifeless matter, I might in process of time (although I now found it impossible)
renew life where death had apparently devoted the body to corruption. . . .
Who shall conceive the horrors of my secret toil, as I dabbled among the un-
hallowed damps of the grave, or tortured the living animal to animate the
lifeless clay? (32)

The prospect of equaling the Creator (the novel is subtitled *The Modern
Prometheus,* and opens with an epigraph from *Paradise Lost:* "Did I request
thee, Maker, from my clay / To mould me man? Did I solicit thee / From
darkness to promote me?—") is both intoxicating and somehow trans-
gressive. All the while Frankenstein locks himself in his "workshop of filthy
creation," he knows he is violating a taboo. He calls Walton's desire to know
the secrets of life and death "madness,"[10] but there is something transcendental about the evils he brings on his head. And yet, there is nothing
magic about his discovery; nothing beyond the bounds of science. Science
itself therefore becomes uncanny, and it is the horror with which Frankenstein greets his creature that indicates where science sins. It is the knowledge
belonging to flawed beings that seeks to rival God's; if Frankenstein had realized how needy and not merely grateful his creature was, he could not
have abandoned him. What he wanted from the creature was his own ag-
grandizement; what he saw in that watery eye was an "other" who made demands on *him.* His object was suddenly a subject, able to make his maker
into an object.

Persons

Chapter Thirteen

Face Value

Here is Roland Barthes, seeing in Garbo's face the epitome and fascination of early cinema:

> It is indeed an admirable face-object. In *Queen Christina* . . . the make-up has the snowy thickness of a mask. . . . Amid all this snow at once fragile and compact, the eyes alone, black like strange soft flesh, but not in the least expressive, are two faintly tremulous wounds. In spite of its extreme beauty, this face [is] not drawn but sculpted. . . .
>
> . . . Garbo offered to one's gaze a sort of Platonic Idea of the human creature. . . . The name given to her, *the Divine*, probably aimed to convey less a superlative state of beauty than the essence of her corporeal person, descended from a heaven where all things are formed and perfected in the clearest light. . .
>
> Garbo's face represents this fragile moment when the cinema is about to draw an existential from an essential beauty, when the archetype leans towards the fascination of mortal faces, when the clarity of the flesh as essence yields its place to a lyricism of woman.[1]

The vestigial description of the statue shows up here in the appeal of cinema. The Mattel company copyrighted Barbie's face as a piece of sculpture.[2]
The focus on the face inspires plastic surgery, whence the expression "face
lift." One practitioner says he has the "hands of a sculptor and the skill of a
surgeon." The human face is not only a *model* for sculpture; it may also be
the *material*.

Without referring to the role of "plastic" in the movie *The Graduate,* the
plastic arts have indeed often functioned as models for plastic surgery. The
performance artist Orlan has made the surgery itself into a performance art.
With only a local anesthetic, leaving her free to perform, she has undergone
many cosmetic surgeries on stage to transform her face into the best of great
European artworks. She is said to have the forehead of the Mona Lisa, the
eyes of a School of Fontainebleau Diana, the nose of Gerome's Psyche, the
lips of Boucher's Europa, and the chin of Botticelli's Venus. In effect, Orlan
is performing her own surgical transformation into a work of art. On a Web
site that includes information about her, one of the sections is called "Re-
facing Orlan," which calls up not only a change of face but a change of *facing*: the change in surfacing accomplished by New England Brickmasters or
Bath Refitters, which may or may not indicate repairs to what is under-
neath. The site on which I found her description was *supervert.org,* a Web
site catering to the perversions (is this, then, a perversion?); it begins, "Is she
the art world's Bride of Frankenstein?" The writer refers to the extensive cin-
ematic tradition that grew out of Mary Shelley's novel. Indeed, early film's
fascination with *Frankenstein,* along with the German films *The Golem* and
Homunculus, is a fascination with its own devices: how do still things come
alive? The being made out of pieces of corpses or statues may come alive
only to bring about the maker's ruin. So, too, might there be something
ghostly about cinema. The early directors were playing with fire.

As filmmakers have always known, people are fascinated by the human
face. Their early and unceasing use of the close-up gives evidence of this fascination. It is a sign of someone's uniqueness—which can be a pathway to
their soul or a device to identify suspects—better than fingerprints, DNA,
or ID cards. Professor Alexander Pentland, working with a team at the MIT
Media Lab, developed a computer that recognizes faces, while working on
the ways in which "perceptual intelligence" must supplement reason in artificial intelligence research. Although most often used for fraud detection,
the computer's ability to recognize faces joins with the "face books" interro-

gated obsessively by people who are part of, or interested in joining, the organization the face books represent. The face thus seems to offer a clue to a person's identity or innermost being. A British celebrity and fashion magazine is called, simply, *The Face.* What is seen and known about a person is the face—the person's ambassador to the realm of visibility.

In a book about the evolution of the human face (after describing how the human ancestor, living in trees, acquired the sight provided by having both eyes facing front, and after describing a baby's eyes as being disproportionately large to inspire a caring response), Terry Landau writes: "We experience identity as a diffuse feeling which is interwoven with all other feelings and which is hard, if not impossible, to describe—that is, until we look in the mirror. And then identity is suddenly personified. It is the face you see reflected. It is you."[3] It is symptomatic that in this passage our identity lies in what is *seen,* not in seeing. The transition from "we" to "you" travels along the same trajectory, but seemingly in the opposite direction. While "we" starts out as a generalization about everyone, "you" is addressed at the end as finding identity in the mirror. Identity is an object, then, without which there would be no subject.

I began this research intrigued by my childhood inability to eat anything with a face on it. The image in my mind was of a face that *did not respond* to a painful stimulus; a face that was inanimate or stony in the present but had an expression of animation sculpted or painted onto it. It was as though I were responding to something that *had been alive* but was now unaware of what was happening; it was alive enough to die, but not alive enough to respond. It might die with an expression of cheery animation, as if the death that overcame it were not related to the animation it expressed. What was spooky about it was that it could still look at me: its aliveness lay neither in its death nor in its smiling face, but in its awareness of *my* face. Something that only *seemed* to look was no different from something that looked, because the taboo in question was *being looked at.* In other words, it was something in *me* and not in the thing.

The words in other languages that mean "face" add to the repertoire of uncanny violence: in French, *visage* and *figure* (both meaning "face") lead to the French verb *dévisager* (to stare) and the English "to disfigure" (to maim). In slightly more recherché English, the term "countenance" leads to the verbs "to countenance" or "discountenance." And in Asian cultures, to "save face" and to "lose face" indicate that "face" can refer to one's appearance *to others,* and not necessarily literally or only to oneself.[4] And finally, "to face" means not only to turn one's countenance toward but also to confront, acknowledge, internalize without dodging. The face can thus be a sign of status, put-togetherness, visibility, tolerance, disconcertedness, or bravery. The variations in the verbs are signs of variations in what a face *is.*

In an influential article by Paul de Man, "Autobiography as Defacement," a reading of Wordsworth's "Essays on Epitaphs" leads a thought about autobiography toward the paradox that the asymptotic relation between a story and a proper name makes the text continue to speak well after the death of the author. The text therefore functions like a prosopopeia, a speaking thing, and the thing that ensures this illusion of speech—writing—is the very thing that deals the fatal blow to the author's biological life. The article concludes: "Death is a displaced name for a linguistic predicament, and the restoration of mortality by autobiography (the prosopopeia of the voice and the name) deprives and disfigures to the precise extent that it restores. Autobiography veils a defacement of the mind of which it is itself the cause."[5] In other words, autobiography is the translation of life into story, and the thing that ensures its lifelikeness—language—is what eliminates the need for biological life.

De Man's etymology of prosopopeia may give us a clue to the nature of this incompatibility between "life" and autobiography: "Voice assumes mouth, eye, and finally face, a chain that is manifest in the etymology of the trope's name, *prosopon poien,* to confer a mask or a face (*prosopon*). Prosopopeia is the trope of autobiography, by which one's name . . . is made as intelligible and memorable as a face. . . . Our topic deals with the giving and taking away of faces, with face and deface, *figure,* figuration and disfiguration."[6]

A mask or a face. De Man's etymology treats these two things as the same. And my childhood prosoponophobia, too, made no distinction between a painted and a living face. Human reactions to patterns featuring two eyes, a nose, and a mouth (or even just two eyes) indicate that what is construed as a look doesn't have to be looking.[7] But even if the eyes blur the distinction, in many cases there *is* a difference between a mask and a face. In fact, that difference is the basis of the story Cecile Pineda tells in her novel *Face.*

Helio Cara, horribly disfigured in a fall into a rocky abyss but not eligible for reconstructive surgery paid for by his insurance because his injury doesn't conflict with his working ("You don't *use* your face, do you?" says the clerk at the rehabilitation window), is nevertheless fired because of his repulsiveness, loses his girlfriend ("I can't make love to a monster," she cries, just before he beats her), and has his shack torched. Despite his inability to pay, he is taken on by a famous plastic surgeon whose office is filled with copies of the journal *Face,* but once his lodgings are burned he has nowhere to live in the city between visits to the surgeon. He travels to the hinterland to his dead mother's house, where, rejected by everyone and working only at night, he performs cosmetic surgery on himself.

At first glance, this would seem like an exemplary story to illustrate "autobiography as de-facement": a character painstakingly reconstructs his own face after a disfigurement just as an autobiographer reconstructs, in writing, the events of his life from the perspective of its end. But the first discordant note between the novel and the essay is the unacceptability of a mask as a substitute for the face:

> "When they discharged you, you were issued a mask?"
> "Yes."
> "A *facial* mask?"
> "Yes. Why?"
> "What happened to it?"
> "I don't have it."
> "You can't be seen here without the mask."
> "Why not?"
> The Oriental becomes impatient. "Everyone who joins the program has to have a mask."
> "It didn't let me breathe."[8]

The mask is incompatible with life, inanimate. Earlier Helio had found it beside him, "shapeless, rust-brown, like a balloon, punctured and inert" (45–46). It is designed for the one looking at him, not for the wearer. As the "Oriental" puts it, "'It's designed to give people seeing it immediate recognition that the wearer is . . .' (he lowers his voice) *'facially impaired'*" (70). The mask thus functions as a sign to the viewer.

More men than ever are availing themselves of plastic surgery, but women still think of it as a way to correct their defects. Its role is similar to an ideal of beauty or a statue: it is that against which the living person measures his or her appearance. Something inanimate always approximates an ideal better than something living. An ideal is not an individual.

But for the wearer in the story, the only thing that matters is whether the mask allows him to breathe, to live. In place of the mask, Helio puts a handkerchief over his disfigurement, hanging from under his hat. Later, smoked out of his home and shot at, Helio decides to make a face for himself. "Not the one he was born with, surely, or one like some hero or movie star. At best, one with just the minimum: a recognizable nose, a mouth with identifiable teeth, eyes whose expression would at the least be reassuring, a kind of utility face" (167). His goal is to "be just like everyone else" (158). As his boss reluctantly fires him from his job at a barber shop, he says of the handkerchief over his scars, "Even with this . . . I'm still the same. . . . Or perhaps not the same" (62).

Designed to be seen, it does not matter whether a mask is animate or inanimate. Audre Lorde heard from a zealous enthusiast of breast prostheses after her mastectomy: "Her message was, you are just as good as you were before because you can look exactly the same. Lambswool now, then a good prosthesis as soon as possible, and nobody'll ever know the difference. But what she said was, '*You'll* never know the difference,' and she lost me right there, because I knew sure as hell *I'd* know the difference."[9] What Helio learns, however, is that the face *does* belong to the viewer: it is because no one can stand his disfigurement that Helio reconstructs a face. The violence against him is caused by his loss: "All because I didn't have a face" (180). "What is there to say about a man without a face?" (165). Without a face, Helio can neither be a topic nor an addressee of language. It is in order to take a place in the human world of discourse that he makes himself a "utility face." Without a face, he is alive, but with a face—animate or inanimate, whether or not it resembles the one he was born with—he can be looked at, addressed. The face speaks about the inside to the outside: what people could not tolerate was having the inside *show* on the outside.

As he turns to leave at the end, Helio examines his new face in a mirror for the first time. "It is unremarkable—like anyone else's. But no. Not like anyone. It is his, his alone. He has built it, alone, sewn it stitch by stitch, with the very thin needle and the thread of gossamer. It has not been given casually by birth, but made by him, by the wearer of it" (192).

The face is the work of art that Helio has made to cover his lack. Again, the work of art "shapes the void" or has "purposiveness without purpose." The work of art suggests that there is a hole somewhere. The inside that showed was not the same inside that a face allows one to presume. Instead of seeking to copy the face he has lost (already deemed impossible when Dr. Godoy rejected his one photograph), he simply fashions a utility face that will serve as his entry pass to the world. While he feels the cool breezes on his new, alive face, for others it might as well be inert: living or not, it will function as a mask, allowing the world to assume the socially acceptable attitudes a face facilitates. The living body becomes as much *material* as the inanimate: social acceptability sculpts the face that will not be seen. As much as we wear our identities on our faces, the goal is to go *un*seen, not to be noticed.

Thus, the first plastic surgeries were designed not only to repair disfigurements but also to reduce "ethnic" characteristics. The most common "aesthetic" surgery, rhinoplasty, reduces the size of a prominent nose, often to create the thinner, turned-up nose said to be more in keeping with white standards. Michael Jackson's numerous reshapings of his face, whatever else they may have accomplished, certainly produced a thinner nose. And Marlo Thomas's nose seems smaller every time she appears in public. Since skin color is less easy to work on surgically than bone, cosmetic surgery has usually confined itself to features. An Asian face, for example, usually undergoes blepharoplasty (eyelid surgery that can make the eye look rounder) if its wearer wants to be a newscaster or an actor. All these changes make diverse faces more alike, so that "morphing" one face into another can be done primarily by changing skin color and by varying a version of features already shaped to a white standard.

The dominant aesthetic of the world, like the force that dominates the global economy, is what appears as an ideal to white people: not whiteness itself, but an ideal that white people, too, are striving for, or differences seen as most naturalizable to white people. As a computer-imaging technician examines and whittles away at his nose, the writer of an article on cosmetic surgery published in the *New York Times Magazine* comments on "what even I . . . recognized to be some ideal—by Western Civilization's standards, at least—of a perfectly proportioned nose."[10]

This is especially true of youthfulness, the look aimed for as improvements in imaging techniques and surgical procedures have brought plastic surgery within the financial reach of more people. Botox injections eliminate the need for surgery altogether: they undo wrinkles by paralyzing facial tissue, but the effect lasts only about six months. After six months, when the paralysis wears off, the patient has to be injected anew. The injections temporarily make the living body into a statue, but unfortunately life, with all its imperfections, comes back. Reductions in size (liposuction, gastric bypass surgery, or breast reduction) are directly related to Western culture's prizing of thinness—another way in which an ideal torments and disciplines Western citizens (and sells products).

A text that transforms a life into writing—*Face* would seem the perfect example of "autobiography as de-facement." Except that it is not an autobiography. Could it have been?

Going back to Benveniste's dictum about pronouns, it reads, in part, "'Person' belongs only to *I/you* and is lacking in *he*."[11] The novel, then, treats Helio Cara as a thing. That is, the story of Helio's face is narrated entirely from the outside (unlike, for instance, Lucy Grealy's book about living with the disfigurements of cancer, *Autobiography of a Face*). Rather than being told by a person (I), it is told about a non-person (he). If it had been told in the first person, the reasons for telling it would have been shaped by the I/you context. That is, we would always have suspected that the "I" had rhetorical designs on us.[12] In the third person, the thing is *acted upon* but does not act (rhetorically, at least). This enables the narrative to avoid dealing with self-consciousness or self-pity. (The same problems arise when one tries to translate classroom jokes into writing. In the classroom, the teacher can function like a thing: her apparent cluelessness is what's funny. But it is impossible to narrate this in the first person—to say that one is clueless is not the same as *being* clueless.) The pathos and heroism of Helio's story depend on his saying nothing about them himself. A face confers addressability, but on condition that it be inanimate. The silence of a thing makes it have no awareness or irony to interfere with the addressee's animation. The human ideal of the person is therefore the thing.

The living face, though, signifies for Levinas the ethical claims of the human Other, who enounces prohibitions and toward whom I am supposed to respond. The face in front of me represents my responsibility for the Other. Because it is not covered or masked, Levinas sees it as humanity at its most destitute. "The face is exposed, menaced, as if inviting us to an act of violence. At the same time, the face is what forbids us to kill."[13] In Western civilization, in fact, the face is usually naked, not masked, in contrast to the rest of the body. Instead of representing inanimateness or disguise, a mask would represent protection or modesty, as conveyed in the following anecdote:

> A white Christian missionary is trying to make his native charges more modest. "Why are you so shameless about being naked?" he asks.
>
> "What is this?" asks an indigenous child, pointing to the missionary's forehead.

"My face," says the missionary.

"Here, this is all face," replies the child, gesturing toward the whole of his body.

The Western face does not function as a sexual thing but as the open, public greeting of the Other. It is exposed to the one who could do violence to it, but at the same time, emitting prohibitions, it invites speech and ethics. It acknowledges any violence done to *it* as its own.

This moves the face closer to religious discourse than to psychology. And indeed, both testaments of the Judeo-Christian Bible have things to say about the face. At first, God converses with Moses "face to face, as a man speaketh unto his friend" (Exodus 33:11). But when Moses wants to make God an object of knowledge, or insists on God's displays of divinity for His people, God replies.

And he said, Thou canst not see my face: for there shall no man see me, and live.

And the Lord said, Behold, there is a place by me, and thou shalt stand upon a rock:

And it shall come to pass, while my glory passeth by, that I will put thee in a clift of the rock, and will cover thee with my hand while I pass by:

And I will take away mine hand, and thou shalt see my back parts: but my face shall not be seen. (Exodus 33:20–23)

Moses comes down from the mountain carrying the first tables of testimony, his face beaming with light,[14] and the children of Israel are afraid to look at him, and he wears a veil over his face from that moment until his death on Mount Nebo.

In the New Testament, Paul tells the Corinthians: "For now we see through a glass, darkly; but then face to face" (I Corinthians 13:12). Face-to-face contact is human contact; a veil or a hand protects the human from seeing the divine; the only time a human can have face-to-face contact with God is when he takes him for a human being. Thus, humans aim at a divine sight that they cannot "know" at all. Divinity and human knowledge are incompatible. Something religious or non-objective about this forbidden knowledge, something about the taboo and imperative of this embrace, lingers in Levinas's ethical sense of the face.

Chapter Fourteen

Anthropomorphism in Lyric and Law

Anthropomorphism. n. Attribution of human motivation, characteristics, or behavior to inanimate objects, animals, or natural phenomena.

—*American Heritage Dictionary*

Through a singular ambiguity, through a kind of transposition or intellectual quid pro quo, you will feel yourself evaporating, and you will attribute to your . . . tobacco, the strange ability to *smoke you.*

—Baudelaire, *Artificial Paradises*

Recent discussions of the relations between law and literature have tended to focus on prose—novels, short stories, autobiographies, even plays—rather than on lyric poetry.[1] Literature has been seen as a locus of plots and situations that parallel legal cases or problems, either to shed light on complexities not always acknowledged by the ordinary practice of legal discourse, or to shed light on cultural crises and debates that historically underlie and inform literary texts. But in a sense, this focus on prose is surprising, since lyric poetry has at least historically been the more law-abiding or rule-bound of the genres. Indeed, the sonnet form has been compared to a prison (Wordsworth),[2] or at least to a bound woman (Keats),[3] and Baudelaire's portraits of lyric depression ("Spleen")[4] are often written as if from behind bars. What are the relations between the laws of genre and the laws of the state?[5] This chapter might be seen as asking the question through the juxtaposition, as it happens, between two sonnets and a prisoners' association.

More profoundly, though, lyric and law might be seen as two very different ways of instating what a "person" is. There appears to be the greatest possible discrepancy between a lyric "person"—emotive, subjective, individual—and a legal "person"—rational, rights bearing, institutional. In this chapter I wish to show, through the question of anthropomorphism, how these two "persons" can illuminate each other.

My argument develops out of the juxtaposition of two texts: Paul de Man's essay "Anthropomorphism and Trope in the Lyric,"[6] in which I try to understand why for de Man the question of anthropomorphism is at the heart of the lyric, and the text of a Supreme Court opinion from 1993, *Rowland v. California Men's Colony, Unit II Men's Advisory Council.*[7] This case has not become a household name like *Roe v. Wade* or *Brown v. Board of Education,* and probably with good reason. What is at stake in it appears trivial—at bottom, it is about an association of prisoners suing for the right to have free cigarette privileges restored. But the Supreme Court's task was not to decide whether the prisoners have the right to smoke (an increasingly contested right, as it happens, in the United States today). The case came before the Court to resolve the question of whether their council can be counted as a juridical "person" under the law. What is at stake, then, in both the legal and the lyric texts is the question: What is a person?

I

I will begin by discussing the article by Paul de Man, which is one of the most difficult, even outrageous, of his essays. Both hyperbolic and elliptical, it makes a number of very strong claims about literary history, lyric pedagogy, and the materiality of "historical modes of language power" (262). Toward the end of his text, de Man somewhat unexpectedly reveals that the essay originated in an invitation to speak on the nature of lyric. But it begins with some general remarks about the relation between epistemology and rhetoric (which can stand as a common contemporary way of framing the relations between law and literature). The transition between the question of the lyric and the question of epistemology and rhetoric is made through the Keatsian chiasmus, "Beauty is truth, truth beauty," which de Man quotes on his way to Nietzsche's short and "better known than understood" essay (239), "On Truth and Lie in an Extra-Moral Sense."[8]

"What is truth?" Nietzsche asks in that essay's most oft-quoted moment: "a mobile army of metaphors, metonymies, and anthropomorphisms." Thus it would seem that Nietzsche has answered, "Truth is trope, trope truth" or

"Epistemology is rhetoric, rhetoric epistemology." But de Man wants to show in what ways Nietzsche is *not* saying simply this. First, the list of tropes is, he says, "odd." While metaphor and metonymy are the names of tropes that designate a pure structure of relation (metaphor is a relation of similarity between two entities, while metonymy is a relation of contiguity), de Man claims that anthropomorphism, although structured similarly, is not a trope. It is not the name of a pure rhetorical structure but the name of a comparison, one of whose terms is treated as a given (as epistemologically resolved). To use an anthropomorphism is to treat as *known* the properties of the human. "'Anthropomorphism' is not just a trope but an identification on the level of substance. It takes one entity for another and thus implies the constitution of specific entities prior to their confusion, the taking of something for something else that can then be assumed to be given. Anthropomorphism freezes the infinite chain of tropological transformations and propositions into one single assertion or essence which, as such, excludes all others. It is no longer a proposition but a proper name" (241).

Why does he call this a proper name? Shouldn't the essence that is taken as given be a concept? If "man" is what is assumed as a given, why call it a proper name? (This question is particularly vexed when the theorist's proper name is "de Man"). The answer, I think, is that "man" as concept would imply the possibility of a proposition. "Man" would be subject to definition, and thus transformation or trope. But proper names are not subjects of definition: they are what they are. If "man" is taken as a given, then, it can only be because it is out of the loop of qualification. It is presupposed, not defined.

Yet the examples of proper names de Man gives are surprising: Narcissus and Daphne. Nietzsche's triumvirate of metaphor, metonymy, and anthropomorphism then functions like the plot of an Ovidian metamorphosis: from a mythological world in which man and nature appear to be in metaphorical and metonymic harmony, there occurs a crisis wherein, by a process of seamless transformation, a break nevertheless occurs in the system of correspondences, leaving a residue that escapes and remains: the proper name. De Man's discussion of Baudelaire's sonnets will in fact be haunted by Ovidian presences: Echo is lurking behind every mention of Narcissus, while one of the recurring cruxes is whether there is a human substance in a tree. It is perhaps not an accident that the figures that occupy the margins of de Man's discussion are female. If de Man's enduring question is whether linguistic structures and epistemological claims can be presumed to be compatible, the question of gender cannot be located exclusively either in language (where the gender of pronouns, and often of nouns, is inherent in each language) or in the world. By extension, the present discussion of the nature of "man" cannot fail to be haunted by the question of gender.

The term "anthropomorphism" in Nietzsche's list thus indicates that a *given* is being forced into what otherwise would function as a pure structure of relation. In addition, Nietzsche calls truth an *army* of tropes, thus introducing more explicitly the notion of power, force, or violence. This is not a notion that can fit into the oppositions between epistemology and rhetoric; rather, it disrupts the system. In the text of the Supreme Court decision that I will discuss in a moment, such a disruption is introduced when the opposition on which the case is based, the opposition between natural person and artificial entity, opens out onto the question of policy. There, too, it is a question of truth and power, of the separation of the constative (what does the law say?) from the performative (what does it do?).

The bulk of de Man's essay is devoted to a reading of two sonnets by Baudelaire: "Correspondances" and "Obsession," which are reproduced here.[9]

"CORRESPONDANCES"
La Nature est un temple où de vivants piliers
Laissent parfois sortir de confuses paroles;
L'homme y passe à travers des forêts de symboles
Qui l'observent avec des regards familiers.

Comme de longs échos qui de loin se confondent
Dans une ténébreuse et profonde unité,
Vaste comme la nuit et comme la clarté,
Les parfums, les couleurs et les sons se répondent.

Il est des parfums frais comme des chairs d'enfants,
Doux comme les hautbois, verts comme les prairies,
—Et d'autres, corrompus, riches et triomphants,

Ayant l'expansion des choses infinies,
Comme l'ambre, le musc, le benjoin et l'encens,
Qui chantent les transports de l'esprit et des sens.

*　*　*

"CORRESPONDENCES"

Nature is a temple, where the living pillars
Sometimes utter indistinguishable words;
Man passes through these forests of symbols
Which regard him with familiar looks.

Like long echoes that blend in the distance
Into a unity obscure and profound,
Vast as the night and as the light,
The perfumes, colors, and sounds correspond.

There are some perfumes fresh as a baby's skin,
Mellow as oboes, verdant as prairies,
—And others, corrupt, rich, and triumphant,

With all the expansiveness of infinite things,
Like ambergris, musk, benjamin, incense,
That sing the transports of spirit and sense.

"OBSESSION"

Grands bois, vous m'effrayez comme des cathédrales;
Vous hurlez comme l'orgue; et dans nos coeurs maudits,
Chambres d'éternel deuil où vibrent de vieux râles,
Répondent les échos de vos *De profundis*.

Je te hais, Océan! tes bonds et tes tumultes,
Mon esprit les retrouve en lui; ce rire amer
De l'homme vaincu, plein de sanglots et d'insultes,
Je l'entends dans le rire énorme de la mer.

Comme tu me plairais, ô nuit! sans ces étoiles
Dont la lumière parle un langage connu!
Car je cherche le vide, et le noir, et le nu!

Mais les ténèbres sont elles-mêmes des toiles
Où vivent, jaillissant de mon oeil par milliers,
Des êtres disparus aux regards familiers.

*   *   *

"OBSESSION"

You terrify me, forests, like cathedrals;
You roar like organs; and in our cursed hearts,

Chambers of mourning that quiver with our dying,
Your *De profundis* echoes in response.

How I hate you, Ocean! your tumultuous tide
Is flowing in my spirit; this bitter laughter
Of vanquished man, strangled with sobs and insults,
I hear it in the heaving laughter of the sea.

O night, how I would love you without stars,
Whose light can only speak the words I know!
For I seek the void, and the black, and the bare!

But the shadows are themselves a screen
That gathers from my eyes the ones I've lost,
A thousand living things with their familiar looks.

Both poems end up raising "man" as a question—"Correspondances"
looks upon "man" as if from a great distance, as if from the outside; "Obsession" says "I" but then identifies with "vanquished man," whose laugh is
echoed in the sea.

"Correspondances" is probably the most canonical of Baudelaire's poems
in that it has justified the largest number of general statements about
Baudelaire's place in literary history. The possibility of literary history ends
up, in some ways, being the real topic of de Man's essay. De Man will claim
that the use of this sonnet to anchor the history of the "symbolist movement" is based on a reading that ignores a crucial element in the poem, an
element that, if taken seriously, will not allow the edifice of literary history
to be built upon it.

"Correspondances" sets up a series of analogies between nature, man,
symbols, and metaphysical unity, and among manifestations of the different
physical senses, all through the word *comme* ("like"). A traditional reading
of the poem would say that the lateral analogies among the senses (perfumes
fresh as a baby's skin, mellow as oboes, green as prairies) are signs that there
exists an analogy between man and nature, and man and the spiritual realm.

De Man focuses on this analogy-making word, *comme*, and notes an
anomaly in the final instance. Whereas the first uses of *comme* in the poem
equate different things into likeness, the last one just introduces a list of examples—there are perfumes that are rich and corrupt, like musk, ambergris,
and frankincense. This is a tautology—there are perfumes like . . . perfumes.
De Man calls this a stutter. He writes, "Comme then means as much as

'such as, for example'" (249). "Ce Comme n'est pas un comme comme les autres," writes de Man in a sudden access of French (249). His sentence performs the stutter he attributes to the enumeration of the perfumes. Listing examples would seem to be quite different from proposing analogies. If the burden of the analogies in "Correspondances" is to convince us that the metaphorical similarities among the senses point to a higher spiritual unity, then sheer enumeration would disrupt that claim.

There is another, more debatable, suggestion in de Man's reading that attempts to disrupt the anthropomorphism of the forest of symbols. De Man suggests that the trees in the first stanza are a mere metaphor for a city crowd. If the living pillars with their familiar glances are metaphorically a city crowd, then the anthropomorphism of nature is lost. Man is surrounded by tree-like men, not man-like trees. It is not "man" whose attributes are taken on by all of nature, but merely a crowd of men being compared to trees and pillars. De Man notes that everyone resists this reading— as do I—but the intensity with which it is rejected does make visible the seduction of the system that puts nature, God, and man into a perfect unity through the symbol, which is what has made the poem so important for literary history. Similarly, if the last *comme* is sheer enumeration rather than similarity, the transports in the last line of the poem would not get us into a transcendent realm but would be like getting stuck on the French transportation system (which, as de Man points out, uses the word *correspondance* for changes of subway or bus station within the system). All these tropes would not carry us away into the spiritual realm but would be an infinite series of substitutions. The echoes would remain echoes and not merge into a profound unity.

If "Correspondances" is said to place man in the center of a universe that reflects him in harmony with all of nature, the poem "Obsession" places all of nature and the universe inside the psychology of man. Even the senses are projections. "Obsession" is the reading of "Correspondances" as hallucination. While "Correspondances" is entirely declarative, "Obsession" is almost entirely vocative. (Interestingly, de Man does not comment on another anomaly in the meaning of the word *comme*—the *comme* in "Obsession" that means "how!"—which is surprising, since it enacts precisely what he calls "the tropological transformation of analogy into apostrophe" [261]). Nature is addressed as a structure haunted by the subject's obsessions. Everywhere he looks, his own thoughts look back. For psychoanalytically inclined readers, and indeed for de Man himself in an earlier essay, "Obsession" demystifies "Correspondances."[10] There is no profound unity in the world, but only, as Lacan would say, paranoid knowledge.[11] But de Man sees the psychological gloss as another mystification, another anthropomorphism— the very anthropomorphic mystification that it is the duty of lyric, and of lyric pedagogy, to promote. "The lyric is not a genre, but one name among several to designate the defensive motion of understanding" (261). De Man concludes provocatively: "The resulting couple or pair of texts indeed becomes a model for the uneasy combination of funereal monumentality with paranoid fear that characterizes the hermeneutics and the pedagogy of lyric poetry" (259). What comes to be at stake, then, is lyric poetry itself as a poetry of the subject. By juxtaposing lyric and law in this chapter, I am implicitly asking whether there is a relation between the "first person" (the grammatical "I") and the "constitutional person" (the subject of rights).

"Only a subject can understand a meaning," claims Lacan; "conversely, every phenomenon of meaning implies a subject."[12] What de Man seems to be arguing for here is a residue of language or rhetoric that exists neither inside nor outside the "phenomenon of meaning." Does lyric poetry try to give a psychological gloss to disruptions that are purely grammatical? Are the periodizations in literary history, like Parnassian and Romantic, merely names for rhetorical structures that are not historical? For de Man, "Obsession" loses the radical disruption of "Correspondances" by making enumeration into a symptom, which is more reassuring than endless repetition. It is as though de Man were saying that "Obsession," despite or rather because it is so psychologically bleak, falls back within the pleasure principle—that is, the psychological, the human—whereas "Correspondances," which seems so sunny, contains a disruption that goes beyond the pleasure principle. When de Man says that we can get "Obsession" from "Correspondances" but not the other way around, this is a way of repeating Freud's experience of the disruption of the pleasure principle described in *Beyond the Pleasure Principle,* a study in which Freud grappled with the very limits of psychoanalysis.[13] Freud noticed that there were experiences or facts that seemed to contradict his notion of the primacy of the pleasure principle in human life (negative pleasures, the repetition compulsion, the death instinct). As Derrida has shown, Freud kept bringing the beyond back within explainability, and the beyond of Freud's theory kept popping up elsewhere.[14] He could, in effect, get the pleasure principle to explain its beyond but not anticipate it. The beyond of the pleasure principle could exist only as a disruption.

De Man makes the surprising claim that "Correspondances" is *not* a lyric but contains the entire possibility of lyric: "'Obsession,' a text of recollection and elegiac mourning, *adds* remembrance to the flat surface of time in 'Correspondances'—produces at once a hermeneutic, fallacious, lyrical reading of the unintelligible" (262). The act of making intelligible, whether in the lyric or in the terminology of literary history, is for de Man always an act of "resistance and nostalgia, at the furthest remove from the materiality of actual history." This would mean that "actual history" is what escapes and resists intelligibility. Listen to how de Man ends his essay:

> If mourning is called a "chambre d'éternel deuil où vibrent de vieux râles," then this pathos of terror states in fact the desired consciousness of eternity and of temporal harmony as voice and as song. True "mourning" is less deluded. The most *it* can do is to allow for non-comprehension and enumerate non-anthropomorphic, non-elegiac, non-celebratory, non-lyrical, non-poetic, that is to say, prosaic, or, better, *historical* modes of language power. (262)

Earlier in the essay, de Man had said of Nietzsche's general analysis of truth that "truth is always at the very least dialectical, the negative knowledge of error" (242). In another essay, de Man speaks of "literature as the place where this negative knowledge about the reliability of linguistic utterance is made available."[15] Negativity, then, is not an assertion of the negative but a nonpositivity within the possibility of assertion. This final sentence is clearly a version of stating negative knowledge. But it is also a personification. "True 'mourning'" is said to be "less deluded." Emphasizing the word *it* as the agent, he writes, "The most *it* can do is to allow for non-comprehension." "True mourning" becomes the subject of this negative knowledge. The subjectivizations performed by the lyric upon the unintelligible are here rejected, but by a personification of mourning. Is mourning—or rather, "true 'mourning'"—human or inhuman? Or is it what makes it impossible to close the gap between "man" and rhetoric? In other words, does this type of personification presuppose knowledge of human essence, or does it merely confer a kind of rhetorical agency? Is it anthropomorphic? Is there a difference between personification and anthropomorphism? Is the text stating its knowledge as if it were a human, or is it just performing the inescapability of the structures it is casting off? Has de Man's conclusion really eliminated anthropomorphism and reduced it to the trope of personification, or is anthropomorphism inescapable in the notion of mourning? Is this what lyric poetry—so often structured around the relation between loss and rhetoric—must decide? Or finesse? The least we can say is that de Man has given the last word in his own text to a personification.

II

> That which henceforth is to be "truth" is now fixed; that is to say, a uniformly valid and binding designation of things is invented and the legislature of language also gives the first laws of truth: since here, for the first time, originates the contrast between truth and falsity. The liar uses the valid designations, the words, in order to make the unreal appear as real, e.g., he says, "I am rich," whereas the right designation of his state would be "poor."
>
> —Nietzsche, "Truth and Falsity in an Ultramoral Sense"

The case of *Rowland v. California Men's Colony, Unit II Men's Advisory Council* is based on a provision in the United States legal code permitting a "person" to appear in court *in forma pauperis*. The relevant legislation reads in part: "Any court of the United States may authorize the commencement, prosecution or defense of any suit, action, or proceeding, civil or criminal, or appeal therein, without prepayment of fees and costs or security therefor, by a person who makes affidavit that he is unable to pay such costs or give security therefor."[16] In other words, a "person" may go to court without prepayment of fees if the "person" can demonstrate indigence. The question to be decided by the court is whether this provision applies to artificial persons like corporations or councils, or whether it is meant to apply only to individuals. In the case that led to *Rowland v. California Men's Colony, Unit II Men's Advisory Council,* a council of prisoners in California tried to bring suit against the correctional officers of the prison for the restoration of the practice of providing free cigarettes for indigent prisoners, which was discontinued. They tried to sue *in forma pauperis* on the grounds that the warden forbids the council to hold funds of its own. The court found that they had not sufficiently proven indigence. They were allowed to appeal *in forma pauperis* in order to enable the court to decide whether the council, as an artificial legal person, is entitled to sue *in forma pauperis.* The appeals court decided that they were so entitled, but this conflicted with another court ruling in another case. Thus the U.S. Supreme Court got to decide whether the provisions for proceeding *in forma pauperis* should apply only to natural persons or also to legal persons like associations and councils. *Rowland v. California Men's Colony* is therefore about what a person is, and how you can tell the difference between a natural person and an artificial person.

Justice Souter's majority opinion in the Supreme Court's decision begins with something that in many ways resembles de Man's stutter of infinite enumeration.[17] To find out what the legal meaning of "person" is, Souter turns to what is called the Dictionary Act. The Dictionary Act gives instructions about how to read acts of Congress. The Dictionary Act states that: "In determining the meaning of any Act of Congress, unless the context indicates otherwise, the word "person" includes corporations, companies, associations, firms, partnerships, societies, and joint stock companies, as well as individuals" (1 U.S.C. 1). Thus, the word "person" does include artificial entities unless the context indicates otherwise. Now the Court asks, but what does "context" mean? The justices turn to *Webster's New International Dictionary,* where they note that it means "the part or parts of a discourse preceding or following a 'text' or passage or a word, or so intimately associated with it as to throw light on its meaning." The context, then, is the surrounding words of the act. Of course, *Webster's* does offer a second meaning for the word "context": "associated surroundings, whether material or mental"—a reference not to the surrounding text but to the broader reality or intentionality—but Souter dismisses this by saying, "We doubt that the broader sense applies here." Why? Because "if Congress had meant to point further afield, as to legislative history, for example, it would have been natural to use a more spacious phrase, like 'evidence of congressional intent,' in place of 'context'" (4062).

The word "natural," which is precisely at issue, since we are trying to find out whether the statute applies only to natural persons, is here applied precisely to an artificial person, Congress, which is personified as having natural intentionality—"If Congress had meant." The Court's decision repeatedly relies on this type of personification. It is as though Souter has to treat Congress as an entity with intentions, even natural intentions, in order to say that Congress could not have meant to include artificial entities in its ruling. There is a personification of an artificial entity, Congress, embedded in the very project of interpreting how far the law will allow for artificial entities to be considered persons.

Turning to the Dictionary Act for "person" and to Merriam-Webster's dictionary for "context," Souter also notes that he has to define "indicates." The difficulty of doing so pushes him into a volley of rhetorical flourishes: "A contrary 'indication' may raise a specter short of inanity, and with something less than syllogistic force" (4062). "Indicates," it seems, means more than nonsense but less than logical necessity. In other words, the task of reading becomes an infinite regress of glossing terms that are themselves supposed to be determinants of meaning. De Man's linguistic stutter returns here as the repeated effort to throw language outside itself. We could read a text, this implies, only if we were sure of the meaning of the words "context" and "indicate." But those are precisely the words that raise the question of meaning in its most general form—they cannot be glossed with any finality because they name the process of glossing itself.

Souter's text, in fact, is most anthropomorphic at those points where the infinite regress of language is most threatening. Congress is endowed with "natural" intentionality in order to sweep away the abyss of reference. Souter's dismissal of the prisoners' council as an "amorphous legal creature" (4063) is the counterpart to the need to reinforce the anthropomorphizability of the artificial legal creature, Congress.[18]

Souter's opinion proceeds to detail the ways in which he thinks the *in forma pauperis* ruling should apply only to natural persons. If an affidavit alleging poverty is required for a person to proceed *in forma pauperis,* then can an artificial entity plead poverty? Souter again turns to Webster's dictionary to find that poverty is a human condition, to be "wanting in material riches or goods; lacking in the comforts of life; needy." Souter also refers to a previous ruling, which holds that poverty involves being unable to provide for the "necessities of life." It is as though only natural persons can have "life," and that life is defined as the capacity to lack necessities and comforts. "Artificial entities may be insolvent," writes Souter, "but they are not well spoken of as 'poor'" (4063). An artificial entity cannot lack the necessities and comforts of life. Only life can lack. The experience of lack differentiates natural persons from artificial persons. To lack is to be human. In a sense, we have returned to de Man's question about mourning. Is lack human, or just a structure? Whatever the case, the court holds that associations cannot be considered persons for the purpose of the *in forma pauperis* procedure.

The majority was only five to four, however. In a dissenting opinion written by Justice Clarence Thomas, it is argued that there is no reason to restrict the broad definition of "person" to natural persons in this case. Thomas quotes the Court's view of "poverty" as an exclusively "human condition," and comments:

> I am not so sure. "Poverty" may well be a human condition in its "primary sense," but I doubt that using the word in connection with an artificial entity departs in any significant way from settled principles of English usage. . . . Congress itself has used the word "poor" to describe entities other than natural persons, referring in at least two provisions of the United States Code to the world's "Poorest countries"—a term that is used as a synonym for the least developed of the so-called "developing" countries." (4067)

Souter glosses the word "poor" as though speakers of English could use it only literally. Thomas responds by identifying the figurative use of "poor" as included within normal usage. The boundaries between natural persons and artificial persons cannot be determined by usage, because those boundaries have always already been blurred. Indeed, in treating Congress as an entity with natural intentions, Souter has already shown how "natural" the artificial can be.

At another point in his dissent, Thomas takes issue with Souter's discussion of a case in which an association or corporation *is* considered a person despite strong contextual indicators to the contrary. In the case of *Wilson v. Omaha Indian Tribe,* 442 U.S. 653, 666 (1979), it was decided that "white person" could include corporations because the "larger context" and "purpose" of the law was to protect Indians against non-Indian squatters, and it would be frustrated if a "white person" could simply incorporate in order to escape the provision of the law. Souter admits that "because a wholly legal creature has no color, and belongs to no race, the use of the adjective 'white' to describe a 'person' is one of the strongest contextual indicators imaginable that 'person' covers only individuals" (4065). Justice Thomas argues that if the court "was correct in holding that the statutory term 'white person' includes a corporation (because the 'context' does not 'indicate otherwise')—the conclusion that an association is a 'person' for *in forma pauperis* purposes is inescapable." Perhaps another inescapable conclusion is that despite its apparent reference to the physical body, the phrase "white person" is the name not of a natural but of a corporate person.

Justice Thomas refutes the reasons Souter gives for finding that artificial entities are excluded from the *in forma pauperis* provision, noting that there may be sound policy reasons for wanting to exclude them but that the law as written cannot be construed to have done so. The Court's job, he writes, is not to make policy but to interpret a statute. "Congress has created a rule of statutory construction (an association is a 'person') and an exception to that rule (an association is not a 'person' if the 'context indicates otherwise'), but the Court has permitted the exception to devour the rule [a nice personification]" (by treating the rule as if artificial entities were excluded rather than included unless the context indicates otherwise). "Whatever 'unless the context indicates otherwise' means," writes Thomas, "it cannot mean 'unless there are sound policy reasons for concluding otherwise'" (4066).

"Permitting artificial entities to proceed *in forma pauperis* may be unwise, and it may be an inefficient use of the Government's limited resources, but I see nothing in the text of the *in forma pauperis* statute indicating that Congress has chosen to exclude such entities from the benefits of that law" (4066–4067).

Thomas's two conservative instincts are at war with each other in this case: he would like the government not to spend its money, but he would also like to stick to the letter of the law.

The question of what counts as a juridical person has, in fact, been modified over time in the legal code. It was in 1871 (significantly, perhaps, at the beginning of the end of post–Civil War Reconstruction) that the Dictionary Act was first passed by Congress, which held that the word "person" "may extend and be applied to bodies politic and corporate." More recently, the question of fetal personhood has been debated, not only in the *Roe v. Wade* decision, where it was decided that a fetus is not a legal person, but also in *Weaks v. Mounter* (88 Nev. 118), where it was decided that a fetus *is* a person who can sue for intrauterine injuries, but only after birth. Recently, the question of granting patents for forms of life like oil-slick-eating bacteria or genetically altered mice has raised the question of whether a hybrid between humans and close animal relatives can be patented. And of course the question of the ethics and legality of cloning humans has been raised. The law has reached another crisis about the definition of "person." In an article on constitutional personhood, Michael Rivard writes:

> Current law allows patents for genetically-engineered animals but not for human beings. Humans are not patentable subject matter because patents are property rights, and the Thirteenth Amendment forbids any grant of property rights in a human being. Nevertheless, this exclusion for humans will prove impossible to maintain: within ten to thirty years, or perhaps sooner, advances in genetic engineering technology should allow scientists to intermingle the genetic material of humans and animals to produce human-animal hybrids. . . . It may soon be possible to patent—and to enslave—human-animal hybrids who think and feel like humans, but who lack constitutional protection under the Thirteenth Amendment.[19]

The Thirteenth Amendment is the amendment that abolished slavery. The constitutional protection against slavery operates as a constraint on the patent office, but it does so in a paradoxical way. The fear of reinstituting something like slavery, or property in humans, is a reaction to, but also a sign of, what must be an ongoing research goal—to come as close as possible to creating the ownable, enslavable human.[20]

Constitutional personhood has in fact often been defined in proximity to slavery. From the beginning the contradiction between equal rights and chattel slavery led to verbal gymnastics, even in the drafting of the Constitution itself. By not using the word "slavery" in the Constitution, and by revising the text of the original Fugitive Slave Clause to refer to the legality of slavery only at the level of the states, rather than the federal government, the framers built a double intentionality into the very foundation of their law. Douglas Fehrenbacher, studying the egregious understanding of original intent later employed by the Supreme Court in the case of *Dred Scott v. Sanford,* writes of the Constitution: "It is as though the framers were half-consciously trying to frame two constitutions, one for their own time and the other for the ages, with slavery viewed bifocally—that is, plainly visible at their feet, but disappearing when they lifted their eyes."[21] A written text of law can thus contain a double intention, the trace of a compromise between differing opinions. No wonder interpreting the law's intention is so complicated. That intention can always already be multiple. The distinction Justice Thomas made between interpreting the law and making policy cannot hold if the law's ambiguity allows for the possibility that the policy it governs will change.

III

> The "inhuman" is not some kind of mystery, or some kind of secret; the inhuman is: linguistic structures, the play of linguistic tensions, linguistic events that occur, possibilities which are inherent in language—independently of any intent or any drive or any wish or any desire we might have. . . . If one speaks of the inhuman, the fundamental non-human character of language, one also speaks of the fundamental non-definition of the human as such.
>
> —Paul de Man, "Benjamin's 'The Task of the Translator'"

> Only smoking distinguishes humans from the rest of the animals.
>
> —Anonymous (quoted in Richard Klein, *Cigarettes Are Sublime*)

The case of *Rowland v. California Men's Colony, Unit II Men's Advisory Council* was ostensibly about whether a council of inmates could sue prison officials *in forma pauperis* to get their cigarettes back. The details of the case seemed irrelevant to the question of whether an artificial person has the right to sue *in forma pauperis*. Yet perhaps some of those details deserve note. Is it relevant that the suit to decide this question is brought by a council of inmates? The phenomenon of the inmate civil suit has grown to the point where the case law may very well be transformed by it. In a 1995 study of inmate suits in California, it was reported that "for the last fourteen years at least, the federal courts have faced a growing caseload and workload challenge posed by inmate cases. . . . By 1992, these filings numbered nearly 30,000, and constituted 13% of the courts' total civil case filings nationwide."[22] The majority of these suits are filed *in forma pauperis*.[23] The Supreme Court's decision may well have been affected by what Clarence Thomas calls "policy decisions."

If prisoners are affecting the nature of civil proceedings, they are also, at least figuratively, affecting theoretical discussions about the nature of rational choice and the evolution of cooperation. The celebrated "Prisoner's Dilemma" has been central to questions of self-interest and social goods since it was introduced by Albert Tucker in 1950. Max Black has even entitled his discussion of the issues raised "The 'Prisoner's Dilemma' and the Limits of Rationality."[24] Why is it that the theoretical study of rational choice has recourse to "man" conceived as a prisoner? Does this have anything to do with the poets' tendency to see the sonnet form as a prison?

And is it by chance that *Rowland v. California Men's Colony, Unit II Men's Advisory Council* is about cigarettes? On the one hand, it seems paradoxical that the council has to demonstrate its indigence in order to pursue its suit against the prison directors for depriving the prisoners of access to cigarettes, which in prisons function as a form of currency. On the other hand, it seems fitting that the personhood of the association is the counterpart to the humanity of the inmates, which, as common wisdom (quoted above, second epigraph) would have it, is demonstrated by the act of smoking. The prisoners would thus, in a very attenuated way, be suing for their humanity. As Richard Klein has wittily shown, smoking serves no function other than to enact a structure of desire—of human desire for self-transcendence, for repetition, for bodily experience corresponding to something other than the "necessities of life" required for existence alone: in short, desire for the sublime.[25] Far from being what defines natural personhood, then, need for the "necessities of life" alone is precisely what *cannot* define the human.

In the article cited above, Rivard declares that "corporations would be presumed constitutional *non*persons," especially for liberty-related rights, unless the corporation could rebut its non-person status by showing specific natural persons "who would be affected if the corporation were denied these rights."[26] This is the opposite view of the one in the Dictionary Act, which considers a corporation a person "unless the context indicates otherwise." Rivard's article is arguing for the rights of new biological species that can pass the "self-awareness test" (which, in a surprisingly Lacanian move derived from Michael Dennett, he defines as wanting to be different from what one is), and he claims that corporations, by their nature, do not pass this test.

But the question of the nature of corporations as persons has never been a simple one, as Rivard admits. In an article titled "The Personification of the Business Corporation in American Law," Gregory Mark outlines in detail the history of corporate personhood.[27] The relation between corporations and the natural persons who compose them has grown more complicated over time, but in most discussions of the matter it is the "natural" person that functions as the known quantity, and the "artificial" who is either just an "aggregate" of natural persons, or a fiction created by the state, or a mere metaphor, or actually resembles (is *like,* to return to the Baudelairean word) a natural person in that it has a "will" of its own. Such a corporate will is a form of agency separate from that of the natural corporators, who exist behind the "veil" of the corporation. Much of Mark's article concerns the exact rhetorical valence of this personification:

> American law has always recognized that people's activities could be formally organized and that the resulting organizations could be dealt with as units. Personification, however, is important because it became far more than a quaint device making it possible for the law to deal with organized business entities. In American legal and economic history, personification has been vital because it (1) implies a single and unitary source of control over the collective property of the corporation's members, (2) defines, encourages, and legitimates the corporation as an autonomous, creative, self-directed economic being, and (3) captures rights, ultimately even constitutional rights, for corporations thereby giving corporate property unprecedented protection from the state. (1443)

Mark takes seriously the role of language in the evolving history of the corporation. Philosophers and legislators have gone to great lengths to minimize the rhetorical damage, to eliminate personification as far as possible, but he asserts that it is not just a figure of speech to speak of a corporation's "mind," or even its "life." "Practical experience, not just anthropomorphism, fixed the corporate mind in the management hierarchy" (1475). The corporation resembles a human being in its capacity to "take resolves in the midst of conflicting motives," to "will change." Yet the analogy is not perfect. The corporation, for example, unlike its corporators, is potentially immortal. The effect of personification appears to derive its rhetorical force from the ways in which the corporation *resembles* a natural person, yet the corporation's immortality in no way diminishes its personification. When Mark says that it is "not just anthropomorphism" that underpins the agency of the corporation, he still implies that we can know what anthropomorphism is. But his final sentence stands this presupposition on its head. Far from claiming that a corporation's characteristics are derived from a knowable human essence, Mark suggests that what have been claimed to be the essential characteristics of man (especially "economic man") have in fact been borrowed from the nature of the corporation:

> Personification, with its roots in historic theological disputes and modern business necessity, had proved to be a potent symbol to legitimate the autonomous business corporation and its management. Private property rights had been transferred to associations, associations had themselves become politically legitimate, and the combination had helped foster modern political economy. The corporation, once the derivative tool of the state, had become its rival, and the successes of the autonomous corporate management turned the basis for belief in an individualist conception of property on its head. The protests of modern legists notwithstanding, the business corporation had become the quintessential economic man. (1482–1483)

Theories of rationality, naturalness, and the "good," presumed to be grounded in the nature of "man," may in reality be taking their notions of human essence not from "natural man" but from business corporations.

Ambivalence about personification, especially the personification of abstractions, has in fact permeated not only legal but also literary history. Nervousness about the agency of the personified corporation echoes the nervousness Enlightenment writers felt about the personifications dreamed up by the poets. As Steven Knapp puts it in his book *Personification and the Sublime:* "Allegorical personification—the endowing of metaphors with the agency of literal persons—was only the most obvious and extravagant instance of what Enlightenment writers perceived, with a mixture of admiration and uneasiness, as the unique ability of poetic genius to give the force of literal reality to figurative 'inventions.' More important than the incongruous presence of such agents was their contagious effect on the ostensibly literal agents with which they interacted."[28]
The uncanniness of the personification, then, was derived from its way of putting in question what the "natural" or the "literal" might be.

We have finally come back to the question of whether there is a difference between anthropomorphism and personification, which arose at the end of the discussion of the essay by Paul de Man. It can now be seen that everything hangs on this question. Not only does anthropomorphism depend on the givenness of the essence of the human while personification does not, but the mingling of personifications on the same footing as "real" agents threatens to make the lack of certainty about what humanness is come to consciousness. Perhaps the loss of unconsciousness about the lack of humanness is what de Man was calling "true 'mourning.'" Perhaps the "fallacious lyrical reading of the unintelligible" is exactly what legislators count on lyric poetry to provide: the assumption that the human *has been* or *can be* defined so that it can then be presupposed without the question of its definition's being raised as a question—legal or otherwise. Thus the poets would truly be, as Shelley claimed, the "unacknowledged legislators of the world," not because they covertly determine policy, but because it is somehow necessary and useful that there *be* a powerful, presupposable, unacknowledgment. But the very rhetorical sleight of hand that would instate such an unacknowledgment is indistinguishable from the rhetorical structure that would empty it. Lyric and law are two of the most powerful discourses that exist along the fault line of this question.

Chapter Fifteen

Lost Cause

I

When Ferdinand de Saussure gave his groundbreaking course on general linguistics, one of the revolutionary things he said was, "Language is not a substance." In a book on persons and things, it is almost inevitable to treat things as substances, addiction to things as substance abuse. Things appear and are discussed as presences. But are they always? Does the functioning of language change anything?

We have also begun to tackle the ethical question via the face. Could it be that the face that prompts an ethical stance is not a substance either? Could it be that it stands as the *thing addressed,* and that addressing is altogether different from perceiving? At any rate, Jacques Lacan gave a seminar called The Ethics of Psychoanalysis in which he seemed to go back not to Kant's Second Critique but to the first, to the "Ding an sich" that is not a phenomenon, not an object, not a substance.

To tie up this project neatly, we will let Kant's critiques speak to each other here, and make Lacan's ethics stand opposite Winnicott's. But first, let us talk about a few novels in which a linguistic key is not present as a substance. The first example is, unsurprisingly, *Frankenstein.* At the center of its layers, as the cause of the story, as the secret that Frankenstein withholds from Walton, but in whose pursuit he recognizes their similarity, lies the secret of conferring life—becoming equal to the Creator. We know that Mary Shelley would have been hard-pressed to give what she didn't have, but Frankenstein's attribution to it of the evils he has suffered makes his withholding seem like proof that he possesses something he is unwilling to share. The secret, the cause of everything, is absent. It is thus not present as a substance but as an articulation, an inaccessible object.

In Nathaniel Hawthorne's *Marble Faun,* the character Donatello, who resembles the faun of Praxiteles, is the last of the breed of half-animals, half-men if he possesses furry ears. But his ears are hidden beneath his curly locks. When the novel's narrator, in a postscript added to the book's second edition, asks the sculptor Kenyon whether, after all, Donatello had furry ears, Kenyon answers, "I know, but may not tell."[1] Once again, what is supposedly central is withheld from us. In both *Frankenstein* and *The Marble Faun,* the knowledge supposedly *exists* but is not divulged, thus functioning as an absence, an articulation. The Thing that makes the story function does not exist *for us* as a substance.

In his 1966 *Ecrits,* Lacan included an essay entitled "La chose freudienne." What was this Freudian thing? Is it the same "Thing" as *das Ding* in the seminar on ethics? What did "thing" mean in the essay?

Lacan was speaking in Vienna about what a "return to Freud" might mean, and explaining in what way the descendants of Freud, particularly those who had gone to America, had betrayed him. Lacan's intention was to renew the contact with "Freud's discovery" (always in the singular in Lacan). "Freud's discovery," we gather, was the discovery of the unconscious. The psychoanalysts in America had given the "ego" too much importance, equating analytic "success" with an identification of the patient's ego with the analyst's, and saying nothing about any unconscious. A "successful" analysis, in keeping with American ideals of productivity and results, was a better adaptation to reality. In contrast, Lacan wished to emphasize the importance of the unconscious, and to make explicit the relevance of vocabularies not at the time available to Freud.

In his 1959–60 seminar, Lacan then tackled the problem of the ethics of psychoanalysis, making it revolve around *das Ding*. "We are concerned here," he writes, "with the Freudian experience as an ethics, which is to say, at its most fundamental level, since it directs us toward a therapeutic form of action that, whether we like it or not, is included in the register or in the terms of an ethics."[2] But the common understanding of psychoanalytic action has it turn traditional ethics on its head, *undoing* the damage caused by repressive moral values. How, then, can it itself have moral values?

For Lacan, the important thing in analysis is that the patient's "truth"— what the unconscious says—"speaks." In his essay, he makes both the truth and a desk speak, perhaps to show the difference between the Freudian Thing and any old thing. The unconscious, in other words, is not just a prosopopeia. What is speaking addresses itself to the analyst, and the question becomes one of his ability to hear. The unconscious does not respond; it repeats.

Lacan's perhaps more radical assertion is that the unconscious is structured like a language. That is, the analyst has to learn its rules and vocabulary in order to hear what is addressing him. The Freudian Thing is a thing that speaks—but nevertheless a thing. "Modern" linguistics, founded after Freud's "discovery" by the same Ferdinand de Saussure quoted earlier, enables us to discern in its messages its organization by the signifier, not the signified. If symptoms are symbolic, their rhetoric belongs to the same unconscious language. In other words, "hearing," for the analyst, is listening for the signifier, for the vehicle of meaning, not its content. The vehicle, not the content, offers a path to follow to the Thing, without which the Thing would remain unfindable.

For the Freudian Thing is a lost object, able to be refound, but never possessed. I would say it resembles Lacan's *objet a,* but Freud, like Heidegger, puts the notion of "object" in a negative light. In accordance with its etymology, it is something standing "over-against" the subject. "An independent, self-supporting thing may become an object if we place it before us, whether in immediate perception or by bringing it to mind in a recollective re-presentation. However, the thingly character of the thing does not consist in its being a represented object, nor can it be defined in any way in terms of the objectness, the over-againstness, of the object."[3] The object is the counterpart to the subject—something that enters willingly into an opposition. Subject and object are symmetrically opposed, and their grammatical opposition underlines their non-overlapping roles. Subject and object are presupposed separate and different: an object is pure spectacle, not at all a spectator; purely inert, and not at all an agent. It is presumably to shake up such a schema that Francis Ponge speaks of *l'objeu.*

Lacan's *objet a,* however, is precisely not an object in this sense. It is searched for as cause of desire but does not exist except in the unconscious of the subject. It is the mother as imagined by the subject prior to the discovery of sexual difference. But the subject does not imagine the mother prior to sexual difference. If the discovery of anatomical difference is traumatic for the subject, this is because he interprets it as meaning "castrated / not castrated," and he, if the subject is a boy, could lose his penis. The castrated phallus is the mother's: what is lost never existed. But nostalgia for the phallic mother is nostalgia for a time when the mother was "all" to the child, what Baudelaire called "la vie antérieure." The first, incestuous, object, in other words, is presumed to have existed because of the feeling that something has been lost. It can be refound, but was never present.

The phallic mother contributes to the reinforcement of what the subject believes is his Ego. He finds in her approving look the same image *as looked at* that he finds in the mirror stage. It is thus his *own* sense of wholeness that is threatened by the discovery of sexual difference. Poets and psychoanalytic theorists have written about the primal mother's role in the consolidation of the self:

> Bless'd the infant Babe,
> (For with my best conjectures I would trace
> The progress of our being) blest the Babe,
> Nurs'd in his Mother's arms, the Babe who sleeps
> Upon his Mother's breast, who, when his soul
> Claims manifest kindred with an earthly soul,
> Doth gather passion from his Mother's eye!
> . . . . .
> His organs and recipient faculties
> Are quicken'd, are more vigorous, his mind spreads,
> Tenacious of the forms which it receives.
> In one beloved Presence, nay and more,
> In that most apprehensive habitude
> And those sensations which have been deriv'd
> From this beloved Presence, there exists

A virtue which irradiates and exalts
All objects through all intercourse of sense.[4]

The most significant relevant basic interactions between mother and child lie usually in the visual area: the child's bodily display is responded to by the gleam in the mother's eye.[5]

In Lacan's well-known seminar called Four Fundamental Concepts of Psychoanalysis, he does not discuss only the unconscious, repetition, transference, and drives; he also differentiates between the eye and the gaze. The eye *is seen;* the gaze *sees.* The gaze is thus the contribution of the Other to the consolidation of the self (and will be the eventual site of the Superego). Lacan calls his section on visuality: "Of the Gaze as *Objet petit a.*"[6]

Lacan is quite struck by Heidegger's example of a jug as a Thing, and particularly by the idea of shaping the void. As a container, the jug introduces emptiness and fullness into the world. As a vehicle, it functions as a signifier. But it is an empty signifier, the empty square that allows the others to move. The Thing signifies signification itself.[7] If the phallus is the salient thing that organizes desire, the Thing is what is lost and has thereby created the feeling of lack. It also organizes desire, but around something missing: the "navel of the dream," Freud called it; the inaccessible woman in courtly love, says Lacan. In any case, they are all equally unpossessable. Lacan writes in his seminar on ethics:

> Now if you consider the vase from the point of view I first proposed, as an object made to represent the existence of the emptiness at the center of the real that is called the Thing, this emptiness as represented in the representation presents itself as a *nihil,* as nothing. And that is why the potter, just like you to whom I am speaking, creates the vase with his hand around this emptiness, creates it, just like the mythical creator, *ex nihilo,* starting with a hole.
>
> Everyone makes jokes about macaroni, because it is a hole with something around it, or about canons. The fact that we laugh doesn't change the situation, however: the fashioning of the signifier and the introduction of a gap or a hole in the real is identical.[8]

As Lacan says about the phallus, "This is . . . the effect . . . of the turning into signifying form as such, from the fact that it is from the locus of the Other that its message is emitted."[9] In other words, "my" body is "there," not "here," when my needs and desires are subject to demand. I can only express them "there," in the place of the Other, subject to the signifying order. The "gap" in the real is the leap from the empirical to the signifying articulation of the object of desire; it cannot be perceived empirically. It is "nothing."

It is no accident that Lacan refers to Heidegger's *Ding* as a "vase," since he (Lacan) several times uses an optical illusion with a vase and a spherical mirror to talk about the nature of images. He first refers to it in his "Remarque sur le rapport de Daniel Lagache" in 1960, to point out the difference between the "*moi idéal*" and the "*ideal du moi.*"[10] He then returns to it for a more extensive discussion in his 1964 seminar The Four Fundamental Concepts of Psychoanalysis. An upside-down vase in a box, reflected in a spherical mirror, produces a real image of the vase, turned right side up, on top of the box, containing a bouquet that was formerly without a container on top of the box. If this image is then reflected to the subject in a flat mirror, its status is exactly the same as his mirror image described in the *Stade du miroir:* a real image, reflected. But anyone can see that the image is an illusion. It's just that the subject's self-image is no less illusory. This fantasy, however, strictly obeys the laws of optics.

So what, for Lacan, is *das Ding,* and what does it have to do with ethics?

In German, there are two terms that mean "thing": *die Sache* and *das Ding.* After a little dance toward etymology (but nowhere near as extensive as Heidegger's, just long enough to suggest that *Sache, causa, Ding,* and *res* are all derived from the functioning of the law), Lacan writes: "Don't imagine that this use of etymology, these insights, these etymological soundings, are what I prefer to guide myself by—although Freud does remind us all the time that in order to follow the track of the accumulated experience of tradition, of past generations, linguistic inquiry is the surest vehicle of the transmission of a development which marks psychic reality."[11] In Freud's essay "The Unconscious," an opposition is set up by Freud between *Sachvorstellung* (the representation of things) and *Wortvorstellung* (the representation of words). These "things" may be the opposite of words, but their articulation is entirely in function of language. They are language's things, the material counterparts of words considered as names. Words are considered in their meanings, and *Sache* are the things they refer to. Words do not enter into relations with each other through their letters, and what words refer to are parts of the world, not the rules of language. In other words, language is seen through the referent, not the signifier, and it is *language* that is not structured like a language. When Lacan refers to the *Ding* as structured by the signifier, he is referring to the *non*-referential aspects of *das Ding*'s structure. Philology itself tracks the history of changes in the signifier that could not be guessed merely by following the connotations of the signified.

Lacan's illustration of a habit of language that includes a pure signifier as a sign that one is following its rules is, in French, the pleonastic *ne*. Supposedly meaningless, the *ne* in *je crains qu'il ne vienne* means nothing different from *je crains qu'il vienne* (both mean "I'm afraid he'll come"), except for the fact that the former shows that the speaker really knows French. *Ne* is normally a sign of negation, but here there is no conscious intent to negate. But perhaps, suggests Lacan, there is an *unconscious* negation indicated by the signifier, as if his coming were, in the unconscious, under erasure. The network of unconscious meanings attaches to the "meaningless" signifier, which then becomes the signifier of unconscious meanings.

Lacan, still asking what the Thing might be, ends up quoting Saint Paul's epistle to the Romans, substituting "Thing" for "sin":

> Is the Law the Thing? Certainly not. Yet I can only know of the Thing by means of the Law. In effect, I would not have had the idea to covet it [my neighbor's Thing] if the Law hadn't said: "Thou shalt not covet it." But the Thing finds a way by producing in me all kinds of covetousness thanks to the commandment, for without the Law the Thing is dead. But even without the Law, I was once alive. But when the commandment appeared, the Thing flared up, returned once again, I met my death. And for me, the commandment that was supposed to lead to life turned out to lead to death, for the Thing found a way and thanks to the commandment seduced me; through it I came to desire death.[12]

We have finally entered the familiar territory of morals. Desire seems to be *caused* by prohibition. But if desire is *simultaneous* with prohibition, is the moral law repressive? Can the Other repress what it creates, or is creating the same as repressing? In any case, the Ten Commandments are the founding image of the Law, and most of them take the form of a negative command: Thou shalt not kill, bear false witness, covet something belonging to thy neighbor, make graven images, commit adultery, steal, or take the lord's name in vain. But there are three commandments that do not take the form of prohibitions: remember the Sabbath, and keep it holy; honor thy father and thy mother; and thou shalt have no other gods before me. While not explaining what remembering and honoring mean, these commandments, too, point out for moral status one's parents, one's god, and one's Sabbath. They do not tell us what worshipping is, but they do describe rivalry among gods; the belief in other gods is not prohibited, so long as the liberator and lawgiver has first place. The speaker of the Law organizes those subject to the Law around his narcissistic investment in his people.

Whatever is prohibited or pointed to for special honor will define the parameters of sin. Why is it, then, asks Lacan, that sin is so alluring? Lacan entitles the first section of his outline "L'attrait de la faute," which is translated in the English version as "The Attraction of Transgression," but could also be translated "The Appeal of Sin." The commandments tell me what to desire by forbidding it. What is prohibited, then, is what is desired. Yet before the commandments (before the discovery of sexual difference), I have the feeling that I did once desire (live in Paradise with the phallic mother). Nevertheless, when I became subject to the Law (the signifier), I translated my desire into the language of the Other (put my desire into signifying form), and since then I have been subject to the death instinct.

The moral law, then, functions as a constraint. But it comes from a god who prides himself on having freed the Israelites from slavery. It is freedom, not constraint, that ushers in the age of ethical thought—and the age of revolution. The American Declaration of Independence was dated 1776; Kant's *Critique of Practical Reason* was published in 1788; the French Revolution began in 1789. All had different ideas of "freedom." For Kant, it was freedom from natural law that gave "reason" its categorical imperative. The revolutionary movements, inspired by the writings of John Locke, aimed at freeing society from hereditary privileges: in the United States the emphasis was on equality and consent; in France, on brotherhood and rights. Another interpretation of freedom, rights, and consent, published in 1795 and written while the author was for more than twenty-five years a prisoner, was Sade's *Philosophy in the Boudoir*. It, too, was based on an imperative: "Français, encore un effort. . ." ("Frenchmen, just one more effort"). A kind of antimorality derived from libertine thought, Sade's work has always been seen as at the antipodes of Kant's. But both were reactions to the new, Newtonian universe, and they said, according to Lacan, who included an essay called "Kant avec Sade" in his 1966 *Ecrits* and speaks about them at length in his seminar on ethics, pretty much the same thing.

If *das Ding* is not a substance, not a presence, can it participate in the world of matter? If the cause of desire can be found again but never had, is it real?

The prohibition of graven images has led to a veritable flood of research on the meaning of "graven." But what if the prohibition is on "image"? This is all the more likely, since the commandment proscribes *likenesses,* as well. But in the first, abortive, creation story in Genesis, God is said to have made man in his image, after his likeness. In the second story, there is no further mention of images. Lacan writes, "In a nutshell, the elimination of the function of the imaginary presents itself to my mind."[13] Eliminating the imaginary, one eliminates representation as well. In Lacan's theory of the three essential orders (imaginary, symbolic, and real), this leaves the symbolic and the real for the moral law. The symbolic order is the order of the signifier. If *das Ding* is in the symbolic order and nevertheless affects the real, its function is indeed that of an absence, a gap. *Das Ding* is an articulation in the signifying chain, perhaps its origin, the cause of desire. It is that which, in the real, stands as the inaccessible object. It is not available to the senses (not, in Kant's terms, *phenomenon* but *noumenon*), but it is not nothing: it is articulation as matter and mechanism, even though it occupies neither space nor time.

There is a name for language's capacity to create things of language: performative language. Instead of referring *to* the world, performative language acts *in* the world. It creates, ex nihilo, things that would not exist without the rules of language. A commandment is like that: the Law is a particular force of language that confers a sense of obligation or obedience on its subjects. Kant sees the same force in the categorical imperative. Reason, freed from the laws of nature, is all the more shaped by the laws of language. Here is what Kant says about imperatives:

> Now this principle of morality, on account of the universality of its legislation which makes it the formal determining ground of the will . . . includes the Infinite Being as the supreme intelligence. . . . [T]he law has the form of an imperative. The moral law . . . is an imperative, commanding categorically because it is unconditioned.[14]

> Imperatives . . . are valid objectively and are quite distinct from maxims, which are subjective principles. . . . Imperatives themselves. . . , when they are conditional, i.e., when they determine the will not as such but only in respect

to a desired effect, are hypothetical imperatives. . . . Laws must completely determine the will as will.[15]

And we remember that, in the midst of such sober prose, Kant suddenly addressed himself directly to duty.

Apostrophe, too, allows one to create ex nihilo. It allows one to create a thing of language without depending on any referent.

Lacan quoted "Moi, la vérité, je parle." If the truth speaks and Laws given by language create an entity that can be addressed, then interactions consisting of language and created by language constitute both the unconscious and ethics. Even Freud summed up analytic progress in a kind of imperative, saying, "Wo es war, soll ich warden"—"Where it was, there must I come to be." The place from which the subject speaks must come to be the place of what was speaking to the analyst.

Freud was hounded by anti-Semitism, and his succession seems to be in the hands of other Jews. How does Lacan, imbued as he is with Christian culture and having a priest for a brother, but not being (says he) a believer, any more than was Freud (said he), relate to his legacy? Is a return to Freud a return to Judaism or a turn away from it?

In Christianity, the Mosaic commandments are adopted, but Christianity prides itself on boiling its commandments down to two:

> The first of all the commandments is, Hear, O Israel; the Lord our God is one Lord:
>
> And thou shalt love the Lord thy God with all thy heart, and with all thy soul, and with all thy mind, and with all thy strength: this is the first commandment.
>
> And the second is like, namely this, Thou shalt love thy neighbor as thyself. There is none other commandment greater than these. (Mark 12:29–31)

Love thy neighbor as thyself—*Eek,* says Freud, *like myself?* Who should 'scape whipping? The Old law, the Law of the Jews, was spelled out as a series of directives and prohibitions. The New law, the Law of Christianity, thanks mainly to Saint Paul, the former Jew, replaces legality with love. Jesus, like Paul, was born a Jew, and it is not clear that he ever stopped being one, whereas Paul, né Saul, becomes an apologist for the difference between Judaism and Christianity. Difference is no longer written on the body (circumcision) but in the spirit. The split between the literal and the figurative inaugurates a whole new era of allegory. But Christians, after appropriating the Decalogue, call upon "love" as what Christianity preaches toward God and one's fellow man. It is no longer a question of rivalry between gods or men, but of love. But what is love? These commandments (like each other) treat all aggression as resolved. Yet Lacan, taking Freud further, says of the formation of that "self" in the mirror stage: "It is clear that the structural effect of identification with the rival . . . can only be conceived of if the way is prepared for it by a primary identification that structures the subject as a rival with himself."[16] In short, the subject can neutralize or sublimate the aggressiveness that structures his relation with his fellow only if they have accomplished together the murder of their common rival, the father, have forgotten it, and have begun to worship it.

> The notion of aggressivity as a correlative tension of the narcissistic structure in the coming-into-being (*devenir*) of the subject enables us to understand . . . all sorts of accidents. . . .
>
> I shall now say something about how I conceive of the . . . Oedipus complex. . . .
>
> Freud shows us, in fact, that the need to participate, which neutralizes the conflict inscribed after the murder in the situation of rivalry between the brothers, is the basis of the identification with the paternal Totem. Thus the Oedipal identification is that by which the subject transcends the aggressivity that is constitutive of the primary subjective identification. I have stressed elsewhere how it constitutes a step in the establishment of that distance by which, with feelings like respect, is realized a whole affective assumption of one's neighbor. . . .
>
> . . . [O]ne cannot stress too strongly the irreducible character of the narcissistic structure, and the ambiguity of a notion that tends to ignore the constancy of aggressive tension in all moral life that involves subjection to this structure: in fact no notion of oblativity could produce altruism from that structure.[17]

In addition, the need to find a substitute for that first, forbidden Oedipal object is, according to Lacan (after Lévi-Strauss), necessary for there to be language and culture at all.

For there to be love and goodwill among equals, as Christianity and the

French Revolution require, the brothers *have* to have murdered the father. The crucifixion of Christ seems to stand as that act, and the notion of original sin refers obscurely toward it, but the need for the murder in order to have the love is forgotten, as if one could have the love without the murder. The commandments to love god and one's neighbor try to legislate and treat as primary something that is based on an act that the Christian Law tries to make inessential. Christianity is thus founded on and obscures the unneutralized aggression of the mirror stage. As Freud says in *Moses and Monotheism,* it is as though Christians assert of non-Christians, "They will not admit that they killed God, whereas we do and are cleansed from the guilt of it."[18]

II

There are four young friends wandering about in an underground world full of the debris of the past. One of the young people is called Donatello. The story involves a delivery to an unknown address. It is centered on a father figure. What is the text? *Both* the movie *Teenage Mutant Ninja Turtles* and *The Marble Faun.* (In the film, a pizza is delivered to a nonexistent address; in the novel, the painter Miriam entrusts to the painter Hilda a mysterious package to be delivered to the Cenci palace. In the film, the Turtles are afraid their mentor, Splinter, will die; in the novel, the meeting between Miriam and Donatello is blessed by the outstretched bronze arm of the statue of Pope Julius III.)

Like the film, Nathaniel Hawthorne's novel, as we have seen before, is a Darwinian-Ovidian tale of a creature halfway between man and animal. One thread of his novel indeed involves the question of whether Donatello really is a faun or only looks like Praxiteles' statue of one. But another thread is the familiar Hawthornian question of the nature of sin. The novel is centered on the scene of a murder, but the murder is entirely in dumb show, a question of glances. The murder victim seems to be an abject and possibly guilty father figure, too, referred to as Miriam's Model, first encountered in the Roman Catacombs and casting gloom on her thereafter. The lingering question is whether the purity of one who merely witnessed a crime has been stained by it. Let me quote the scene of the murder:

> Looking around, she [Miriam] perceived that all her company of merry friends had retired, and Hilda, too, in whose soft and quiet presence she had

always an indescribable feeling of security. All gone; and only herself and Donatello left hanging over the brow of the ominous precipice!

Not so, however, not entirely alone! In the basement-wall of the palace, shaded from the moon, there was a deep, empty niche, that had probably once contained a statue; not empty, neither; for a figure now came forth from it, and approached Miriam. She must have had cause to dread some unspeakable evil from this strange persecutor, for, as he drew near, such a cold, sick despair crept over her, that it impeded her breath, and benumbed her natural promptitude of thought. Miriam seemed dreamily to remember falling on her knees, but, in her whole recollection of that wild moment, she beheld herself as in a dim show, and could not well distinguish what was done and suffered, no, not even whether she were really an actor and sufferer in the scene.

Hilda, meanwhile, had separated herself from the sculptor, and turned back to rejoin her friend. At a distance, she still heard the mirth of her late companions, who were going down the cityward descent of the Capitoline Hill; they had set up a new stave of melody, in which her own soft voice, as well as the powerful sweetness of Miriam's, was sadly missed.

The door of the little courtyard had swung upon its hinges, and partly closed itself.

Hilda (whose native gentleness pervaded all her movements) was quietly opening it, when she was startled, midway, by the noise of a struggle within, beginning and ending all in one breathless moment. Along with it, or closely succeeding it, was a loud, fearful cry, which quivered upward through the air, and sank quivering downward to the earth. Then, a silence! Poor Hilda had looked into the courtyard, and saw the whole quick passage of a deed, which took but that little time to grave itself in the eternal adamant.[19]

Miriam's experience of the murder shifts rapidly from prospective dread to dream-like retrospection. There is no present—no *conscious* present, at any rate. But Donatello has read clearly what the eyes of Miriam were saying: "'What have you done?' said Miriam. . . . 'I did what ought to be done to a traitor!' he replied. 'I did what your eyes bade me do, when I asked them with mine, as I held the wretch over the precipice!'" (172). This interpretation of what Miriam's eyes "said" seems confirmed by the testimony, a little later, of Hilda:

"After the rest of the party had passed on, I went back to speak to you," she said; "for there seemed to be a trouble on your mind, and I wished to share it with you, if you could permit me. The door of the little courtyard was partly shut; but I pushed it open, and saw you within, and Donatello, and a third person, whom I had before noticed in the shadow of a niche. He approached you, Miriam! You knelt to him! I saw Donatello spring upon him! I would have shrieked; but my throat was dry! I would have rushed forward; but my limbs seemed rooted in the earth! It was all like a flash of lightning. A look passed from your eyes to Donatello's—a look—"

"Yes, Hilda, yes!" exclaimed Miriam, with intense eagerness. "Do not pause now! That look?"

"It revealed all your heart, Miriam!" continued Hilda, covering her eyes as if to shut out the recollection. "A look of hatred, triumph, vengeance, and, as it were, joy at some unhoped-for relief!"

"Ah, Donatello was right, then!" murmured Miriam. (209–210)

The scene of the murder is eclipsed, and filled in with interpretations. Miriam is right to wonder who was its cause—who was active and who passive, who dunnit, who was the agent. Her first question, "What have you done?" addressed to Donatello, implies that she sees *him* as the agent. But he responds, "I was not the agent—*you* were." And Hilda says she *saw* Miriam give the order. If a dream, according to Freud, is the fulfillment of an *unconscious* wish, could it have been visible in Miriam's eyes? Or did Donatello and Hilda *want* Miriam to be the agent of the crime? After all, it was only Miriam who had known the decedent, and both Donatello and Hilda might have wanted him out of the way. Donatello killed for love, removing a rival, but Hilda, too, might have wanted Miriam for herself—or wanted no one to complicate her farewell.

At any rate, in Hawthorne's *text* the agency of the deed is not given. This recalls to my mind two other scenes in which agency is eclipsed. One is the climactic scene between Dorothea and Ladislaw in *Middlemarch*. After hundreds of pages of restraint and misprision, we get this at the turning point: "It was never known which lips were the first to move towards the other lips; but they kissed tremblingly, and then they moved apart."[20] The other scene is closer to the one in Hawthorne but perhaps less well known. It is the scene in Nella Larsen's *Passing* when Clare Kendry either falls or is pushed from a high window. Irene Redfield, jealous and perhaps attracted to Clare, was standing next to her when her enraged husband, John Bellew, came into the room. "What happened next, Irene Redfield never afterwards allowed herself to remember. Never clearly. One moment Clare had been there, a vital glowing thing, like a flame of red and gold. The next she was gone."[21] The novel insists on this eclipse of agency, ending, with Irene down on the ground: "Her quaking knees gave way under her. She moaned and sank down, moaned again. Through the great heaviness that submerged and drowned her she was dimly conscious of strong arms lifting her up. Then everything was dark."[22] In 1971 Macmillan issued an edition of *Passing* in which those lines were succeeded by the following paragraph: "Centuries after, she heard the strange man saying: 'Death by misadventure, I'm inclined to believe. Let's go up and have another look at that window.'"[23]

In the case of both Hawthorne and Larsen, the motivation of the murder seems to be *unconscious:* its first manifestation is a problem with recollection. The deed seems to take but a moment, but it is as if someone infinite were keeping accounts. In one case, it is viewed from "centuries later," and in the other, it is engraved on the "eternal adamant." Adamant is a hard stone, but the word must have attracted Hawthorne for also being associated with strong emotions. In any case, what results is a graven image. Miriam's sin cannot be erased.

What are the ethical implications of this deed? It seems as if no one questions the guilt that binds Donatello together with Miriam. The question shifts, therefore, to Hilda. What is she to do with her guilty knowledge? "It seems a crime to know of such a thing, and to keep it to myself," laments Hilda.[24] Should she report the crime to the police? Only Hilda is free to be besieged with ethical questions. Only Hilda really has a choice.

The "thing"—*chose* or cause—on which the story turns morally is therefore not a substance. Everything points to desire—but someone else's. Donatello's eyes seek in Miriam's eyes the confirmation of an intention he has formed—for her. Hilda beholds in the exchange of glances between Miriam and Donatello an intimacy that leaves no room for others. Hilda's whiteness and purity, emphasized from the beginning, are her first concern. She is worried lest Miriam's sin has stained her purity in the moment of seeing it. Her first question, then, is whether the eyes have let in sin along with knowledge. She expels Miriam from her, but that doesn't restore her sinlessness.

It is easy to be annoyed with Hilda's concern for her purity. The question is whether Hawthorne sets her up as an ideal or an error. Herman Melville, in his "Hawthorne and His Mosses," formulated and created a "Hawthorne problem" that has haunted all later interpreters: "[Hawthorne's] great power of blackness . . . derives its force from its appeals to that Calvinistic sense of

Innate Depravity and Original Sin, from whose visitations, in some shape or other, no deeply thinking man is always wholly free."[25] But is Hawthorne's "Puritanism" religious, psychological, or aesthetic? In other works, Hawthorne tackles, in the midst of Puritan gloom, the harm done by Puritanism. He defends Hester in *The Scarlet Letter* against the town's condemnation, makes her work her "A" into a work of art, describes a whole moral mindset as belonging to the past, but nevertheless makes his novel out of the crushing weight of moral censure upon characters.

Art seems to be made out of sin, but the guilt of sin is in no way diminished thereby. And the question of what is inherited is tied, for Hawthorne, to his Puritan ancestors' persecution of Quakers for witchcraft. As Thomas Connolly says about "Young Goodman Brown," Hawthorne "weaves the themes of man's natural depravity and Hawthorne's ancestral witchcraft guilt into a rich fabric of fiction."[26] Thus the question of Donatello's ears and the question of Miriam's sin go together for Hawthorne—but not so much for *The Marble Faun*.

For Wendy Steiner, at least, Hilda has a central role to play in the Romance temptation. She represents the lure of an aesthetic illusion. Her purity is tied to an aesthetic of form and immobility; an aesthetic that does not admit experience:

> Even such a talented interpreter as Hilda tends to disjoin subjects from their histories. Miriam, observing the sensitivity of Hilda's copy of Guido's *Beatrice,* wonders whether the copy does not indicate a sympathy between Hilda and the wretched Beatrice. But Hilda answers, "I really had quite forgotten Beatrice's history, and was thinking of her only as the picture seems to reveal her character." Hilda's innocence lies in her "gifted simplicity of vision," the very faculty that makes her such a perfect copyist. . . . Innocence, like formalism, is a nonnarrative state.[27]

Steiner is not wrong to see in Hilda an aesthetic of statuesque form that excludes the temporality of life. The Parnassian ideal is also the Romance ideal, and all of Hawthorne's "novels" are called Romances. But the sight of the murder not only brings Hilda into narrative; it brings her into subjectivity. She can no longer so effortlessly serve the Masters she copies.

Once, "the girl was but a finer instrument, a more exquisitely effective piece of mechanism, by the help of which the spirit of some departed Painter now first achieved his ideal, centuries after his own earthly hand, that other tool, had turned to dust."[28] *But now,* whereas once her skill as a copyist lay in her transparency as a medium through which she could "channel" the Old Masters, now she finds herself less transparent and, therefore, more of an obstacle to their thought.

> Like all revelations of the better life, the adequate perception of a great work of art demands a gifted simplicity of vision. In this, and in her self-surrender, and the depth and tenderness of her sympathy, had lain Hilda's remarkable power as a copyist of the Old Masters. And now that her capacity of emotion was choked up with a horrible experience, it inevitably followed that she should seek in vain, among those Friends so venerated and beloved, for the marvels which they had heretofore shown her. In spite of a reverence that lingered longer than her recognition, their poor worshipper became almost an infidel, and sometimes doubted whether the pictorial art be not altogether a delusion.[29]

It is this loss of blankness that Hilda perceives as a stain, and of which she wishes to rid herself. Subjectivity, being oneself the obstacle to another's thought, is itself a sin. The contamination could not enter through the eyes if it were not reinforced by the understanding—conscious or unconscious. What Hilda fears and wants to get rid of is thus the suspicion that something *in her* is guilty. An article by T. Walter Herbert called "The Erotics of Purity: *The Marble Faun* and the Victorian Construction of Sexuality" spells out the double bind faced not so much by Hilda but by Ada Shephard, the governess of Hawthorne's daughters in Rome.[30] One of the daughters, Una, became very sick with malaria, which required regular visits from an Italian physician, Dr. Franco, who at the same time intensified his sexual pursuit of Shepherd. Because the role of women depended on their innate purity, Shepherd was appalled to discover that Dr. Franco's advances excited her. Any sexual response to another's lust gave proof of "sin," not purity. Any sexual encounter was therefore the *woman's* fault, even a rape. Shepherd did not tell the Hawthornes about her sexual assault, knowing that they would treat *her* with moral contempt. Herbert writes:

> The social reality established through the symbolic power of purity may thus be called hysterical; it is constituted by the not-knowing of what is known. . . . [T]he repression that enforces the not-knowing is activated in response to the forbidden impulse when it is felt to be present. An hysterical person thus does not know and feel what he knows and feels; the con-

tours of his conscious awareness bespeak an inward knowing of which he is ignorant.[31]

Another odd quirk of the Victorian mania for female purity was the number of Emperor's-New-Clothes-like statues or paintings or photographs of nude women with which they surrounded themselves. Protected by a veil of meaning, Victorian men could look at nude women as long as they liked. They could respond with unconscious eroticism, and know nothing about it. Herbert's primary example of this dynamic is the most famous statue by an American artist in the nineteenth century: Hiram Powers's *Greek Slave*. This statue, which featured a naked young woman in chains, toured the United States in the late 1840s and was exhibited in London's Crystal Palace in 1851. Not seeing what was clearly there in front of one had more than one advantage: not only did spectators see an image of white womanhood as purity but the statue also enabled them to pity Greek women in chains and not think of the enslaved black women in their midst. This was, of course, right before the Civil War. Not everyone seeing the statue was completely unaware of American slavery, however. Witness the following poem by Elizabeth Barrett Browning, written in 1850:

> They say Ideal Beauty cannot enter
> The house of anguish. On the threshold stands
> An alien image with enshackled hands,
> Called the Greek Slave! As if the artist meant her
> (That passionless perfection which he lent her,
> Shadowed not darkened where the sill expands)
> To so confront man's crimes in different lands
> With man's ideal sense. Pierce to the centre,
> Art's fiery finger, and break up ere long
> The serfdom of this world. Appeal, fair stone,
> From God's pure heights of beauty against man's wrong!
> Catch up in thy divine face, not alone
> East griefs but west, and strike and shame the strong,
> By thunders of white silence, overthrown.

Is Hilda afraid of adult sexuality? It could be that the guilty sight she saw was a sexual look between Miriam and Donatello. But in any case, she rejects *existing*. Becoming a subject means falling from an atemporal paradise into mortal experience. Donatello becomes more of a man, and Hilda seeks a way to return to virginity.[32]

Hilda's lodgings in Rome require her to keep a lamp lit at a shrine to the Virgin Mother. Early in the novel, Miriam asks Hilda whether she ever prays to the Virgin while tending her shrine. Hilda blushingly replies: "Sometimes I have been moved to do so. . . . She was a woman once" (69). Humanness is what unites Catholicism and Protestantism. But Rome is full of works of art inspired by Catholicism, which New Englanders equated with idolatry. Hawthorne is often berated for lacking appreciation for the tourist's view of the art that is available in Rome, but critics don't tend to factor in his resistance to Catholicism. After all, there were hundreds of years of religious wars fought over the difference between Catholics and Protestants. For a New England writer it must have been traumatic to suddenly be surrounded by art as the outcome of that "popery" so reviled by his Puritan ancestors. The character Kenyon marvels at the richness of cathedral walls, and the "holy emblems, such as Catholics judge it necessary to their devotion withal" (255), compared with New England's "formless mode of worship" (346). Forms versus formlessness: had Hawthorne the artist given his life to idolatry? And Hilda, whom Hawthorne always refers to as a New England girl, can that motherless child find comfort in Mary's embrace without also being attracted to Catholicism? "If she knelt—if she prayed—if her oppressed heart besought the sympathy of Divine Womanhood, afar in bliss, but not remote, because forever humanized by the memory of mortal griefs—was Hilda to be blamed? It was not a Catholic, kneeling at an idolatrous shrine, but a child, lifting its tear-stained face to seek comfort from a Mother!" (332).

In the mid-nineteenth century, the divide between Catholic and Protestant cultures springs not from the enormousness of the differences between the religions but from a sense of the incompatibility of their worlds. The writers from England and New England were united in their anti-Catholic feelings and in their Protestant origins. English stock on both sides of the Atlantic was still the dominant cultural force, which perhaps explains why, between two otherwise quite dissimilar cultures, novels like Charlotte Brontë's 1853 *Villette* and Hawthorne's 1860 *Marble Faun,* one finds surprising similarities. In both novels, a Protestant heroine seeks comfort in a Catholic confessional. In *Villette,* the first thing confessed by Lucy Snowe, who has written many pages about feeling out of place in French-speaking,

Catholic Villette, is "je suis Protestante!" In *The Marble Faun,* Hilda, seeing the solace on the faces of people exiting the confessional, and entering the booth marked PRO ANGLIA LINGUA, disburdens herself there of the story of the murder of Miriam's Model—until she is told by her confessor that the seal of the confessional only holds for Catholics, and that it is his duty to report the story to the authorities. But, he adds, she shouldn't feel responsible for any legal pursuit, because he suspects that, among those responsible for meting out justice, the story is already known. The confessor makes one more attempt to reel in a convert, but is rebuffed:

> "You have experienced some little taste of the relief and comfort, which the Church keeps abundantly in store for all its faithful children. Come home, dear child—poor wanderer, who hast caught a glimpse of the heavenly light—come home, and be at rest!"
>
> "Father," said Hilda. . . . "I dare not come a step farther than Providence shall guide me. Do not let it grieve you, therefore, if I never return to the Confessional, never dip my fingers in holy-water; never sign my bosom with the cross. I am a daughter of the Puritans." (362)

(The second surprising similarity between the two works is their preoccupation with Cleopatra—a painting in *Villette,* and a sculpture in *The Marble Faun.* The Egyptian queen represents, for the Victorians, the enigma of seductive, almost obscene, femininity, and also some kind of racial mixture. Writing during the heyday of Egyptomania, Hawthorne describes her "full Nubian lips" [129], while Brontë describes "this huge, dark-complexioned gipsy-queen."[33] Both authors know in vain that Cleopatra was a Ptolemy; the fascination or anxiety about miscegenation cannot help but make the Egyptian queen appear dark. Like Miriam, in fact, Cleopatra's parentage is uncertain; the text several times alludes to Miriam's Jewish ancestors, once hypothesizes Miriam's "drop of burning African blood" [23], and it is never known what kind of hold the Model has over her. All that is known is that Miriam is haunted by a past she cannot control, and in Victorian culture, a woman with a past is not pure.)

As soon as Hilda removes her "stain" by confessing what she witnessed, she is aware of the sacrifices that have sustained her purity. To keep contamination away, she has banished her dearest friend. "'Miriam loved me well,' thought Hilda remorsefully, 'and I failed her at her sorest need!!'" (386).

Hilda thus faces an ethical dilemma: to constantly maintain her isolated purity or to abandon the frantic cleansing of her image and give herself to relationships. She must choose between concern for her own perfection and love for her friend. That is, concern for her *image* and interaction with the other. The time when the friend most needs support may be when she seems to sin the most. The sculptural ideal is incompatible with interaction: one must be ready to lose not only perfection but also the self as an ethical *image* if one is to act truly ethically.

Epilogue

The question of things turns out to be a question of things *for people*. This book has been less interested in why, as a bumper sticker has it, "He who has the most toys when he dies wins," and more interested in how the dynamics of identification and idealization are mediated by people's relations to things. It is a question, in other words, of psychology (that is, rhetoric) rather than economics. Although one can never be sure where the separation might lie.

My interest in this topic was doubtless piqued by Paul de Man's repeated and somehow necessary encounters with something inanimate at the heart of what we think is ourselves. Whether it is Milton's line on Shakespeare— "doth make us marble with too much conceiving"—or his conviction that, at the bottom of language, there is something "inhuman," non-life seems to lie behind what is considered most deeply human. And yet, witness the use of the word "human" in the following exchange:

> *Meyer Abrams:* I want to go back to the question that Neil, Professor Neil
> Hertz, raised about language being somehow opposed to the human.

. what about beyond language?

And the grounds on which one makes such a claim. I want to do what I
did yesterday. . .

De Man: Sure.

Abrams: . . . not to oppose your claim, not even to complement it, but simply to provide a different perspective, just so we can settle the matter in
another way. And that perspective won't surprise you because you've
heard it before and expect it from me.

De Man: That's very human.[1]

This reply uses the word "human" in its colloquial sense of "dear" or "under-
standable." It implies a recognition of foibles or characteristics that make
human beings dearer, and are considered beyond the ken of a machine.
"*Very* human" is the way in which value inheres in what makes people other
than things. Used in this way, the word puts de Man squarely in the tradition he is questioning.

But nevertheless, de Man goes on to argue that the "folk" understanding
of language puts the "human" in question:

Abrams: Suppose I should say, as many people have said before me, that instead of being the nonhuman, language is the most human of all the
things we find in the world. In that language is entirely the product of
human beings. . . . [A]ll I want to do is present the humanistic perspective, as an alternative, which appeals to me. Instinctively, it appeals to
me.

De Man: Well, it appeals to me also, greatly; and there is no question of its
appeal, and its desirability. . . . [But it is said that] language is not human, it is God-given: it is the logos . . . this whole notion of language as
natural process, versus language as divinely revealed . . . indicates a constant problem about the nature of language as being either human or
nonhuman. That there is a nonhuman aspect of language is a perennial
awareness from which we cannot escape, because language does things
which are so radically out of our control that they cannot be assimilated
to the human at all. . . . Things happen in the world which cannot be ac-
counted for in terms of the human conception of language.[2]

There are two aspects of this discussion that are important for our purposes.
One is that the non-human is as likely to involve the divine as the mechanical. Hence the fascination with statues coming alive, or the animation of

[handwritten margin notes:]
"Very human"
Humanism of Language
Historical Debate on Language as Natural or Divine (Logos) is indicative of tension in the nature of language

"god-bodies."[2] The other is that *things happen in the world* that seem willed, but not by humans. The human is in the realm of desire ("there is no question of its desirability"), and the non-human lies somewhere beyond the pleasure principle. Whether what happens is caused by God or by the rules of a language, something is willing things that is not human.

Paul de Man always fascinated people when he quoted a passage about digging up a statue, as he does with the epigraph by Thomas Hardy to "Shelley Disfigured": "While digging in the grounds for the new foundation, the broken fragments of a marble statue were unearthed. They were submitted to various antiquaries, who said that, so far as the damaged pieces would allow them to form an opinion, the statue seemed to be that of a mutilated Roman satyr, or, if not, an allegorical figure of Death. Only one or two old inhabitants guessed whose statue those fragments had composed."[3] This passage contains many narrative enticements—which won't be followed up. Already the reader has been put in a receptive mood, though, by expecting an analysis of Shelley's "The Triumph of Life" and thinking about Shelley's untimely death. But the uncanniness of digging in the ground—will one find a corpse or a treasure?—always grabs readers. Even writers with very different projects—a book on the Renaissance called *Unearthing the Past,* for instance—make use of the same figure.[4] Digging shows up prominently in the Henry James story that Hillis Miller devotes considerable time to. But no matter how hard he tries to become a faithful follower of de Man, Miller always moves to the positive side of the fantasy, calling his book *Versions of Pygmalion.*[5] De Man seems to be one of the few people for whom the idea remains unredemptive.

While Paul de Man is using the non-human—God or the thing—to de-idealize the human, Jacques Lacan, as we have seen, considers the non-human as the very basis for selfhood. In his essay "The Mirror Stage," he speaks as though the self *needs* its "armour of alienating identity" to become human. The self then suffers from the gap between its trembling or flawed self and the ideal self it has perceived in the mirror. His suffering comes from the *failure to become a thing.* The kind of stasis that only a thing can have becomes a perfection the human being will never achieve—life itself becomes a flaw the human being strives to deny.

The combination of these two ideas—thing as demystification versus thing as ideal—in not being *entirely* contradictory but seeming so, poses a challenge this book has tried to tackle. The more I thought about this topic,

×it reassures us and simultaneously, as Cortazar puts it, creates a ful....

or the utopic impulse, that if it were to be actualized would be a dystopic hell. to be truly above.

232   *Epilogue*

Problem of
inter-personal
relations...

the more it seemed to me that people *wanted* other people to be things so
that they could be dealt with. In other words, it is treating other people as
things that we normally do, and that reassures us. But that still leaves treating other people as people in the realm of the unknown. Grammar is no
help here, and may reinforce the problem: wherever the subject looks, he
sees only objects. A book called *Persons and Things* implies that there is a difference, even an opposition. But what if things are all we know? If we consider ourselves persons, then the relation between persons and things can
contain only one person, and the problem of treating persons as persons becomes one of having a person come face to face with another person.

This book offers no help in treating persons as persons, but it does explore the richness of a human being's relation to things. Although often
hotly denied, people's relations with things contain or embody the hopes
and fears they think belong to their relations with people. It is by studying
the complexity of those relations that I have hoped to shed light on the "human"—even when there is *nothing* where the "thing" is presumed to be.

* what if persons (subjects) are exactly — the uknown?

Notes

1. Toys R Us

1. Emile Benveniste, *Problems in General Linguistics,* trans. Mary Elizabeth Meek (Coral Gables, FL: University of Miami Press, 1971), 217.

2. *American Heritage Dictionary,* 3rd ed. (Boston: Houghton Mifflin, 1992). *Princeton Encyclopedia of Poetry and Poetics* (Princeton, NJ: Princeton University Press, 1974).

3. Paul de Man, "Lyrical Voice in Contemporary Theory: Riffaterre and Jauss," in *Lyric Poetry: Beyond New Criticism,* ed. Chaviva Hošek and Patricia Parker (Ithaca: Cornell University Press, 1985), 61.

4. Stéphane Mallarmé, "Crise de vers," in Mallarmé, *Oeuvres complètes,* ed. Henri Mondor and G. Jean-Aubry (Paris: Gallimard, 1945), 364; translation and italics mine.

5. S. T. Coleridge, "The Eolian Harp," in *The Portable Coleridge,* ed. I. A. Richards (New York: Viking, 1950), 66.

6. Jonathan Culler, *The Pursuit of Signs* (Ithaca: Cornell University Press, 1981), 135.

7. Ibid.

8. Jean-Jacques Rousseau, *Essay on the Origin of Languages,* trans. John H.

Moran, in Moran, ed., *On the Origin of Language* (Chicago: University of Chicago Press, 1966), 22.

9. William Wordsworth, *Poetry and Prose* (Cambridge, MA: Harvard University Press, 1963), 616.

10. Emily Dickinson, *The Complete Poems* (Boston: Little, Brown, 1960), 216.

11. Audre Lorde, *The Collected Poems of Audre Lorde* (New York: Norton, 1997), 409.

12. Toni Morrison, *Beloved* (New York: Knopf, 1987), 4–5.

13. Paul de Man, "Autobiography as De-facement," in *The Rhetoric of Romanticism* (New York: Columbia University Press, 1984), 76.

14. Samuel Johnson, *The Major Works* (Oxford: Oxford University Press, 1984), 96.

15. Wordsworth, *Poetry and Prose,* 605.

16. De Man, "Autobiography as De-facement," 55.

17. Dickinson, *Complete Poems.*

18. John Berryman, *The Dream Songs* (New York: Farrar, Straus and Giroux, 1969), vi.

19. Alice Walker, *The Color Purple* (New York: Harcourt Brace Jovanovich, 1982), 165–167.

20. *American Heritage Dictionary,* s.v. "personification."

21. Karl Marx, *Capital,* vol. 1, in *Marx-Engels Reader* (New York: Norton, 1978), 320.

22. Walter Benjamin, *The Arcades Project* (Cambridge, MA: Harvard University Press, 1999).

23. *A Dictionary of Marxist Thought,* ed. Tom Bottomore (Cambridge, MA: Harvard University Press, 1983).

24. Walter Benjamin, letter to Max Horkheimer, in *The Correspondence of Walter Benjamin,* trans. Manfred R. Jacobson and Evelyn M. Jacobson, ed. Gershom Scholem and Theodor W. Adorno (Chicago: University of Chicago Press, 1994).

25. Benjamin, *Arcades Project,* 864.

26. Aimé Césaire, *Discourse on Colonialism,* trans. Joan Pinkham (New York: Monthly Review Press, 1972), 21.

2. The Poetics of Things

1. Marianne Moore, *The Complete Poems* (New York: Macmillan/Viking, 1967), 84.

2. Francis Ponge, *Le parti pris des choses* (Paris: Gallimard, 1942), 43.

3. Francis Ponge, *The Voice of Things,* trans. Beth Archer (New York: McGraw-Hill, 1972), 37.

4. *Entretiens de Francis Ponge avec Philippe Sollers* (Paris: Gallimard/Seuil, 1972), 112. Translations from the interview are my own.

5. Ibid., 110.

6. Ibid., 114.

3. Monuments

1. Sylvia Plath, *The Collected Poems* (New York: Harper and Row Publishers, 1981), 129.

2. Paul de Man, *The Rhetoric of Romanticism* (New York: Columbia University Press, 1984), 78.

3. Gwendolyn Brooks, *The Black Poets* (New York: Bantam Books, 1972), 169.

4. Elizabeth Bishop, "The Monument," *The Complete Poems, 1927–1979* (New York: Farrar, Straus and Giroux, 1983), 23.

5. It is interesting that these two marvels of the modern world (of 1886), these two functionless monuments that people love to hate, the Eiffel Tower and the Statue of Liberty, have become the symbols of their cities for tourists, and the basis of the most extravagant kitsch in the world.

6. Marina Warner, *Monuments and Maidens* (New York: Atheneum, 1985), 7.

7. Plath, *Collected Poems,* 129.

8. Ibid., 158–159.

9. It is no longer possible for visitors to climb the stairway inside the statue.

10. Warner, *Monuments and Maidens,* 3.

11. This is the ideology, not always the reality.

4. Ego Sum Game

1. Heinz Kohut, *The Analysis of the Self* (New York: International Universities Press, 1983), xv.

2. Ovid, *Metamorphoses,* trans. Frank Justus Miller, Loeb Classical Library (Cambridge, MA: Harvard University Press, 1971), 154–155.

3. René Descartes, "Second Meditation," in Descartes, *Philosophical Essays* (Indianapolis: Bobbs Merrill, 1964), 82.

4. Ibid., 89.

5. Jacques Lacan, "Le stade du miroir comme formateur de la function du *Je* telle qu'elle nous est révélée dans l'expérience psychanalytique," in Lacan, *Ecrits* (Paris: Editions du Seuil, 1966), 93.

6. Jacques Lacan, "The Mirror Stage as Formative of the Function of the *I* as Revealed in Psychoanalytic Experience," in Lacan, *Ecrits: A Selection,* trans. Alan Sheridan (New York: W. W. Norton, 1977), 1.

7. In Jacques Lacan, *L'éthique de la psychanalyse, 1959–1960,* ed. Jacques-Alain Miller (Paris: Editions du Seuil, 1986); *The Ethics of Psychoanalysis,* trans. with notes by Dennis Porter (New York: Norton, 1992).

8. Sylvia Plath, "Edge," in Plath, *The Collected Poems* (New York: Harper and Row Publishers, 1981).

9. *Le roman de la rose,* 112, line 1568.

10. Heinrich von Kleist, *An Abyss Deep Enough: Letters of Heinrich von Kleist, with a Selection of Essays and Anecdotes,* ed., trans., and introduction by Phillip B. Miller (New York: Dutton, 1982), 214–215.

5. They Urn It

1. Martin Heidegger, "The Origin of the Work of Art," in Heidegger, *Poetry, Language, and Thought,* trans. Albert Hofstadter (New York: Harper and Row, 1971), 23–24.

2. Ibid., 18.

3. Ibid., 29.

4. Martin Heidegger, "The Thing," in Heidegger, *Poetry, Language, and Thought,* trans. Albert Hofstadter (New York: Harper and Row, 1971), 166–169.

5. Heidegger, "Origin of the Work of Art," 71, footnote by Hofstadter: "Thrownness, *Geworfenheit,* is understood in *Being and Time* as an existential characteristic of *Dasein,* human being, its thatness, its 'that it is,' and it refers to the facticity of human being's being handed over to itself, its being on its own responsibility; as long as human being is what it is, it is thrown, cast, 'im Wurf.'"

6. G. E. Lessing, *Laocoön,* trans. Edward Allen McCormick (Baltimore: Johns Hopkins University Press, 1984), 17.

7. On Van Gogh's painting of shoes, in Heidegger, "Origin of the Work of Art."

8. Immanuel Kant, *Critique of Judgement* (New York: Hafner, 1951), 73.

9. Ibid., 65.

10. Heidegger, "The Thing," 173.

11. Stéphane Mallarmé, "La fausse entrée des sorcières dans *Macbeth,*" in Mallarmé, *Oeuvres complètes* (Paris: Pléiade, 1945), 351. "The curtain goes up simply a minute too soon, betraying fateful agencies" (translation mine).

12. Jon Stallworthy, "Versification," in Alexander W. Allison, ed., *The Norton Anthology of Poetry,* 3rd ed. (New York: Norton, 1983), 1405.

13. Frank Lentriccia, *Critical Terms for Literary Study* (Chicago: University of Chicago Press, 1995), 439.

14. Jacques Derrida, *The Ear of the Other,* trans. Peggy Kamuf and Avital Ronell, ed. Christie McDonald (New York: Schocken, 1985), 33.

15. Shakespeare, *Hamlet,* I.v, lines 59–67.

16. Carolyn Forché, *The Country between Us* (New York: Harper and Row, 1981), 16.

17. Elizabeth Cropper, "On Beautiful Women, Parmigianino, *Petrarchismo,* and the Vernacular Style," *Art Bulletin* 58, no. 3 (1999): 376–377.

18. Kant, *Critique of Judgement.*

19. Heidegger, "Origin of the Work of Art," 21.

20. Shakespeare, *Hamlet,* III.ii, lines 112–121.

21. Ann Petry, *The Street* (Boston: Beacon Press, 1974), 235.

22. Ovid, *Metamorphoses,* trans. Frank Justus Miller, Loeb Classical Library (Cambridge, MA: Harvard University Press, 1971), 41.

23. Jorie Graham, "Self-Portrait as Apollo and Daphne," in *Dream of the Unified Field* (Hopewell, NJ: Ecco Press, 1995), 70–73.

24. Peter Sacks, *The English Elegy* (Baltimore: Johns Hopkins University Press, 1985), 4–5.

25. Christopher Braider, *Apollonian Eros and the Fruits of Failure in the Poetic Pursuit of Being* (Netherlands: Kluwer, 1990), 325.

26. Rachilde, *The Juggler,* trans. Melanie C. Hawthorne (New Brunswick, NJ: Rutgers University Press, 1990), 18. The play on words, in English, that makes the "jug" into a "juggler" is not, alas, present in Rachilde's *Jongleuse* or in Heidegger's *Krug.*

27. Ibid., 20–23.

28. Ibid., 21.

29. Anne Sexton, *The Complete Poems* (Boston: Houghton Mifflin, 1981), 17.

30. Sylvia Plath, *The Collected Poems* (New York: Harper and Row, 1981), 81–82.

6. Puppets and Prostheses

1. Heinrich von Kleist, "Über das Marionettentheater," in Kleist, *An Abyss Deep Enough: A Selection of Essays and Anecdotes,* trans. Philip Miller (New York: Dutton, 1982), 211.

2. Ibid., 214.

3. Quoted in Harold B. Segal, *Pinocchio's Progeny: Puppets, Marionnettes, Automatons, and Robots in Modernist and Avante-garde Drama* (Baltimore: Johns Hopkins University Press, 1995), 100.

4. Ibid., 81.

5. Sigmund Freud, "The Uncanny," in Freud, *The Standard Edition of the Complete Psychological Works,* ed. James Strachey (London: Hogarth, 1917–1919), vol. 17, 240–241.

6. Victoria Nelson, *The Secret Life of Puppets* (Cambridge, MA: Harvard University Press, 2001), 30–31.

7. Kleist, "Über das Marionettentheater," 216.

8. Edward Gordon Craig, "The Actor and the Über-marionette," in Craig, *On the Art of the Theatre* (Chicago: Browne's Bookstore, 1911), 56.

9. Quoted in Segal, *Pinocchio's Progeny,* 48.

10. Kleist, "Über das Marionettentheater," 214.

11. David Wills, *Prosthesis* (Stanford: Stanford University Press, 1995), xx.

12. Ibid.

13. Ibid., 10.

14. Ibid., 3.

15. E. T. A. Hoffmann, *The Best Tales of Hoffmann,* trans. E. F. Bleiler (New York: Dover, 1967), 212.

16. Ernest Jones, *The Life and Work of Sigmund Freud,* one-volume edition (New York: Basic Books, 1961), 443.

17. Herman Melville, *Moby-Dick,* Norton Critical Edition (New York: Norton, 1967), 160–162.

18. Charles Dickens, *Our Mutual Friend* (New York: Modern Library, 1960), 46.

19. Ibid., 48.

7. Using People

1. See Emmanuel Levinas, *Ethics and Infinity,* trans. Richard A. Cohen (Pittsburgh, PA: Duquesne University Press, 1985). Levinas himself avoids thus grounding ethics in *restraint* by defining the subject not in isolation but always in relation to the Other, for whom and to whom the subject is responsible, without any prior intactness or guarantee. My quarrel here is more with a sort of "Levinas effect" than with any particular writing, whether by Levinas or others.

2. Immanuel Kant, *Critique of Practical Reason,* trans. Lewis White Beck (London: Macmillan, 1956), 136.

3. Heinz Kohut, *The Analysis of the Self* (New York: International Universities Press, 1971), 33.

4. To give you an idea of the horror of a transitional object that *would* be a mirror double, I refer you to My Twinn, a company that makes dolls "individually crafted to look like your daughter," now available online. The proud parent is invited to choose among skin tones, eye colors, hair color and style, and to diagram birthmarks, moles, and freckles. Renaissance blazons that dismembered the female body were nothing compared to this parental dissection and commodification of the living child. Suppose the girl gets one for her birthday, and the dog eats it? Wouldn't the doll require a kind of protection that is the very model for enslavement to the ideal *I?* As if the daughter does not have enough trouble with the mirror stage, she must be haunted by this Dorian Gray–like perfect unchanging object as she herself grows up, gets pimples, falls into puberty.

5. D. W. Winnicott, *Playing and Reality* (London: Tavistock, 1971), xi–xii. Page numbers in parentheses refer to this volume.

6. Immanuel Kant, *Foundation of the Metaphysics of Morals,* Section 1, footnote.

7. "Summary of Special Qualities in the Relationship," in Winnicott, *Playing and Reality,* 5.

8. Kant, *Critique of Practical Reason,* 89.

9. Ibid.

10. For an excellent feminist critique of Winnicott's image of motherhood, see

Carolyn Dever, *Death and the Mother from Dickens to Freud* (Cambridge: Cambridge University Press, 1998), chap. 2, "Psychoanalytic Cannibalism."

8. Romancing the Stone

1. "The imagination, supplying what is missing, adds to the beauty that remains a certain amount of beauty it hypothesizes. When the object is whole, it gives the mind something finished. That's all there is." Many details of this story are taken from the unpublished dissertation of Matthew Gumpert, Harvard University.

2. Many details of this story come from the unpublished dissertation of Noah Heringman, Harvard University; the *Guardian* (March 10, 1994); and the *New York Times* (February 5, 1998), A1.

3. Théophile Gautier, *Mademoiselle de Maupin,* trans. Joanna Richardson (Harmondsworth, England: Penguin, 1981), 142.

4. Ovid, *Metamorphoses,* trans. Frank Justus Miller, Loeb Classical Library (Cambridge, MA: Harvard University Press, 1971), vol. 2, 83.

5. Ibid., 85.

6. Paul de Man, *The Rhetoric of Romanticism* (New York: Columbia University Press, 1984), 78.

7. Charles Baudelaire on Théophile Gautier, in *Oeuvres complètes* (Paris: Pléiade, 1976), vol. 2, 114 (translation mine).

8. Ibid., 113.

9. Gautier, *Mademoiselle de Maupin,* 39.

10. Sylvia Plath, *The Collected Poems* (New York: Harper and Row, 1981), 272. Plath's "Symphony in White Major" is called "Moonrise" and concerns not blushing but pregnancy. The arrival of a baby is described as a "New statue. / In a drafty museum" (157), while a "Barren Woman" is a "museum without statues" (157). "Moonrise" is about mulberries ripening, turning from white to red. There are at least two uses of the word "white" for every three lines. The poem ends: "The berries purple / And bleed. The white stomach may ripen yet." Achieving sexual reproduction and achieving sexual responsiveness may be very different, but infusing red into a white statue is the starting point of each. Another study of whiteness is Plath's poem "In Plaster," where whiteness stands for perfection and death, while color stands for imperfection and life.

11. Rachilde, *The Juggler,* trans. Melanie C. Hawthorne (New Brunswick, NJ: Rutgers University Press, 1990), 10. Wilhelm Jensen, *Gradiva, and Delusion and Dream in Wilhelm Jensen's Gradiva,* trans. Helen M. Downey, one-volume edition (Los Angeles: Sun and Moon Press, 1993), 29.

12. Charles Baudelaire, *The Parisian Prowler,* trans. Edward K. Kaplan (Athens: University of Georgia Press, 1989), 11.

13. Personal communication.

14. Henry James, "The Last of the Valerii," in *The Complete Tales of Henry James,* ed. Leon Edel (Philadelphia: J. B. Lippincott Company, 1962), vol. 3, 122.

15. Villiers de l'Isle-Adam, *Eve of the Future Eden,* trans. Marilyn Gaddis Rose (Lawrence, KS: Coronado Press, 1981), 31ff.

16. Nathaniel Hawthorne, *The Marble Faun* (New York: Penguin, 1990), 120.

9. Surmounted Beliefs

1. Charles Baudelaire, "The Vampire," in *The Flowers of Evil,* trans. James McGowan (New York: Oxford University Press, 1993), 65.

2. Ibid., 155, 157.

3. Leopold von Sacher-Masoch, *Venus in Furs,* in *Masochism: "An Interpretation of Coldness and Cruelty," by Gilles Deleuze, Together with the Entire Text of "Venus in Furs," by Leopold von Sacher-Masoch* (New York: Zone Books, 1991; orig. pub. Braziller, 1971), 145.

4. Frederick Douglass, *My Bondage and My Freedom* (Chicago: University of Illinois Press, 1987), 146–147.

5. Charles Baudelaire, "Salon de 1846," in *Oeuvres complètes* (Paris: Gallimard, 1976), vol. 2, 487.

6. Karl Marx, *The Marx-Engels Reader,* ed. Robert C. Tucker (New York: Norton, 1978), 98–99 (manuscripts of 1844).

7. Sigmund Freud, *The Standard Edition of the Complete Psychological Works of Sigmund Freud,* ed. James Strachey (London: Hogarth Press, 1953–1974), vol. 7, 153.

8. William Pietz, "The Problem of the Fetish: I," *Res* 9 (Spring 1985), 5.

9. Karl Marx, *Capital* (New York: International Publishers, 1967), vol. 1, 72.

10. Freud, *Complete Psychological Works,* vol. 21, 152–153.

11. Jacques Lacan, *Ecrits: A Selection,* trans. Alan Sheridan (New York: W. W. Norton, 1977), 290.

12. Walter Benjamin, *The Arcades Project,* trans. Howard Eiland and Kevin McLaughlin (Cambridge, MA: Belknap Press of Harvard University Press, 1999), 55.

13. Walter Benjamin, letter to Max Horkheimer (April 16, 1938), in *The Correspondence of Walter Benjamin,* trans. Manfred R. Jacobson and Evelyn M. Jacobson, ed. Gershom Scholem and Theodor W. Adorno (Chicago: University of Chicago Press, 1994), 557.

14. Benjamin, *Arcades Project.*

15. Sigmund Freud, *Delusion and Dream in Wilhelm Jensen's Gradiva,* in Wilhelm Jensen, *Gradiva, and Delusion and Dream in Wilhelm Jensen's Gradiva,* trans. Helen M. Downey, one-volume edition (Los Angeles: Sun and Moon Press, 1993), 173–174.

16. Ibid., 163.

17. Wilhelm Jensen, *Gradiva,* in *Gradiva, and Delusion and Dream in Wilhelm Jensen's Gradiva,* trans. Helen M. Downey (Los Angeles: Sun and Moon Press, 1993), 33–34.

18. Freud, *Delusion and Dream in Wilhelm Jensen's Gradiva,* 174.

19. Ibid., 201.

20. Ibid., 122.

21. Ibid., 123.

22. Jensen, *Gradiva,* 117–118.

23. Freud, *Delusion and Dream in Wilhelm Jensen's Gradiva,* 242.

10. Artificial Life

1. *Boston Globe,* February 17, 1996.

2. Richard Powers, "A Game We Couldn't Lose," *New York Times,* February 18, 1996.

3. Bruce Weber, "Computer's Ability against Chess Champion Has Surprised and Intrigued," *New York Times,* February 18, 1996.

4. Quoted in Bruce Weber, "A Mean Chess-Playing Computer Tears at the Meaning of Thought," *New York Times,* February 19, 1996.

5. Sherry Turkle, *Life on the Screen* (New York: Simon and Schuster, 1995), 105. The section including ELIZA is called, incidentally, "The New Pygmalion."

6. E. W. Bonabeau and G. Theraulaz, "Why Do We Need Artificial Life?" in Christopher G. Langton, ed., *Artificial Life: An Overview* (Cambridge, MA: MIT Press, 1995), 322.

7. T. S. Ray, "An Evolutionary Approach to Synthetic Biology: Zen and the Art of Creating Life," in Langton, *Artificial Life,* 192.

8. Adapted from Langton, *Artificial Life,* and from Claus Emmeche, *The Garden in the Machine: The Emerging Science of Artificial Life,* trans. Steven Sampson (Princeton, NJ: Princeton University Press, 1994).

9. Emmeche, *The Garden in the Machine,* viii.

10. Mary Shelley, *Frankenstein* (New York: W. W. Norton, 1996), 29.

11. Turkle, *Life on the Screen,* 136.

12. Gareth Cook, "Making Sense: Robot Research Eyes Emotion," *Boston Globe,* April 30, 2001.

13. See Philip Fisher, *Hard Facts: Setting and Form in the American Novel* (New York: Oxford University Press, 1985), esp. 87–127 (chap. 2, "Making a Thing into a Man").

11. Real Dolls

1. Sigmund Freud, *The Standard Edition of the Complete Psychological Works of Sigmund Freud,* ed. James Strachey (London: Hogarth Press, 1953–1974), vol. 17, 233.

2. Terry Castle, *The Female Thermometer: Eighteenth-Century Culture and the Invention of the Uncanny* (New York: Oxford University Press, 1995), 10.

3. This was still an aesthetic commonplace in Yeats's day, as witness the following part of his poem "Upon a Dying Lady" (the section is entitled "Certain Artists Bring Her Dolls and Drawings"):

> Bring where our Beauty lies
> A new modeled doll, or drawing;
> With a friend's or an enemy's
> Features, or maybe showing
> Her features when a tress
> Of dull red hair was flowing
> Over some silken dress
> Cut in the Turkish fashion,
> Or, it may be, like a boy's.
> We have given the world our passion,
> We have nought for death but toys.

4. See, for example, Elisabeth Bronfen, *Over Her Dead Body: Death, Femininity and the Aesthetic* (New York: Routledge, 1992).

5. Bella English, "Fenway-Bound? Take a Hatpin," *Boston Globe,* June 19, 1991, 21.

6. Jill Goldsmith, "A $2 Billion Doll Celebrates Her 40th without a Wrinkle," *Boston Globe,* February 10, 1999.

7. M. G. Lord, *Forever Barbie: The Unauthorized Biography of a Real Doll* (New York: William Morrow, 1994).

8. Ann Ducille, "Dyes and Dolls: Multicultural Barbie and the Merchandizing of Difference," *Differences* 6, no. 1 (1994): 46–67.

9. See, for example, Maya Angelou, *I Know Why the Caged Bird Sings* (Toronto: Bantam, 1969), 1.

10. Toni Morrison, *The Bluest Eye,* in Sandra Gilbert and Susan Gubar, eds., *The Norton Anthology of Literature by Women* (New York: Norton, 1985), 2076–2077.

11. Angelou, *I Know Why the Caged Bird Sings,* 43–44.

12. Ibid., 2.

13. Ducille, "Dyes and Dolls," 65.

12. Animation

1. Ann Ducille, "Dyes and Dolls: Multicultural Barbie and the Merchandizing of Difference," *Differences* 6, no. 1 (1994): 66.

2. Nadar (Félix Tournachon), quoted in Walter Benjamin, *The Arcades Project* (Cambridge, MA: Harvard University Press, 1999), 673–674.

3. *New York Times,* Saturday, October 17, 1992.

4. Peter Watson, "Aladdin Is Not an Actor," *New York Times,* February 15, 1993, A15.

5. Ibid.

6. Villiers de l'Isle-Adam, *L'Eve future* (Paris: José Cortí, 1987), 16; translation mine.

7. Ibid., 18, translation mine.

8. Christopher G. Langton, ed., *Artificial Life: An Overview* (Cambridge, MA: MIT Press, 1995), xi.

9. Mary Shelley, *Frankenstein* (New York: W. W. Norton, 1996), 17.

10. See ibid., 146: "Are you mad, my friend? Or whither does your senseless curiosity lead you?"

13. Face Value

1. Roland Barthes, *Mythologies,* trans. Annette Lavers (New York: Hill and Wang, 1972), 56–57.

2. M. G. Lord, *Forever Barbie: The Unauthorized Biography of a Real Doll* (New York: William Morrow, 1994), 73.

3. Terry Landau, *About Faces* (New York: Doubleday, 1989), 31.

4. The title of this chapter, "Face Value," in fact alludes to a play written, but never officially released, by David Henry Huang soon after his success with *M. Butterfly,* that chews over the links between this sense of "face" and racial traits.

5. Paul de Man, "Autobiography as De-facement," in *The Rhetoric of Romanticism* (New York: Columbia University Press, 1981), 81.

6. Ibid., 76.

7. See Jacques Lacan's discussion of the circles on the wings of a moth as a false face.

8. Cecile Pineda, *Face* (New York: Penguin Books, 1985), 70.

9. Audre Lorde, *The Cancer Journals* (Argyle, NY: Spinsters, Ink, 1980), 42.

10. Charles Siebert, "The Cuts That Go Deeper," *New York Times Magazine,* July 7, 1996, 22.

11. Emile Benveniste, *Problems in General Linguistics,* trans. Mary Elizabeth Meek (Coral Gables, FL: University of Miami Press, 1971), 217.

12. The idea for this discussion came from Richard Moran, "Interpretation Theory and the First Person," *Philosophical Quarterly* 44, no. 175 (1994): 154–173.

13. Emmanuel Levinas, *Ethics and Infinity,* trans. Richard A. Cohen (Pittsburgh, PA: Duquesne University Press, 1985), 86.

14. According to Jonathan Kirsch, the tradition of representing Moses with horns

comes from a mistranslation of this "divine radiation burn." See Jonathan Kirsch, *Moses* (New York: Ballantine, 1998), 5.

14. Anthropomorphism in Lyric and Law

1. I am thinking of Richard Posner, *Law and Literature* (Cambridge, MA: Harvard University Press, 1988); Richard Weisberg, *The Failure of the Word: The Protagonist as Lawyer in Modern Fiction* (New Haven, CT: Yale University Press, 1984); and other works. But for a legal approach that *does* address poetry, see the interesting discussion of Wallace Stevens in Thomas Grey, "Steel against Intimidation: The Motive for Metaphor in Wallace Stevens, Esq." *Yale Journal of Law and the Humanities* 2, no. 2 (Summer 1990): 231, as well as the more extended treatment of Wallace Stevens in Thomas Grey, *The Wallace Stevens Case: Law and the Practice of Poetry* (Cambridge, MA: Harvard University Press, 1991).

2. William Wordsworth's sonnet "Nuns Fret Not at Their Convent's Narrow Room" contains the lines, "In truth the prison, into which we doom / Ourselves, no prison is: and hence for me, / In sundry moods, 'twas pastime to be bound / Within the Sonnet's scanty plot of ground." *The Selected Poetry and Prose of Wordsworth,* ed. Geoffrey H. Hartman (New York: Signet, 1970), 169.

3. John Keats's sonnet on the sonnet begins, "If by dull rhymes our English must be chained, / And, like Andromeda, the sonnet sweet / Fettered." *The Selected Poetry of Keats,* ed. Paul de Man (New York: New American Library, Signet Classic, 1966), 264.

4. One of several poems by Baudelaire entitled "Spleen" describes a mood produced by or analogized to a rainy day: "Quand la pluie étalant ses immenses traînées / D'une vaste prison imite les barreaux" (When the rain imitates the bars of a vast prison, spreading its huge drifts [translation mine]). Charles Baudelaire, *Oeuvres complètes,* vol. 1 (Paris: Pleiade, 1975), 75.

5. For a suggestive discussion of what it means for a text to obey the law of genre, see Jacques Derrida, "The Law of Genre," in Derrida, *Acts of Literature,* ed. Derek Attridge (New York: Routledge, 1992).

6. Paul de Man, "Anthropomorphism and Trope in the Lyric," in de Man, *The Rhetoric of Romanticism* (New York: Columbia University Press, 1984). Page numbers in parentheses refer to this essay.

7. *United States Law Week* 61, no. 25 (January 12, 1993).

8. The allusion to Keats's "Ode on a Grecian Urn" stands in for the premise of the compatibility of literary aesthetics with linguistic structures, and of linguistic structures with perceptual or intuitive knowledge, that de Man is often at pains to contest. See his remarks on the pedagogical model of the *trivium* in the titular essay in *The Resistance to Theory* (Minneapolis: University of Minnesota Press, 1986). Friedrich Nietzsche, "Truth and Falsity in an Ultramoral [*sic*] Sense," trans. Mazemilian A. Mügge, in Hazard Adams, ed., *Critical Theory since Plato,* rev. ed.

(Forth Worth: Harcourt Brace Jovanovich College Publishers, 1992; orig. pub. 1971), 634–639. If the Keats poem stands as the claim that aesthetic and epistemological structures are compatible, Nietzsche's text, for de Man, stands as a parody of that claim.

9. The translations are mine, for the purpose of bringing out those aspects of the poems that are relevant to my discussion.

10. Paul de Man, "Allegory and Irony in Baudelaire," in de Man, *Romanticism and Contemporary Criticism: The Gauss Seminar and Other Papers,* ed. E. S. Burt, Kevin Newmark, and Andrzej Warminski (Baltimore: Johns Hopkins University Press, 1993). This essay is part of the Gauss Seminar given by de Man in 1967.

11. Jacques Lacan, "Agressivity in Psychoanalysis," in Lacan, *Ecrits,* trans. Alan Sheridan (New York: Norton, 1977), 17: "What I have called paranoic knowledge is shown, therefore, to correspond in its more or less archaic forms to certain critical moments that mark the history of man's mental genesis, each representing a stage in objectifying identification."

12. Ibid., 9.

13. Sigmund Freud, *Beyond the Pleasure Principle,* trans. James Strachey (New York: W. W. Norton, 1961).

14. Jacques Derrida, "Freud's Legacy," in Derrida, *The Post Card: From Socrates to Freud and Beyond,* trans. Alan Bass (Chicago: University of Chicago Press, 1987).

15. Paul de Man, *The Resistance to Theory* (Minneapolis: University of Minnesota Press, 2006), 10.

16. *United States Code* (1994), vol. 15, 438.

17. *United States Law Week,* 61, no. 25 (January 12, 1993): 4060–4068. Page numbers in parentheses refer to this text.

18. In a response to this chapter when I gave it as paper at the Yale Law School, Shoshana Felman made the brilliant suggestion that Souter would have wanted to re-write Baudelaire's "Correspondances" as: "Le Congrès est un temple où de vivants pilliers laissent parfois sortir de confuses paroles." The neoclassical, Parnassian architecture of official Washington, D.C., and the common metaphorical expression "pillars of the community," add piquancy to this suggestion.

19. Michael D. Rivard, "Toward a General Theory of Constitutional Personhood: A Theory of Constitutional Personhood for Transgenic Humanoid Species," *UCLA Law Review* 39, no. 5 (June 1992): 1428–1429.

20. See A. Leon Higginbotham, Jr., and Barbara Kopytoff, "Property First, Humanity Second: The Recognition of the Slave's Human Nature in Virginia Civil Law," *Ohio State Law Journal* 50, no. 3 (June 1989): 520: "The humanity of the slave, requiring that he be treated with the care due other humans and not like other forms of property, became *part* of the owner's property rights."

21. Douglas E. Fehrenbacher, *Slavery, Law, and Politics: The Dred Scott Case in Historical Perspective* (Oxford: Oxford University Press, 1981), 15.

22. Kim Mueller, "Inmates' Civil Rights Cases and the Federal Courts: Insights Derived from a Field Research Project in the Eastern District of California," *Creighton Law Review* 28, no. 1255 (June 1995): 1258–1259. In the Eastern District of California, inmates' civil rights actions constituted nearly 30 percent of the case filings. (California Men's Colony is not in the Eastern District; it is in San Luis Obispo.)

23. Ibid., 1276 and 1281.

24. Max Black, *Perplexities* (Ithaca, NY: Cornell University Press, 1990). See also Robert Axelrod, *The Evolution of Cooperation* (New York: Basic Books, 1984).

25. Richard Klein, *Cigarettes Are Sublime* (Durham, NC: Duke University Press, 1993). Klein notes, incidentally, that Baudelaire is one of the first French writers to use the word "cigarette" in print (in his *Salons de 1848*); ibid., 8.

26. Rivard, "Toward a General Theory of Constitutional Personhood," 1501–1502.

27. Gregory A. Mark, "The Personification of the Business Corporation in American Law," *University of Chicago Law Review* 54 (Fall 1987): 1441.

28. Steven Knapp, *Personification and the Sublime: Milton to Coleridge* (Cambridge, MA: Harvard University Press, 1985), 2.

15. Lost Cause

1. Nathaniel Hawthorne, *The Marble Faun* (New York: Penguin, 1990), 467.

2. Jacques Lacan, *The Ethics of Psychoanalysis,* trans. Dennis Porter (New York: Norton, 1992), 133.

3. Martin Heidegger, *Poetry, Language, Thought,* trans. Albert Hofstadter (New York: Harper and Row, 1971), 167 ("The Thing").

4. William Wordsworth, *The Prelude* [1805] (Oxford: Oxford University Press, 1959), 56.

5. Heinz Kohut, *The Analysis of the Self* (New York: International Universities Press, 1971), 117.

6. Jacques Lacan, *The Four Fundamental Concepts of Psychoanalysis,* trans. Alan Sheridan (New York: W. W. Norton, 1981).

7. See Jacques Lacan, "La signification du phallus," in Lacan, *Ecrits* (Paris: Editions du Seuil, 1966).

8. Lacan, *Ethics of Psychoanalysis,* 121.

9. Ibid., 286.

10. Jacques Lacan, "Remarque sur le rapport de Daniel Lagache," in Lacan, *Ecrits,* 673–675.

11. Lacan, *Ethics of Psychoanalysis,* 43.

12. Ibid., 83.

13. Ibid., 81.

14. Immanuel Kant, *Critique of Practical Reason,* trans. Lewis White Beck (New York: Macmillan, 1956), 32.

15. Ibid., 18.

16. Jacques Lacan, "Aggressivity in Psychoanalysis," in Lacan, *Ecrits: A Selection,* trans. Alan Sheridan (New York: W. W. Norton, 1977), 22.

17. Ibid., 22–24.

18. Sigmund Freud, *Moses and Monotheism,* trans. Katherine Jones (New York: Vintage, 1967), 176.

19. Hawthorne, *The Marble Faun,* 170–171.

20. George Eliot, *Middlemarch* (New York: Penguin, 1965), 869.

21. Nella Larsen, *Quicksand and Passing* (New Brunswick, NJ: Rutgers University Press, 1986), 237.

22. Ibid., 242.

23. Ibid., 246.

24. Hawthorne, *The Marble Faun,* 210.

25. Quoted in Michael J. Colacurcio, *The Province of Piety* (Cambridge, MA: Harvard University Press, 1984), 5.

26. Thomas Connolly, in Nathaniel Hawthorne, *The Scarlet Letter and Selected Tales* (New York: Penguin, 1970), 24.

27. Wendy Steiner, *Pictures of Romance* (Chicago: University of Chicago Press, 1988), 98–99.

28. Hawthorne, *The Marble Faun,* 59.

29. Ibid., 335–336.

30. T. Walter Herbert, "The Erotics of Purity: *The Marble Faun* and the Victorian Construction of Sexuality," *Representations* 36 (Fall 1991).

31. Ibid., 121–122.

32. Hawthorne, *The Marble Faun,* 172–177 (chapter titled "The Faun's Transformation").

33. Charlotte Brontë, *Villette* (New York: Penguin, 1979), 276.

Epilogue

1. Paul de Man, *The Resistance to Theory* (Minneapolis: University of Minnesota Press, 1986), 99, discussion after his lecture on Walter Benjamin's essay "The Task of the Translator."

2. Ibid., 99–101.

3. Paul de Man, *The Rhetoric of Romanticism* (New York: Columbia University Press, 1984), 93.

4. Leonard Barkan, *Unearthing the Past: Archaeology and Aesthetics in the Making of Renaissance Culture* (New Haven, CT: Yale University Press, 1999).

5. J. Hillis Miller, *Versions of Pygmalion* (Cambridge, MA: Harvard University Press, 1990).

Acknowledgments

Two essays in this book have been published before: Chapter 7 appeared as "Using People," in Marjorie Garber, Beatrice Hanssen, and Rebecca L. Walkowitz, eds., *The Turn to Ethics* (New York: Routledge, 2000); and Chapter 14 appeared as "Anthropomorphism in Lyric and Law," *Yale Journal of Law and the Humanities* (Summer 1998), 10, no. 2. The author is grateful to the publishers for permission to reprint.

In addition, the following works are quoted with permission:

Elizabeth Bishop, excerpt from "The Monument," from *The Complete Poems, 1927–1979,* by Elizabeth Bishop. Copyright © 1979, 1983 by Alice Helen Methfessel. Reprinted by permission of Farrar Straus and Giroux, LLC.

Gwendolyn Brooks, "The Chicago Picasso." Reprinted by consent of Brooks Permissions.

Carolyn Forché, "The Colonel," from *The Country between Us,* by Caroline Forché, copyright © 1981 by Carolyn Forché. Originally appeared in *Women's International Resource Exchange*. Reprinted by permission of HarperCollins Publishers; and by permission of the William Morris Agency, LLC, on behalf of the Author.

Marianne Moore, "To a Steam Roller," from *The Complete Poems of Marianne*

Moore, reprinted with the permission of Scribner, a division of Simon & Schuster, Inc., from *The Complete Poems of Marianne Moore,* by Marianne Moore, copyright © 1935 by Marianne Moore, copyright renewed © 1963 by Marianne Moore and T. S. Eliot, all rights reserved.

Sylvia Plath, "The Colossus," from *The Colossus and Other Poems,* by Sylvia Plath, copyright © 1957, 1958, 1959, 1960, 1961, 1962 by Sylvia Plath. Used by permission of Alfred A. Knopf, a division of Random House, Inc.; and by permission of Faber and Faber Ltd and © The Estate of Sylvia Plath.

Sylvia Plath, "Edge," from *Ariel,* by Sylvia Plath. Copyright © 1963 by Ted Hughes. Reprinted by permission of HarperCollins Publishers; and by permission of Faber and Faber Ltd and © The Estate of Sylvia Plath.

Sylvia Plath, "In Plaster," from *Crossing the Water,* by Sylvia Plath. Copyright © 1971 by Ted Hughes. Reprinted by permission of HarperCollins Publishers; and by permission of Faber and Faber Ltd and © The Estate of Sylvia Plath.

Sylvia Plath, "Virgin in a Tree," from *The Collected Poems of Sylvia Plath,* edited by Ted Hughes. Copyright © 1960, 1965, 1971, 1981 by The Estate of Sylvia Plath. Editorial material copyright © 1981 by Ted Hughes. Reprinted by permission of HarperCollins Publishers; and by permission of Faber and Faber Ltd and © The Estate of Sylvia Plath.

Francis Ponge, "L'Huître," from *Le Parti pris des choses,* copyright © 1942 by Editions Gallimard, reprinted by permission of Editions Gallimard. English translation by Beth Archer Brombert from *The Voice of Things,* her complete translation of *Le Partis pris des choses* and other works by Francis Ponge; reprinted with the permission of the translator.

Anne Sexton, "Where I Live in This Honorable House of the Laurel Tree," from *To Bedlam and Part Way Back,* by Anne Sexton. Copyright © 1960 by Anne Sexton, renewed 1988 by Linda G. Sexton. Reprinted by permission of Houghton Mifflin Company. All rights reserved.

Wallace Stevens, "Anecdote of the Jar," from *The Collected Poems of Wallace Stevens,* by Wallace Stevens, copyright © 1954 by Wallace Stevens and renewed in 1982 by Holly Stevens. Used by permission of Alfred A. Knopf, a division of Random House, Inc.

W. B. Yeats, "Upon a Dying Lady," section entitled "Certain Artists Bring Her Dolls and Drawings," from W. B. Yeats, *The Poems,* New Edition (London: J. M. Dent, 1994), reprinted by permission of A. P. Watt Ltd on behalf of Gráinne Yeats.

Index